E.S,
It was my distict pleasure
with you at SAP, and I a
appreciated the great advice an
counsel I received from you. I wish
you all the best in your future.

M000297054

THE INVISIBLE ECONOMY
OF CONSUMER ENGAGEMENT

THE INVISIBLE ECONOMY
OF CONSUMER ENGAGEMENT

Uncovering, Defining and Optimizing the Ocean of
Trade Promotion and Channel Incentives Money
That Drives Consumer Engagement

Robert L. Hand, Jr.

HPM TradeScope Press

Cover Design: Hayley Hand

Copyright © 2021 by HPM TradeScope™ Press. All rights reserved.

Published by: HPM TradeScope™ Press

No part of this publication may be reproduced, stored in a retrieval system, or transmitted in any form or by any means, electronic, mechanical, photocopying, recording, scanning, or otherwise, except as permitted under Section 107c or 108 of the 1976 United States Copyright Act, without either the prior written permission of the Author/Publisher. Requests to the Author/Publisher for permission should be addressed to:

HPM TradeScope™ Press
1101 Monterrey Oak Circle
Marble Falls, TX 78654

Or send your permission requests to info@handpromotion.com

Limit of Liability/Disclaimer of Warranty: While the publisher and author have used their best efforts in preparing this book, they make no representations or warranties with respect to the accuracy or completeness of the contents of this book and specifically disclaim any implied warranties or merchantability or fitness for a particular purpose. No warranty may be created or extended by sales representatives or written sales materials. The advice and strategies contained herein may not be suitable for your situation. You should consult with a professional where appropriate. Neither the publisher nor author shall be liable for any loss of profit or any other commercial damages, including but not limited to special, incidental, consequential, or other damages.

For general information on our other products and services or for tech support, please contact our Customer Care Department within the United States at info@handpromotion.com

Hand, Jr., Robert L.

Full title: The Invisible Economy of Consumer Engagement

Pages: 292

Endnotes; Index

ISBN 978-1-7377879-0-7 (hardback); ISBN 978-1-7377879-1-4 (paperback); ISBN 978-1-7377879-2-1 (ebook)   1. Business Marketing   I. Hand, Jr., Robert L.   II. Title

Library of Congress Control Number: 2021922906

Printed in the United States of America

10 9 8 7 6 5 4 3 2 1

DEDICATION

Dedicated to Gina, Hayley, and Renée

CONTENTS

Foreword xi

Preface xiii

Acknowledgements xv

Endorsements xvii

Eureka! 1

All This Money... for *What*, Exactly?. 7
    Big Business. 8
    The Second Largest Financial Line Item 9
    The Path to Success 11

The World's Third-Oldest Profession. 15
    The Rise of Co-op Advertising and Channel Incentives Growth 16
    The Roots of Trade Channel Promotion 17
    "It's a Free Concert Now." 20
    Evolving the Promotion Plan 25

The Consumer Chain 31
    The Day the Earth (and my retail grocery store) Stood Still 32
    Addressing the Consumer. 33
    Impacting the Links of the Consumer Chain 35
    Identifying the Need 35
    Researching the Product 39
    Researching the Optimal Shopping Experience 41
    Making the Decision to Purchase 43
    How Will I Purchase? 44
    Pull the Trigger 46
    Transfer of Ownership 48
    The Product Experience 50
    The Verdict 51
    Thumbs Up or Down? 52
    Show and Tell 53
    The Follow-Up 55
    The Reprise 56

The Shell Game. 59
    What's the Deal? 61
    The Sell-Out 65
    Where's the Pea? 66
    Over and Above 67
    Expanding the Game. 69

The Battle for Hearts and Minds (and Shelf, Basket, and Pantry) . . 73
    Tactical Failure 74
    Trade Channel Promotion Tactics. 78
    Plugging a Decades-Old Gap 83
    The Ground Game 84
    RGM to the Rescue 87
    Flags of Truce 89

Digital DEFCON 1 . . . . **95**
   Digitally Transforming the Invisible Economy 96
   Emergence of the Omnichannel 118
   An Immovable Object vs. an Unstoppable Force. 119
   If You Can't Beat 'Em, Join 'Em—A Challenging Détente 121
   Internet-of-(All)-Things 124
Real-Time Telemetry in the 4TH Dimension **127**
   Beyond the "Big Data" Initiatives 128
   Creating the Corporate Infrastructure—The CDO 129
   The Metrics of Data Initiatives. 130
   Strengthening the "Spokes" 132
   The Data Value Vector 134
   The Data Value Vector Decision Workshop 136
   Controlling the Data Value 137
   The Cost of Data (COD) 139
   Figure 8.3 The Business & Operations Data Flow Measuring the Cost of
   Data (COD) 140
Attaining the Dimensions of Knowledge **143**
   Crossing the Rubicon 143
   THE 1ST DIMENSION: FOUNDATIONAL 144
   Forecast, Demand Plan, Shipments, and Baselines 147
   Promotion Plan Timing, Tactics, Products and Costs 150
   Post-promotion Volume, Revenue and Profitability 155
   Simple Calculation of Promotion ROI 156
   Syndicated Consumption Intelligence 157
   THE 2ND DIMENSION: OPTIMIZED. 158
   AI- and ML-Driven Predictive Analytics 159
   Increased POS Data to Provide Near Real-time Visibility 160
   Integrated and Aligned Consumer Marketing Planning 163
   Integrated Near Real-Time Retail Execution Compliance Data . . . 164
   Pricing, Assortment and Logistics Data in Promo Planning. 166
   THE 3RD DIMENSION: PRESCRIPTIVE 171
   Time-Tested Algorithms Shared by Channel and Marketing 172
   Increased Data Capture from All Promotions and Events 173
   Daily, Near-100% POS Data Capture and Reporting 174
   Dynamic Inventory Alerts and Threshold Monitoring 176
   Social Sentiment and Real-Time E-commerce Integration 177
   THE 4TH DIMENSION: ENGAGED 179
   Integrated Consumer-Driven RGM-Based Promotions 180
   IoT-Based Monitoring and Consumer Demand Sensing 181
   Real-Time Dynamic Baseline Adjustment 182
   Enrichment of Causal Data Driving Marketing Mix 183
   Predictive Supplier, Materials and Value Chain Optimization 184
Taking It to the Streets. **187**
   Another Fine Mess You Got Me Into 188
   Begging for Attention 189
   What's the Big Deal? 191

The Extent of the REX Problem 193
Who Executes the Execution? 198
Tools of the Trade 200

A New Chip Off the Old Blockchain **203**
Is This for Real? 204
Most Likely Use Cases 208
POS, POP, and POW! 211
Cryptopromotion 213
Pros and Cons for Blockchain Applications in Trade Channel Promotion 215

How Do We Get to the Endgame? **223**
Are We There Yet? 224
Data Excellence 227
Baseline Excellence 228
Analytics Excellence 232
Trade Promotion Management & Execution (TPx) Excellence 235
Optimization Excellence 244
Collaboration Excellence 245
Execution Excellence 248
Consumer Excellence 248
Managing the Change 249
Have We Arrived? 251

About the Author **255**
Endnotes **257**
Index **261**

FOREWORD

Having worked with Rob for over 20 years, there is not anyone better to examine Trade Promotion issues let alone Revenue Growth Management topics. With Rob, there is one huge difference, his solutions are never esoteric. They are prudent, ROI-driven answers to actual problems.

I have learned from one of the best, and Rob has worked on the industry's largest Sales, Marketing and Supply Chain issues. This book provides fascinating real-life examples of creating lifelong consumer engagement touchpoints via Trade Promotions. His "start with the consumer and work backwards" approach and simplification of extremely complex and critical issues in Trade Promotion is a must-read for every consultant, software developer, student, and industry professional trying to better understand the intricacies of Trade Promotions.

Whether it's Trade Promotion Management, Excellence or Optimization, Rob not only understands the business, processes, and technologies, he educates everyone and shares his lifelong passion on cultivating better collaboration between the supplier and the consumer.

I am honored and humbled to write this foreword for a friend. I am certain that every reader will want to memorize this book. It's the first comprehensive overview of trade promotions ever published written by the "godfather of Trade Promotion, let alone Revenue Growth" – Mi Amigo, Rob Hand.

John Rossi

CEO, Retail Velocity, Inc.

PREFACE

"Write the book, Rob."

That is what I have been hearing for the past two decades from so many people from a cross-section of industries, analyst firms and academia. I've always wanted to, but with ADHD being so much a part of me, it was always hard to imagine sitting down for more than a month, much less the full year it took to make that possible.

But the timing could not have been more appropriate than now.

Even before this awful pandemic we've dealt with, the importance of trade channel promotion management and execution began to rise to the top of the C-suite as a major priority focus in the quest for consumer engagement excellence. Trade promotion, co-op advertising, and market development funded spending in the channels of distribution, especially retail, has reached new heights as a percentage of gross revenues, and is most often the second largest line item in a consumer products company's financials. And yet, according to many of the leading analysts and consulting experts, it fails more than half of the time to achieve a positive return.

Throughout most of my career in this channel incentives business, the practices of trade promotion, co-op advertising, and market development fund management has been called a "necessary evil," with little attention paid to the execution and analysis of this mission-critical process. It seemed that the grassroots management of this money was relegated to lower managerial and supervisory staff positions who had the difficult jobs of claim and deduction settlement processing, report development, and overall fund accounting, while the sales reps and key account managers spent literally hundreds of billions of dollars globally to ensure meeting their forecasts.

Thanks to the advent of new technology, the explosion of e-commerce, and the emergence of corporate mandates to engage in digital transformation, senior corporate management has followed the money only to learn what those of us who have been in this business for years already knew.

Channel promotion management is a top priority and vital to the success of the company.

Now, I am seeing the consumer products industry focus on trade promotion and co-op advertising like never before. Blogs, podcasts, white papers, and webinars have all increased in scope and frequency. Trade organizations now have several events throughout the year, attended by higher level executives, and dedicated to trade promotion and channel marketing—and on a truly global scope. Trade promotion management, execution, and analytics is now a growth industry.

And yet, you can't find a book on this subject that seems to cover the end-to-end process, practice, and technology of what we all now call "modern trade promotion."

Even today, university level curricula seem to ignore trade promotion, even though the chances are high that a recent graduate just beginning his or her career in marketing, supply chain, advertising, or even finance may actually find themselves deep into the management organization supporting trade promotion.

There is so much to know, so much to understand, and so many ways that trade promotion and its associated family of channel incentives programs impacts the success of every consumer goods company that sells products through the distribution channels. I found a few college thesis papers and doctoral dissertations formally published on some aspects of channel promotion, but not enough to give someone a true and comprehensive understanding of what trade promotion is all about.

This book is detailed and, by necessity, often seems redundant in places; but that is only because so much of the work that has to be done spans so many areas of the corporate consumer goods value chain. There will be areas of disagreement within this book that people smarter than me might question, but that may be exactly what this industry needs—vigorous debate which leads to better ideas, technologies, and in the end, more effective consumer engagement.

What I have intended for the book is my point of view about what it takes to win the consumer's loyalty, trust, and a sustained relationship, even though trade promotion, as a practice, has not often been directly associated with the consumer. But in the end, it is exactly what trade promotion and co-op advertising management, execution, and analytics are intended to deliver.

My belief, based on my long experience, is that the tools, technology, and science we have today can turn those awful records of achievement of trade spending from more than a 50% failure rate to a 100% success rate. Some say it's not possible. I say, read this book. Then tell me it's not.

The time is right for this book. If what I have written can help someone elevate this practice of trade promotion to new heights of success for themselves and/or their company, then I will have accomplished my objective.

Thank you for buying this book, and I hope you will enjoy it.

ACKNOWLEDGEMENTS

I have to thank God for blessing me with all that I have.

I want to thank my wonderful wife Gina, who has had to put up with my "book brain" as I wander around my house, left-brained from hours of writing. She is my mate in every sense of the word.

I am grateful to my children, Hayley, and Renée, for putting up with the sometimes ranting and raving. Dad has been guilty of doing that long before taking on this mission of writing a book.

The only way this could have happened was because my best friend and editor, Michael Hambrick, has the patience of Job (truly) and walked and talked me through an incredible last couple of years as we took on this mission. His guidance, counsel and advice has not only educated me but inspired me to make this happen.

So many people helped me along the way and contributed to the words in this book. I want to thank my longtime friend and colleague, John Rossi for the kind words in the *Foreword*, and his domain expertise I have heavily depended upon throughout our association.

I have to thank Hans Van Delden and Mark Osborn for their input, as well as Timo Wagenblatt, who was one of those people pushing me to write this book for so many years. I want to especially thank Jeff Beckett for his contributions and the exciting phone calls he and I have had over the years as we have attempted to solve the world's problems. There are also so many people who contributed stories and interviews that asked for anonymity—you know who you are, and you must know I could not have had the content I do without you.

Albert Guffanti and the team at Consumer Goods Technology and EnsembleIQ have worked tirelessly in this industry to bring about many of the changes I have said needed to happen.

Promotion Optimization Institute, and especially their chief commercial officer, Pam Brown provided me with excellent content. Pam is one of those people who grew up in the trenches in this business and has a wealth of experience about consumer packaged goods and trade promotion in particular. She honed her skills doing just about everything one can do in the management of trade promotion for some of the largest, most powerful CPG companies on Earth.

One of the most valuable business and friendship associations I have had is with my longtime friend and business partner, Tim Moore. I met Tim when I came to Texas in 1983 and he inspired me to create our first business, MEDIANET, here in Austin, Texas. Tim's common sense approach, orderly and practical application of technology and process inspired us to grow MEDIANET to one of the most innovative channel incentive management service firms in the business. The company has been through a couple of acquisitions, and is now part of BrandMuscle, Inc., but still operating in Austin, Texas.

Thanks have to go to Harris Fogel for his longtime relationship and the trust that I could discuss anything with him and always get a strong answer to any issue I presented.

A special thank you has to go to my friend Dale Hagemeyer, former vice president of Gartner who managed their consumer goods practice for so many years. Dale always told me I should "write the book," and so I have. Dale left the industry and pursued his mission of support and help to the Mexican people he embraced for so many years. Dale's guidance and knowledge certainly accelerated my own thinking and gave me significant confidence in my own abilities.

There are also those who no longer grace us with their presence I want to thank who, in so many ways helped me through this work and who many of us had the opportunity and pleasure to work with. My long time business colleague and good friend, the late Bob Houk, who authored one of the most recent books about modern co-op advertising always provided insight and domain expertise that I grew from, as so many of my fellow industry people did.

You can't write a book about anything consumer goods without input from one of the most important people this industry has had, Roddy Martin, who recently passed away. I thank him for his help last year spurring me on to write the book and giving me some great quotes.

Another wonderful person—a pioneer in this industry—was Rick Pensa, founder, and CEO of CPGToolBox, who we lost to Covid-19 last January. He and I became close friends, and I always appreciated his wisdom and clarity in this mission.

I wish I could name and thank every client and every person I've worked with, but of course that's not possible. I have had the extraordinary honor to work with the men and women of this and other industries who gave me the opportunities to help them grow and expand the functionality and capabilities of their trade promotion and co-op advertising programs. To all of them I say, "Thank you for giving me the opportunity to work with you and your fine organizations," and to partner in the development of some very cool technology and business processes.

Rob

ENDORSEMENTS

"Finally … Rob publishes THE book about Trade Promotion. I recommend the book to anyone who wants to understand what drives consumer engagement globally. The book provides it all, the history, the status quo, and the inspiration and guidance required for a successful future. The Invisible Economy of Consumer Engagement underlines Rob's thought leadership of the last decades."

Timo Wagenblatt—Product Manager, Google Merchant Shopping

"The Intelligent Deployment of capital will be critical to future differentiation between leaders and laggers in the Consumer Goods Industry; in order to win, companies will need to overhaul their Trade Promotion and Revenue Growth Management strategies. Rob Hand's book captures all you need to know as to why this is the case and delivers actionable steps for implementing the essential changes you need to make now."

Dominick Dinardo—CEO, Founder, Aforza, Inc.

"Here is a business book you won't give away. The "been there - done it" stories and straight forward folk-talk pulls you in to this largely invisible world all while you reach for a highlighter for the plethora of insights and how-tos he backs up with facts and clear examples. I dog ear bookmarked page after page and the other pages are covered in yellow highlights. Insightful and exceptionally fun to read. Thanks Rob!"

Larry Layden—Senior Vice President, UCBOS

"Always leading so thoroughly on the critical topic of trade promotion, Rob Hand provides the foundation, vision and proposes the solution here. "The Invisible Economy of Consumer Goods" is both guide to the future successful strategies and the single point of truth on the subject! Grab a pen you're going to be taking a lot of notes!"

William Deakin—SVP Growth & Ecommerce, Sprecher Brewing Co.

"Rob has championed the use of better tools to get real ROI from promotions for years. There is no better person to write the definitive guide on improving the effectiveness of trade promotions spending."

John Bermudez—Vice President Product Marketing, TraceLink

"We've had seminal moments in the past that have changed everything. Rob has painted a bold picture, while providing a most useful roadmap, for us to see what's next, and deliver what's required."

Michael Forhez—Global Managing Director, Industry Strategy Group, Oracle Corporation

"I often say that Rob has "written the book" on trade promotions. And now he has. In this book you will find the first in-depth and documented source of everything you need to know about modern trade promotion. I highly recommend it as a reference for best practices in this ever changing world of consumer relationships."

Keith Costello—General Manager, Global SAP Business, IBM

CHAPTER 1

EUREKA!

For me, growing up in the smallest of Tennessee towns was full of wonder. New Johnsonville, Tennessee is an exceedingly small industrial town on the east bank of the Tennessee River and was one of those towns where the city limits sign could really have been on two sides of the same post. My father worked for DuPont and was transferred there when I was eight years old.

But it was a cool little place to have a childhood. The river, with its large lakes and backwaters, made it a perfect place to hunt, fish, explore, sail, and swim. We were so cut off from the outside world that much of the news of the day never reached us at all. Nestled out of reach of the two nearest TV markets of Nashville and Jackson, we barely had TV reception and so most people found their lives existing outside of the glare of the TV screen.

Radio, on the other hand, was a big deal for me. Boy Scout campouts, neighborhood back yard campouts, and winding down in my bed at night found my ear glued to a transistor radio listening to WLS in Chicago, and those amazing disc jockey personalities like Dick Biondi, Art Roberts, and Ron Riley. For most of my life up to that point, I wanted to be a doctor. But listening to these guys derailed that dream and set me on a path to rock and roll and broadcasting.

I found out early I had a talent for music. I was part of a trio at the age of 13 performing folk music ballads with two of my friends at local events and at scout

1

camps and jamborees. I played bass for a local rock band where we found ourselves performing all over and recording on Nashville's Music Row. I was in the high school band and played a pretty mean trumpet, enough to earn a scholarship to Memphis State University.

In the late '60s, Memphis was an ideal place for me. Not only was the MSU band one of the coolest college bands in the world, but the city of Memphis was home to the blues, Stax Records, Sun Records, Elvis, and all the music that grew out of the Mississippi Delta sound. Plus, it was a super-hot radio market, with the likes of George Klein, Rick Dees and a host of other personalities and stations. WHBQ, the home of Sam Phillips and the first to play Elvis Presley became my first professional gig.

Throughout my college career with internships and stints on the campus radio station, it quickly became evident I would not have the "voice" for radio. I graduated with a degree in Radio-TV-Film and immediately became the lead sales guy for the FM unit of WHBQ. I loved this job. As the only sales guy at the station, I also enjoyed the opportunity to generate the amount of revenue I did—every sale made at the station was MY sale, and MY commission!

But alas, that didn't last long. My draft board sent the "Greetings from your President" letter and I found myself being sworn into the United States Naval Air Reserve two days later! My broadcast career would have to wait a bit. I had to complete my active duty, and when I returned, things were different. There was a new hotshot sales guy on board, and he was building momentum on my old accounts. I was left scrambling with the task of starting all over.

There was no doubt I was going to be nowhere near the revenue stream I had built up for the station before my active-duty service, so I had to work with the little businesses, taking ridiculously small chunks of change and being more creative. One such situation occurred with a small Kawasaki dealer who sold motorcycles out of the living room of his house in North Memphis. The owner converted his living room into a small showroom and used his garage as the service bay.

After more sales calls than I could muster, I gave up trying to sell him radio time. He told me he didn't think motorcycles sold on radio, and I was wasting his time. But after a couple of months, he called me.

"I have some money I just found, and it is supposed to be used for radio, I think." he said. "I gave you a call because I know how many times you've tried to pitch me radio, and you are the only radio guy I know."

He *found* money? Well, I figured since he called me, the least I should do is check this out. So, I went down to his shop, and he showed me a statement of some kind. It had a Kawasaki corporate logo on the top of the page and showed he had earned a

$5,000 balance of accrued *co-op advertising* funds available to him from the company. I had never seen anything like this, but if he thought he had the money from this official document from Kawasaki, who was I to dispute it?

The statement mentioned that to receive the money, he had to send a copy of the radio station invoice, a notarized copy of the script, and fill out a claim form. Easy. So, I told him it appeared that he had this money to spend and that it would not cost him any additional money to run the advertising. On the strength of that statement, he decided to give it a go.

I sat down with the program director, and we created a great promotion. We set up a contest which was based on listeners spelling K-A-W-A-S-A-K-I with the first letter of highlighted songs we played throughout the day. The first listener to identify every song, and the time they played, that spelled *KAWASAKI* won a 75cc Kawasaki minibike. The promotion lasted for four weeks.

The promotion was a huge success, not only for the station's ratings, but for the owner of the Kawasaki shop. He sold out of all his motorcycles in a week and had to drive up to Michigan to bring back more bikes to sell. In fact, over the next few weeks, he sold out every week, and when the promotion ended and we had a winner, he was featured on a local TV news station and in the newspaper. Eventually, the owner bought an old automobile dealership building and was quickly one of the top Kawasaki dealers in the south. He was an incredibly happy client.

That was a great success story, but the most important aspect of the story is what *I* learned from it. Six weeks after the contest ended, I was paid for my monthly commissions and noticed that my check did not include the commissions from the promotional sale. I quickly learned that the owner of the dealership had not paid his bill and he was about to go 60-days past due! Since collecting past due bills was one of my least favorite functions, I dreaded the call I was going to have to make.

When I knocked on the door to his office, he greeted me with a big bear hug and a smile. I told him why I was there, and he changed his state quickly to an almost fierce response.

"I'm not paying for this!" he said. "You told me that this statement I showed you said I had $5,000 from the Kawasaki company, and you were wrong," he nearly yelled. "So here," he said as he threw me the paper report he'd received showing his request for the money from Kawasaki was denied. "You get them to pay me, and I'll pay you!" he exclaimed.

Escaping his wrath, I took the letter and report back to my office and looked at it. There were two documents. The first one was an audit report showing the amount claimed and a couple of comments of denial. The second was a form letter saying that the request for reimbursement was denied because the dealer failed to get "prior approval" which was required for any broadcast co-op advertising.

What? Prior Approval? Co-op Advertising?

At the bottom of the letter was a toll-free number you could call to ask questions. So, I made the call.

Thinking that I was calling Kawasaki in Los Angeles, I actually called the service firm that administered the Kawasaki co-op advertising program.

I asked, "Is this Kawasaki?"

"Actually, we handle the Kawasaki program, may I help you?" the person replied.

I went through the process of describing what I wanted, and how I did not know about a prior approval. The account manager told me if I had the dealer resubmit the claim with a request for prior approval, and a description of the success of the promotion, she felt quite sure they would reimburse the claim. So that is what we did, and sure enough, the claim was reimbursed for the full amount and my station was paid.

And I was paid.

This whole experience gave me pause. What was this? And what in the world was co-op advertising? Initially, I figured if I knew of other products offering these kinds of financial incentives, I may have a way to build up my small account base.

After a few days, I called the number at the bottom of the Kawasaki Co-op Advertising Program audit report and spoke to another individual there. It turns out the office I called was the San Francisco office of a national outsource company which managed co-operative advertising programs for hundreds of manufacturers across all consumer products sectors. I ended up speaking to one of the managers there who quickly told me that the company had a large office right there in downtown Memphis and gave me the name of the manager there for me to talk with.

I visited the office and was astounded at what I saw. Three floors of people sitting at desks reading newspapers, processing stacks of co-op advertising claims submitted by retailers and distributors all over the country.

I found out how this service firm administered co-op advertising programs; and more importantly, learned what co-op advertising *really* was.

It hooked me. The amount of money spent on local media advertising was a huge figure, even then. But, to think that virtually 80% of that money came from manufacturer co-op advertising funds and allowance programs was a staggering fact which boggled my mind.

Manufacturers and suppliers provide billions of dollars in subsidized promotional funding to their channel customers (e.g., retailers, wholesalers, distributors, and other storefront resellers). The purpose of these offers is to enable local promotion of the manufacturer's products without them having to place and execute local advertising and marketing campaigns, which would be virtually impossible to do because of cost and labor intensive efforts to cover the entire country or world, for that matter.

Who knew? I didn't.

I had so many advertising, marketing, and journalism classes in college and grad school, and never had I heard of such a program. The phrase *co-operative advertising* was something new to me, and I would have bet it was new to most advertising and marketing students and professionals as well. And I was right.

I had to be part of this. Never mind trying to sell radio or TV time, generating the thousands of dollars of revenue for the station. This was an opportunity to work across multiple exciting companies in every consumer industry, and deal with billions of dollars in channel promotion funds. I went to work for that company in April 1972, and there began my career in co-op advertising and trade channel promotion.

Today, after nearly fifty years in this business, I still see that channel promotions are defined in many ways. The most common nomenclature is *trade promotion*, which really applies to the processes, policies, and procedures of manufacturer-supplied funding to customers in any channel of distribution across all consumer products sectors. These programs are offered by all manufacturers which sell their products through these channels of distribution.

This book will concentrate more on the *fast-moving consumer goods* (FMCG) sector which is defined as products that are sold on a high frequency basis that are typically lower in price and more akin to commodities. Examples include any and all products sold in supermarkets, mass merchandisers and so-called club stores (such as Costco and Sam's in the USA). The most widely used definition for this consumer products sector is *consumer packaged goods* which is broadly defined with the acronym "CPG."

Even back in 1972, when I began my career, the flow of this money accrued by retailers as a percentage of net purchases of products, spent by the manufacturers reimbursing hundreds of billions of dollars of promotional ads, rebates, and other types of promotional tactics, was already an underground ocean of financial transactions.

Unbelievably higher than anyone would typically know.

Unseen.

Invisible.

CHAPTER 2

ALL THIS MONEY... FOR *WHAT*, EXACTLY?

Most sane shoppers know that products are sold at a discount at some point throughout their lifecycle, and that these discounts or "sales deals" are generally offered by the retailer, e-commerce site, distributor, or wholesaler who sells them. The phrase, "On Sale" denotes a temporary price reduction for some specific period of time and/or for some specific reason. In the consumer goods industry, this is the most widely used tactical practice to attract potential buyers.

Whether the price reduction is a strategic play to promote a new product, help move excess inventory from a previously failed promotion, reduce the inventory of obsolete or soon-to-be-discontinued product, or just to take advantage of attracting shoppers' attention to a popular or frequently demanded product, one thing is certain: the difference between the usual price and the reduced price is paid by the manufacturer and/or the supplier. The retailer, wholesaler, distributor or any class of channel resellers will simply not eat that cost delta unless they are going out of business. Most people do not know that. For instance, they most likely believe the retailer drops the price hoping to recover the cost of the discount with a higher volume of products crossing the check-out scanner.

Over the years I have had to explain the business I am in. Trade channel promotion, co-op advertising, market development funding, or any other moniker you give it, is as alien as trying to explain Einstein's theory of relativity to a third grader. Even now, I get glazed eyes and a sort of "Gee, that's pretty cool... I think I will get another drink, so if you will excuse me?"

Forget trying to tell them how the money is used, I've lost them at "trade channel promotion." Oh, and more often than not, they are in some form of marketing discipline!

So, if you want to simplify what all of this means, think of when you see all those tags on the shelf showing discounts, all the ads promoting a "short time only" sale price, or even the person handing out samples of food and drink in your store, offering you a slice of this or a small cup of that, think about where the money comes from and how much it must cost to pay for those promotional activities. That is what I am talking about in a nutshell.

Big Business

The estimated sales within the consumer packaged goods (CPG) industry in the United States alone in 2020 was $860 billion (USD).[1] Globally, the CPG industry revenues exceed $1.9 trillion (USD).[2] Considering that the average spending on all trade promotion represents more than 19% of gross revenues for CPG companies,[3] and almost 30% for the largest revenue tier of CPG companies, you can imagine we are talking about a lot of money. If you take the government statistics on retail sales and apply these percentages representing trade spending, it means fast-moving consumer goods (FMCG) companies in North America alone spend more than $500 billion and globally, more than $700 billion every year on trade promotion! This represents the second largest line item in the corporate financials after cost of goods. The projections for trade spending are almost a trillion dollars globally by 2025. One *Trillion* dollars!

Throughout this book, the phrase "trade channel" is used to denote the various ways and locations a consumer can purchase a product—from a physical brick-and-mortar storefront location or online via e-commerce sites like Amazon. Within the various consumer products industry sectors, the channels can vary from grocery stores like Kroger, big box retailers like Best Buy, mass merchandisers like Walmart, or fashion and department stores like Macy's. They can also be convenience stores, auto parts stores, and warehouse or club stores like Sam's and Costco. Then, think about the fact that this trade promotion spending data I just mentioned applies to only one industry sector—FMCG, which is often interchangeably characterized as "CPG."

Consider what it would be if you added trade channel spending for fashion, consumer electronics, automotive aftermarket, hardware/DIY, sporting goods, appliances, and home furnishings. This is serious cash, and the average shopping consumer has no idea of the immense amount of money spent every year in channel incentives—the overarching category definition of all these types of expenses as well as what we will characterize as "trade promotion," or "trade channel promotion" from this point on.

It can also encompass co-op advertising, market development fund programs and other business-to-business rebates or financial incentives.

Now, imagine you are the chief financial officer of a major CPG company who must deliver the annual financial report to the board of directors. You wear your best suit, power tie, and spit-shined shoes, and you walk in with some of the most beautiful graphics presentations you have ever had created for you.

It doesn't take you long to get to the second line item in your expense chart—trade promotion spending. You report that this past year, your company spent 19% of the gross revenue on trade promotions with your retail customers. One of the sharp board members asks you why we spend so much. After giving him a brief clinic on trade promotion and the amount of money spent by CPG companies, his eyes widened. He asks if the promotions are successful. "What is our ROI for this money," he asks.

All of the sudden, your collar feels too tight, your hands are perspiring, and you look at your latest figures from your revenue growth management and trade promotion team, and you say, "Uh, our retail customers typically do not sell everything we ship, so while we make money on the sell-in, the final result is that the promotion does not always create a positive ROI—uh, at least for our retail partner." You read off the chart, "It appears our ROI is about 65%."

Everyone in the room is looking at each other and, in unison, turns their heads to you. "So, you are saying that we spend 19% of our gross revenue, and on average, 35% of that money fails to generate positive ROI?" asks the chairman. You glance over at the executive vice president of sales, who is set to present after you, and you mumble something about industry averages and how your company is right in line with the industry statistics. Then you point out that this should be a conversation to have with the Chief Sales Officer when she comes up to present. After all, you've already had these conversations with her, and these deals are created by her team, not your financial people.

The collective gathering begins to flip their folders over to the sales sections and make notes. You present the remaining financial data and take your seat, with the sound of the approaching bus, under which your sales colleague is about to be thrown, as she slowly approaches the podium giving you a "Thanks a lot!" stare as she walks by you.

The Second Largest Financial Line Item

According to Nielsen, the global research firm that tracks billions of promotions every year, the actual figure of failure rate for trade spending is even worse—as high as 71%. This is up from an average of 67% in 2015.[4]

So, why would any company allow this dreadful result to continue to rise year on year? Simple. It has been the result of a longstanding practice by both retailers and

CPG companies to concentrate financial incentives on two primary goals:

1. The retailer depends upon this money to fuel a large portion of its profitability; and,

2. The CPG sales account executive depends on it to provide an incentive for the retailer to buy the products he needs to sell to achieve his forecast.

Historically, both of these goals are the result of long agonizing policies, practices and processes that have evolved since manufacturers began providing financial incentives. We will delve deeper into this history in the next chapter; but essentially, the retailers have begun to depend upon trade promotion funds to replace the loss of margin they suffer when their products are sold at discounted prices. The average net profit margin by grocery retailers in 2020 was 1.48%.[5] Pure product margins are even significantly less, so the money earned through trade promotion deals made across the entire portfolio of CPG suppliers provides a very large percentage of what the grocery retailers' profitability will be for any given year.

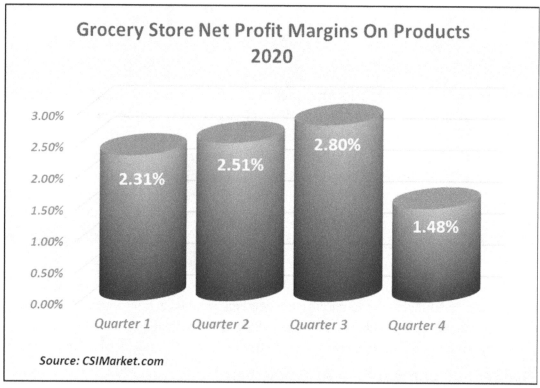

Figure 2.1 Retail Grocery Average Profits on Product Sales 2020

In the CPG industry in particular, the practice of allocation of funds is highly discretionary. Historically, in this CPG industry sector, the practice of determining what funds go to which retail account has evolved from the calculation of a percentage of net purchases of product to a far more complex formula that is a blend of the projection of the annual marketing budget, the retailer's demand for specific amounts of money and the manufacturer's account representative's need to achieve the volume required to meet his/her forecast.

All too often, the final agreement for allocated funding is based disproportionately on non-consumer engagement-driven factors like the need to meet a profit or product sell-in volume objective instead of meeting specific consumer demands.

This has long been a controversial issue, especially for the smaller independent grocery competitors. It has begun to open up some inquiries in the United States into certain practices by large mass retailers and CPG brand companies. In one March 2021 white paper released by the National Grocers Association, a coalition of more than 21,000 independent grocery retailers, the group was calling for federal investigation and oversight into these practices that they consider to be discriminatory.[6] The claim centers around behavior during the Covid-19 pandemic of 2020-21 where they claimed that the largest retail chains were able to get inventory of key household essentials and even their distributors charged more per product than they could get buying from their mass market competitors; but this action signaled a resurgence in the anti-competitive concerns that have existed for more than 70 years.

If you have any doubt that trade promotion money is at the heart of these large-scale business dealings in an industry that you, as a consumer are part of every day of your life, you can be sure it is the life blood of consumer goods, not just in America, but globally as well.

So, for now, this answers the question, "All this money…for *what*, exactly?"

Further details regarding both of those "goals" are dealt with comprehensively in the pages to come; but clearly, wondering about what this has to do with retailer profitability has to give you pause, right?

The Path to Success

What this book is about is how to improve the success rate of trade promotions from what is essentially one of the most expensive ongoing failures in global business history to produce a near 100% *success* rate in promotion return on investment.

To accomplish this, we will take an in-depth look at what this practice is, how it is managed, why it has evolved as it has and what it takes to turn the numbers around. People in general, and even many of those involved in global consumer goods, have far too little visibility to this problem, and therein lies the problem.

Promotions are about one thing—communicating the details of an offer, product quality, price, and location to the consumer. This is the essence of consumer engagement, which is the ultimate purpose of all this money. The value it brings runs the length of the entire supply chain from the nugget of an idea for a product to the disposition of a product that is at the end of its lifecycle. Everyone in this so-called *Value Chain* must work together to ensure success of any product; but all too often the consumer gets lost in the maze of daily workloads and processes.

Certainly, the lack of concern about the success of a promotion (and that is exactly what it has been) is responsible for the awful statistical performance of trade channel promotion ROI over the years.

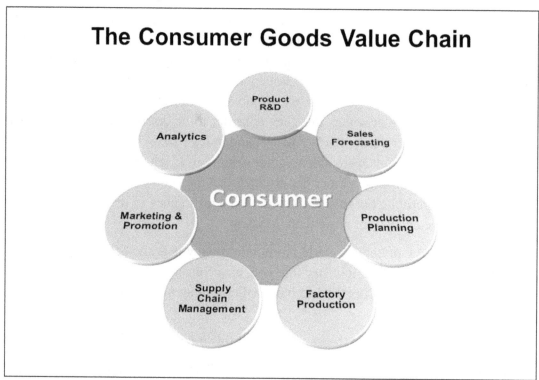

Figure 2.2 Functional Components of the Consumer Goods Value Chain

The *Value Chain* is the combination of the key processes that form the product lifecycle. The problem with many consumer products companies is that this series of functions and processes are often siloed, disconnected and dysfunctional. When operated properly, each component process is both linked and dependent upon every other process in the Value Chain cycle. For instance, *Sales Forecasting* is a starting point that springs from the corporate strategic plan that dictates targeted revenues, which will also include the allocation of budget to support execution of the operational plan. The decisions for sales and operations, factory production and supply chain management spring from those early forecasting plans. Marketing and promotion planning are derived from the forecast and once executed, analyzing the performance results is the critical function that drives future product planning, research, and development.

Strategic alignment between all these functions is difficult to achieve in this business environment for several reasons. Chief among those reasons is the failure to define and align the functional goals and objectives of each process to the ultimate corporate execution of engaging with the consumer to convert them to a loyal customer and maintain this relationship throughout the life cycle of the product.

This means that to be successful, the *Consumer* should be front and **center**—in the middle of the Value Chain. However, all too often the core Value Chain component process linkage is missing this element. The result is dysfunctional operations that all too often end up with failure to achieve the corporate strategic objectives.

The good news is that this is quickly becoming one of the most important focus areas in corporate executive management circles. The realization of something so simple as putting the consumer in first place of every strategic and operational decision in the Value Chain is gaining traction with both the major channel retailers and the consumer goods manufacturers.

In the chapters that follow, we will dissect the Value Chain, relating and breaking down every mission critical aspect of trade promotion management, execution, and performance measurement. Our objective will be to define and overhaul those many areas where the consumer products company and channel leadership can collaborate effectively to produce dramatically successful promotions every time.

We will expose the practices and processes and illuminate the money trails and regimen of selling and promoting products in this modern age of digital consumerism. This book will include deep probes into current methods, policies and procedures that have contributed to these failures over the years. We will examine the way trade promotions are created, planned, executed, and measured as well as the best practices we see in the marketplace today.

This book will not answer every question, to be sure; but it will shine a very bright light on areas of all consumer products trade and channel promotion practices that we hope can drive true transformation and help optimize the monumentally high cost of promotion in every channel of distribution. The intended objective is that you will have a better understanding of how to contribute your particular talent to the ongoing effort of achievement of 100% success rate in trade promotion effectiveness.

I refuse to accept that this cannot be done; and given the previous horrible year with Covid-19 and the geo-political fear, supply chain disruption and overarching control of consumers, we should drive the stake in the ground now to be more effective and efficient.

With the arguably high success rate of many consumer products companies now despite the failure rate of trade and channel promotion, imagine how it could be when the key performance indicators are reversed and promotions actually do what they are supposed to do—sell your products, make money and make your consumers happy and loyal.

CHAPTER 3

THE WORLD'S THIRD-OLDEST PROFESSION

In a Los Angeles business conference on March 2, 1977, Ronald Reagan gave us one of the most famous of presidential quotes, "Politics is supposed to be the second-oldest profession. I have come to realize that it bears an awfully close resemblance to the first."[7] And we all know what the oldest profession in the world is. But if politics is the second oldest, then this strange and invisible practice of billions paid by manufacturers to retailers, distributors, and resellers must be the third.

The history of retail is as old as mankind. The need for the things of life has driven people from their domiciles out to wherever they can find the "stuff" they need. The earliest caravans of goods making their way across the wilderness of the Middle East and North Africa 4,000 years ago were the first "points of sale" for the people of the small villages and tribal camps. At some point, someone figured out they could set up their tents, and store the goods bought in bulk from these traders to provide a more permanent place for people to get what they needed WHEN they needed it.

From that point forward, human ingenuity and innovative thinking began to find ways to *attract* the people to their stalls, booths, and later small shops to buy *more* than what they needed. Throughout the genesis of retailing, the "trick of the trade" was to incite people to come in and buy something, regardless of whether they needed it or not. In Charles Dickens' *A Christmas Carol*, Ebenezer Scrooge yells down from his apartment to a boy in the street asking if the prize turkey is still hanging in the poulterer's shop down on the corner, to which the boy responds, "It's hanging there now!" The "prize turkey" was an advertisement. The poulterer must have purchased it after it won the prize, and decided to make that point known—to everyone who walked past his shop.

The pressure, even in those early days, of selling to the consumer was high. And as the retail mercantile industries grew, the suppliers knew they had to do all they could to help their retail customers sell their products, turn that inventory faster, and buy more product.

The Rise of Co-op Advertising and Channel Incentives Growth

The idea of a manufacturer or supplier providing some tangible incentive to their retailer or distributor, to help promote their products to the buying public, is as old as mercantile itself. Important tasks like inventory management, employee training, and advertising were often supported by an array of tools and information provided to the reseller by the manufacturer. Early in the 18th century, manufacturers would provide preproduced printing plates of product illustrations and descriptions to ensure consistency in the promotion of their products in the local marketplace. While there is no record of any financial payments, clearly this represents a value to both the retailer for not having to pay for the expensive typesetting, and the manufacturer who could be sure the message and product illustration was consistent and accurate throughout the local markets.

As multitier distribution began, manufacturers were unable to keep up with the explosive growth of small town retailers who carried their products and wanted to promote them in their hometown newspapers—also experiencing a monumental growth themselves. Manufacturers found themselves unable to afford to buy advertising in each of these publications, so they had to be selective and only advertise in the largest newspapers in the big cities. This meant they could no longer effectively reach the local market consumers to promote their products.

In 1786, William Taylor established the first advertising agency in London.[8] Volney Palmer opened the first advertising agency in the United States in Philadelphia in 1841.[9] The advertising agency could now produce the advertising and act as the broker/agent for the manufacturer to purchase space in the newspapers.

Many of the larger newspapers across the region began offering rates per agate line of space at a discount from the so-called "national rates" which were usually charged to the manufacturers. This expanded the number of ads the manufacturer could run in the newspapers for the budget they had, but still meant the growing population in more rural areas and small towns would not have visibility to the manufacturer's advertising other than the possible mention of the products advertised by the local retailers.

The services offered by the expanding ad agency industry included the verification of performance—making sure the advertising placed ran in accordance with the size, date, and content paid for. Newspapers had to provide *proof of performance* to the agencies which included the invoiced cost and an actual page of the newspaper on which the advertisement appeared. The ad agency would package this information and create reports which would be sent to the manufacturer's marketing organization in order to be paid for the ad placement services—the primitive beginnings of proof of performance.

Throughout the period from 1840 to 1900, newspapers grew more technically capable in the areas of illustrations, pictures, and lithography. This meant that even small town papers began providing local retailers with the ability to advertise pictures and illustrations of the products they carried. As ad agencies began dominating the space running manufacturer's ads, such as Procter & Gamble's Ivory Soap in 1882, smaller local retailers were unable to compete with large agencies placing ads for national manufacturers. Newspapers began changing pricing structures by segmenting individual rate cards according to the type of advertising placed. National placement pricing was the highest rate, with local advertising benefiting from a much lower discounted rate. The difference between the rates the agencies and/or national manufacturers would pay ranged between 15 and 40% higher on average.

As the newspapers continued to expand their advertising content, the cost the agencies and manufacturers had to pay began to tax their marketing budgets significantly. At the same time, retailers took advantage of the lower local discounted rates and increased ad placement, quickly becoming the largest revenue source for the newspapers. Local retailers began to promote specific products to attract more customers through a broader portfolio of product lines carried in their stores.

The Roots of Trade Channel Promotion

At this point in time, two intervening forces came together to create one of the most important and historic changes in the global consumer products business—the explosive growth of local product advertising, and the development of the first formal channel promotion incentive programs. There is no historical recording of the people, time, and place of this fusion of ideas, but the best possibility is it most probably happened in the period of post-Civil War America.

Retailers demanded that the manufacturer/suppliers begin providing financial assistance to them for promoting their products—both in the newspapers and inside their stores with displays and store signage. The arguments made to their manufacturer sales rep was that it was unfair to place the full burden of cost to the retailer for promoting the manufacturer's product in their local area. They demanded some financial help to defray the cost of promotion.

At the same time, corporate marketing and advertising executives of major consumer products companies struggled with thousands of pages of newspaper tearsheets and reams of paper reports produced by the agencies to show where the ads appeared and where they failed to appear. This was literally a dirty and expensive process which often took months to generate and required the agencies to communicate and gather tearsheets from every newspaper in every market within which the placed ads appeared. This was the process employed by the ad agencies until after the turn of the century.

Seeking a way to expand the ad budgets, or at least stretch the budget to expand the reach into the local markets, advertising and marketing executives began to explore alternatives to high-cost, agency-placed newspaper advertising. Whether the product promotion complaints of the retailers received in the field made it to the executive suites, or the coincidence of brilliance occurred, the idea of leveraging the retailers' ability to buy newspaper ads at a significantly lower price than their agency became an extremely attractive concept.

Shortly after 1900, manufacturers began to set aside a percentage of the net cost of products purchased by the retailers as an allowance they could use to help defray the cost of advertising in local markets. Early programs like this, called *cooperative advertising,* began to spring up across the fast moving consumer packaged goods industry. These allowances, earned from these small percentages of net purchases, were maintained and managed by the manufacturer, either in the marketing or finance departments. The retailers could draw from these allowances (funds) by submitting a claim for their advertising costs, supported by proof of performance in the form of the actual tearsheet showing the ad, the invoice from the newspaper or magazine, and then be reimbursed based on an audit of the documentation by the manufacturer to ensure compliance with the terms and conditions of the co-op advertising program. The manufacturer would keep the record of payments and accounting of the funds to ensure against overpayment of earned allowances. Although the amounts of money accrued from product purchases for most of these programs were rarely published, it was typically an extremely low percentage of around 1% of net purchases.[10]

The die was cast. This began what is now considered to be the second largest line item on the corporate financials for consumer products companies—the spending of trade channel promotion and co-op advertising allowance funds. Now manufacturers could use their wholesale goods price margin to build an entirely new budget, which could be defrayed by slight increases in margin, and take advantage of lower-cost local advertising now placed and managed by their thousands of retail customers across the country. Not only was this a new phenomenon in the USA, but similar provisions were being made by European manufacturers and retailers as well, marking a completely new form of consumer promotion globally.

In the early 20th century, new companies began to spring up to provide services to verify advertising performance in newspapers and magazines by physically receiving, storing and scanning actual tearsheets (the term used to describe an actual page of the newspaper or magazine on which the advertising appeared).

Page after page of ad content were meticulously checked against program requirements to provide proof of performance to the manufacturer so the retailer could be reimbursed.

One such company was the first company I worked for in the industry and mentioned back in Chapter 1.

Because newspaper advertising dominated the promotional tactics in the first half of the 20th century, services provided by companies like this clearly found the sweet spot—verification of performance and an incredible visibility to critical marketing concerns like pricing, product promotion, and ad spending. This expanded marketing intelligence not only paved the way for smarter insights into how to reach the consumer, but it also set the stage for the next level of anticompetitive practices, like price discrimination and disproportionate allocation of incentives.

By the mid-1910s most major product manufacturers were already offering some sort of financial incentive in the form of cooperative advertising allowances earned from product purchases.

In addition to the allowance funding terms, the rather primitive programs which appeared around this time also included basic requirements for content, consisting of instructions on how to describe and define products, what the product illustrations could and could not be, minimum sizes in some cases, and pricing (not a specific price, but the mandate of having a price on the ad).

These "requirements" became the basic genesis of the terms, conditions, and guidelines found in today's modern co-op advertising and trade channel promotion programs. The major areas of governance were:

- Eligibility for participation
- Basis, timing, and requirements for accruing promotional funds
- Advertising media, and cost covered and approved
- Percentage of reimbursement
- Payment

Of course, the most critical and controversial area of concern was *how much money* each retailer or distributor would receive. It did not take long for the retail and distribution companies to begin questioning the policies of allocation of funding, specifically weighing their own size, stature, and reputations in the local marketplace as legitimate drivers of a need for more money than some other smaller retailer or distributor. The manufacturers began listening to these arguments and were pressured by both their customers and internal sales executives to consider practical responses to these demands.

While these newly published programs represented attempts to regulate fairness in funding and payment policies, it did not stop the less visible practices of financial offers of higher fund accrual rates, and flat amount payments to the largest retail customers. Pandora's Box was located, cobwebs brushed off, and latches disengaged.

"It's a Free Concert Now."

In August 1969, the famous Woodstock Music and Art Fair took place in a beautiful setting of rolling hills owned by farmer Max Yasgur near Bethel, NY. Thirty-two acts of some of the greatest rock and roll artists in history performed over a three-day period during sporadic thundershowers. The promoters erected fences around the venue with ticket gates at multiple locations to control entry into the concert.

Before the event even officially started, more than 50,000 people crammed into the area in front of the stage, and just several hours into the event, people had trampled down the fences to get in. The public address announcer casually announced, "It's a free concert now,"[11] eliminating the ticket rules and creating one of the most expensive losses in music history. A similar fate has befallen trade promotion.

Since the early 1900s, the pattern of discriminatory practices around advertising allowances had been a major cause for so many legal actions brought by plaintiffs who were financially injured due to unfair offerings of money and services to larger channel customers. In today's modern co-operative advertising and trade promotion practices of consumer products industries, great care is taken to ensure the terms and conditions of supplier programs are not only fair but enforced equally and proportionately across all competing channel customers.

After more than 50 years of discriminatory practices around trade promotion and advertising allowances, the 1970s brought a huge influx of changes into the consumer products industries. But none seemed more disrupting than the transfer of control of payment transactions from the manufacturers that received, processed, and reimbursed the claims to the large retail chains, who began deducting claim amounts directly off of the checks they paid to the manufacturers and suppliers for product. The promotion program rules that established the governance for payment of claims were being ignored.

The "fences" were coming down, and manufacturers were slowly losing control of not only the actual reimbursement of promotion claims, but soon to come, the entire content of the promotion. How could this happen with a supposedly active Federal

Trade Commission who recently won a couple of important judgments against retailers and manufacturers for anticompetitive practices, and was now focused on advertising allowances as a major source of discriminatory action?

Universally across industries, the terms for trade promotion, co-op advertising, and market development funding programs were rather straightforward. Channel customers were to conduct promotions within the scope of approved tactical activities, submit indisputable proof of performance with actual copies or representations of the advertisement, invoices with actual net costs, and be paid *only* for those costs—nothing more, nothing less.

On top of that proof of performance and cost, the submitting channel reseller is paid *to the limit of the funds earned and no more.*

The exception to this practice is the modern fast-moving consumer goods, or consumer packaged goods industry (CPG).

I use the term *modern* in this description because the CPG industry channel incentive practices began with the same policies and procedures as all other consumer products programs up to the early 1980s in America. Claims were submitted with proof of performance and cost documentation, and CPG manufacturers would audit the documentation and provide payment at rates of reimbursement in the 50% range generally.

Today's CPG trade promotion practices have evolved in a completely unique and different manner than all other industries. This evolution was not a wholesale rejection of the usual standard practices of claim documentation, submission, and settlement. Rather, it was a result of financial pressures that resulted from the combination of rapidly declining margins on product and lengthy turnaround times for ad and promotion claims processing by the CPG manufacturers and suppliers.

As stated in Chapter 2, the high product turnover, inventory velocity, and competitive price actions resulted in some of the lowest, if not THE lowest, product profit margins in any consumer products industry sector. The intensity of shelf space competition and the speed of product turns among the top CPG brands generally required the manufacturers' field sales reps and key account managers (KAMs) to help with immediate support of certain locally initiated activities, such as local instore flyers and the placement of displays.

This usually involved a small amount of funds within a checking account from which, at their discretion, the rep or KAM could write a small check to help cover more immediate, yet small ancillary costs. Generally, these checks would be less than two hundred dollars—but the practice set up a discretionary funding mechanism through which the sales reps and KAMs could control and disburse.

Because of the nature of the speed and frequency of product promotions in the predominantly grocery retail chains, the number of claims that had to be prepared, documented, and submitted to the manufacturers for reimbursement soon overwhelmed the internal teams at the CPG manufacturer's headquarters. This created a huge backlog of claim processing and often led to great delays in reimbursement, as much as 90 to 120 days. This meant the retailers, already suffering huge margin hits, often went into the red awaiting reimbursement. Whether via check payments or credits against future orders, the retailers' open-to-buy ratios (the amount of money and product inventory volume they would be able to afford in a specific time period) dropped below safety thresholds which ensured enough inventory in each store to generate revenues by adequately stocking shelves and supporting promotional offers to the consumers.

The combination of the delayed reimbursement, and the growing costs of the retailers' own internal personnel to assemble documentation, log, submit, and track status of claims to CPG suppliers for the potentially more than 28,000 individual products they carry in their retail stores,[12] soon forced one of the most significant changes to the business practice of trade promotion in history—the *deduction of promotional cost* from the payment for goods to the manufacturer. Initially, this action was taken for specific claims that were more than 90 days old, but soon became standard operating procedure in the CPG channels.

The failure of the manufacturers to clear and pay claims within a reasonable timeframe created an increasingly untenable situation for retailers and was beginning to impact corporate financial sustainability. Costs for promotions were real—cost of media advertising placement and production, overhead cost to erect and manage displays, and of course the cost of price reductions on products placed on promotion. Even by 1980s figures, $1 billion dollars of product purchases annually would generate $130,000,000 in promotion allowances. If interest rates were around 1% per month, the difference in receiving reimbursement in 30 days or less, versus 90 to 120 days, would be more than $1,300,000 annually.[13] So the pain felt by all major retailers awaiting lengthy claim turnaround times by the manufacturer was real.

The practice of deducting certain costs and expenses by retailers was not new. Retailers would deduct for many reasons including missing shipments, incorrect product shipped, spoils, and so on. But the idea of deducting for promotional costs without first furnishing documented proof of cost and performance was novel. And bold.

This became one of the many issues tackled by the Food Marketing Institute (FMI) when it was formed in 1977.[14] The company recently rebranded using the "FMI" acronym to signify *Food Marketplace Inc.* and focuses on the retailer as the primary "heart" of the food industry. In a seminar in 1991, Timothy M. Hammonds, then Executive Vice President for Research and Education of the FMI, stated "Approximately 80% of invoice deductions are caused by not understanding the terms and conditions of promotional programs."[15] While there was no doubt there were situations where retailers were confused with certain CPG programs which were often vaguer in their requirements and guidelines, I would have to challenge Mr. Hammonds' statement.

Because I sat on the front lines of this fight, in my experience, deductions were taken to avoid the massive delays in reimbursement by the manufacturers/suppliers. The manufacturers reacted with a mass of complaints and challenges to the FTC.[16] The deduction practice grew despite recommendations against such practices by the FTC.

At MEDIANET, we managed one of the most active and largest trade promotion programs for one of the world's top CPG companies, and the volume of claims received was truly overwhelming. As efficient and quick as we were in turning claims around, it still took between 45 and 60 days to audit, respond to questions, seek help from the retailers, and work through unauthorized deductions before we could clear and pay the claims. We had sophisticated technology to manage high volumes of complex ad and promotion claims, so it is easy to understand how manufacturers, with nothing but spreadsheets and primitive database management systems, could take 90-120 days to reimburse the retailers for their claims.

Right here. Right. Here. This is where the practice of deduction from merchandise remittances as the primary settlement methodology for promotions in the consumer packaged goods industry began. Buoyed by the pressure from major retail chains constituting huge percentages of CPG manufacturer revenues along with industry trade groups like FMI, the justification for these deviations became universal.

In fact, the ability to take the deduction and recoup the cost of promotions immediately became an attractive new standard for promotion settlement. Retailers began to change their internal practices of documenting and submitting claims and began informing the CPG manufacturers and suppliers that the amount of the claim would be *automatically* deducted from the next check for products and that the manufacturer was *always welcome* to come into the HQ location and conduct their audits of that documentation themselves.

The CPG manufacturers cried foul, sent complaints to the FTC, and threatened to cut off some of their best customers. Accounts receivables executives were on the warpath, hunting down the field sales reps and key account managers to explain why these huge sums of money were being deducted and what, exactly, they were. The largest CPG companies were scrambling to set up entire departments of people dedicated to tracking down the source and reasons for the deductions.

Throughout the 1980s the practice of deductions grew to become standard operating procedure for promotional settlements. By the beginning of 1990, every CPG company had formalized *deduction management teams* who did nothing but research and clear deducted amounts for promotions. It was a full-blown industry norm now, and the numerical statistics associated with deduction management were beginning to be viewable from space.

In 1990, the Grocery Manufacturers Association (now known as the Consumer Brands Association) partnered with FMI to create the Joint Industry Committee on Deductions. This was the first real attempt to quantify the issue of deduction management and to identify and hopefully resolve some of the sticky issues that surrounded this controversial process:[17]

- Invoice deductions represented 3% to 7% of a manufacturer's sales, on average, adding up to more than $10 billion USD in sales annually.

- During the 1980s, the deductions grew between 15% and 20% annually.

- Direct costs to the industry for processing and transacting deductions were estimated at 0.10% of sales, or the equivalent of hundreds of millions of dollars annually.

- The administrative costs of managing deductions were averaging as high as $3 million to $4 million annually.

- Buyers, key account managers, and sales representatives were reportedly spending between 10% and 50% of their time in each appointment dealing with deduction issues.

Twenty-five years later, in a 2015 survey,[18] Attain Consulting Group produced a sweeping examination of the deduction issue across multiple industries. In fact, the practice of deductions has moved into most consumer products industries including fashion, hardware/DIY, consumer electronics, toys, HVAC, office products, home furnishings, software, pharma, cosmetics and just about any sector that sells products through a channel of distribution.

According to the survey, more than 500 respondents reported that nearly half (48%) of their primary customers were retailers with another 25% being wholesale/distributors, so this is the heart of the source of deductions for consumer products. There are other reasons for a channel customer deducting off-invoice for merchandise payments, but advertising and promotional discounts represent far and away the lion's share of deductions received.[19]

When deducting from check payments to manufacturers became virtually standard operating procedure for promotional settlements in consumer products, it set off a wave of new practices which further strained the channel-supplier relationships. Retailers began to look back at prior-year promotional activity and identified promotions which they either were not able to claim or were paid at less than the claimed amounts.

They began to deduct these charges as well, sending newly organized deduction management teams digging back into past activities to attempt to understand and reconcile these deductions. The funding year was closed, so these deductions were without funding or allocation of budget, driving the overall trade spending through the roof.

The new practice was called "Post-audit Deductions" and was soon to become the bane of many CFOs. In a 1994 conversation with the CFO of one of today's top-ten CPG companies, I addressed the problem of post audit deductions. He turned every shade of red when I brought it up and would have probably spit on the floor if it was a nice hardwood surface. "I'll tell you what," he said. "If someone comes in here and tells me I have to pay for an ad or display that they say we missed two years ago, my first inclination is to call security!" He said that, for the first time, his post-audit deductions totaled almost 25% of the total deductions received, and he and his team had to take action with the customers themselves.

"In a conference call with our counterpart CFOs of our top ten retail customers, I made it clear that post-audit deductions would not be tolerated any longer." He paused, looked up and closed his eyes for a moment, then looked me squarely in the eyes. "You know what they said? They said that they were not going to stop, and that it was unfair to them that these promotions were not paid for, and certainly not our place to reduce the amounts they say they spent."

This was the story across the country, and so much so that several companies started full service practices representing the retailers by going into their files and digging out old promotions to deduct. Today, these companies are going strong, and as with the entire deduction process itself, post-audit deductions are a widely accepted practice. Most CPG companies have created strict rules governing the way the post-audit deductions are being handled. One of the better and more detailed policies are those of Johnsonville, LLC where the rules for acceptance of post-audit deductions include definitions, timelines, documentation, and compliance policies for promotion, non-promotion and shipping post-audit deductions.[20]

Evolving the Promotion Plan

With the rapid growth of mass merchandising and expansion of chain store locations, the retail industry not only had the power, but wielded it heavily, despite the continued paper tiger enforcement from the FTC of Robinson-Patman Act sections 2(d) and 2(e). Even an updated and amended publication of the "Guides," now sporting a tacit approval of deductions providing that they did not create an anticompetitive environment or condition in the market, seemed to favor the growing deduction practice. The CPG manufacturers were split internally, with field sales forces supporting the practices, even though they were spending so much time tracking, tracing, and identifying the basis for the unauthorized deductions.

Another transition took hold in the consumer packaged goods industry around the way promotions were planned and executed. Unlike historical practices of documented claim submissions and accounts payable transactions, the *planning* of promotions became an extremely critical process, especially in view of the need to validate a deduction. Because deductions were being taken without documentation, the responsibility for validating proof of performance was clearly in the manufacturer's/ supplier's court.[21]

Few, if any, manufacturers took up the mantle of going on-site at the retailer's headquarters and researching cost and performance documentation. As a result, the alternative was to adopt the "honor system" of sorts and change the rigors of compliance from the receipt and audit of documented claims to using field sales reps and field merchandising teams to do representative checks of retailer locations to validate that the promotions were in place with displays, advertising, price discounts, and other visible tactical activities which correlated and aligned with the "plan."

The *promotion plan* was becoming a detailed document which specified customer account, promotion timing, product, tactics, and costs. Costs, by the way, became an entirely new form. Instead of the hard net costs of promotional media, production, and distribution, that would have been documented in a claim, *cost* for each tactic became whatever the retailer said it was. Sales reps and key account managers (KAMs) generally accepted this new methodology, and the process of planning between the reps and their retail buyer and merchandising counterparts began to take on a split visibility to benefit—retailer desiring enough money to guarantee a successful promotion and the KAM wanting to get the volume at a margin that supports his/her forecast requirement.

With the mounting pressure on field sales reps and (KAMs) to grow the volume, traditional forecast objectives became even more intense amidst the heavy competition within the category and brand. The retailer's ability to dictate and mandate cost terms quickly grew trade promotion spending demands annually, driving the trade promotion budget higher than the corporate marketing budgets for most CPG companies. The focus was on volume—driven by the need to achieve forecast and the retailers' increased appetite for funding to help drive consumers into the stores and increase the overall profitability. KAMs were less focused on the latter, concentrating their budget allocations on higher incentives for the retailer to purchase larger volumes of product.

This combination of retailer-driven mandates for more promotional funding, and the willingness of account sales executives to relent and make the money available, caused an explosion of exponential proportions, increasing the average trade promotion spending from 4% in 1930 to over 20% by 2019.[21,22] For major CPG companies, this can be as high as 30% of gross revenue today.

Promotion plans, whether done on spreadsheets, home-grown technology, or vendor trade promotion management and execution (TPx) technology, formed the entire basis of compliance when the retailers deducted or, in a reducing number of cases, claims submitted for payment. The structure of most common promotion plans included information about the product shipping dates (to support the anticipated sales response), the individual tactics or promotional activities, the amount of cost for each activity, and the total cost of the promotion or "deal."

BASIC PROMOTION PLAN FORM

PROMO ID   246887

ACCOUNT   Any Store
TERRITORY   Southwest

SHIPPING DATE: 8/15/2021

FROM DATE	TO DATE	TACTIC/ACTIVITY	DESCRIPTION	COST	
10/1/2021	10/6/2021	Price Reduction	$1.00 off	$	12,000.00
10/1/2021	10/6/2021	Display	End Cap	$	2,500.00
10/1/2021	10/6/2021	Advertisement	Instore Flyer	$	5,000.00
			TOTAL PLAN	$	19,500.00

Figure 3.1 Basic Components of the Promotional Planning Form

Ideally, the typical promotion plan form was designed to provide two key functions. First, it serves as the contract between the CPG supplier and the retailer, wholesale/distributor, or reseller which contains both the details and the joint commitment for purchase of product and provision of the funding incentive to promote to the consumer.

Second, it would form the basis of compliance verification by enabling field merchandiser reps to know what to look for when they make their instore visits, and for the deduction management personnel to research when the deduction would be received.

As a legal document, however, the promotion plan forms lack the terms, conditions, and language binding the retailer to the negotiated *deal*.

Because of numerous real unplanned market or business issues, the retailer could, and often did, change the promotional event dates, change the order for product, omit or fail to perform one or more of the tactics and change the cost.

Key account managers had to stay vigilant and monitor promotions to ensure the order was fulfilled, and the event was held as committed. The retailer suffered as well, with missing products in the shipment, missing or failed shipping schedules, and conflicting corporate marketing offers on the same products they were promoting in the store events.

The promotion plan, as a *proof of performance* basis, was supposed to guide the validation and settlement of deductions. Practically, it did little of that. Early deduction management processes rarely included any data on the check with the deduction that pointed to any of this data. Outside of a valid starting point, the early promotion plans were often inadequate to validate or audit for compliance and proof of performance.

This was a typical complaint from both the trade promotion management and financial executives. Between 1980 and 2000, the deduction processes improved dramatically, with better technology, retailer systems able to sync the deduction identification to specific promotion plan line items, and of course more rigorous (and overly expensive) instore field merchandising audits.

All this change in the so-called co-op advertising foundational paradigms of channel incentive operations changed the course of business in consumer goods forever, especially for FMCG.

The incredible rise in trade promotion funding and spending in the past fifty years, coupled with the new way of working together in trade channel promotion planning, execution, and settlement was, at the end of the day, necessary given the rapid pace of change in the consumer shopping habits and the channels of distribution that serve them.

There were, and still are, abuses on both sides of the consumer packaged goods channel, and the amounts of money transacted and managed to engage the consumer dwarfs any other single industry sector. The federal authorities have done little over the years to enforce any regulatory statutes that impact the way business is done, and the opportunity for a small independent food products retailer to survive in today's economy is virtually zero.

This chapter is entitled "The World's Third-Oldest Profession" because as with prostitution, political abuses, harsh criminal behavior like murder, extortion and treason, no matter what seemingly well-intended law, regulation or "guideline" is derived from the legislative process, operational interpretations of resulting practices around trade promotion and channel incentives can be controversial and questionable. As consumers, we want the low cost, convenient and attractive environments when we shop. For brick and mortar retailers, this means continuing to leverage this trade promotion money to build profit and to incite the shopper to visit rather than order online. That means the deals must continue, the trade promotion funds will certainly continue to be the majority of the manufacturers' corporate marketing budgets, and the invisible ocean of money it takes to keep prices low on the shelf will continue to rise.

Amidst those dire consequences and frankly scary scenarios, however, the good news is that trade promotion in all its forms of channel incentives has become a critical mission in the quest for consumer engagement. New technologies are creating collaborative platforms which can and will maximize efficiency and optimize the shopping experience for the retailer, the manufacturer/supplier, and the consumer.

CHAPTER 4

THE CONSUMER CHAIN

The staggering level of money which drives the Invisible Economy of consumer engagement has begun to shift from a traditional focus on the business-to-business relationship and the need to drive pure sales volumes back to the consumer—again.

The original intention of modern trade promotion, co-op advertising, and most all other channel incentives may have always been ostensibly on supporting the retailer, wholesaler, or distributor attraction of the consumer to shop and purchase in their stores. However, as we documented in Chapter 3, the consumer seemed to become a secondary objective over the past 60 years. However, with the erupting digital economy and the impact of social media, e-commerce, and mobile communications, it's a whole new ballgame.

For consumer products manufacturing companies, the processes and functions which begin with the production of the product in the factory (or harvesting of produce in the fields) and ends on the retailer shelf or online listing are collectively called the *supply chain*. The supply chain includes the combined processes of demand planning, manufacturing, warehousing, shipping, receiving, stocking, and inventory management. Modern analysts may also include procurement of raw materials in that definition as well.

The intent of the supply chain is to define the consumer demand and get the right products to the right retailers in the right quantities and at the right time to ensure meeting the sales forecast. Most manufacturers work hard to understand what we consumers want and when, where, and how much we will spend to buy their products. With all the billions of dollars spent on consumer marketing, and especially trade channel promotion, why are they only marginally successful at creating sustainable loyalty?

Perhaps it is because they do not truly understand, or at least effectively respond to, how a consumer moves from a *need* to a *buy*, to *satisfaction*.

The Day the Earth (and my retail grocery store) Stood Still

The Covid-19 pandemic of 2020 was one of the most significant non-wartime disruptions of the supply chain in the modern history of humanity. As consumers, we stood in long lines, wearing masks, keeping six-feet apart, and waiting for a chance to get inside to take our small one-package allocation of toilet tissue and shop the near empty shelves of whatever else we could drop into our shopping baskets. Clearly a lot of people found themselves consuming a menu variety based on *availability of products* rather than a desire for what to eat for dinner. This is the total opposite intention of an efficient and responsive supply chain.

Fears of death and lockdowns (in that order) clearly caused panic buying which quickly cleared the shelves and limited or shut down manufacturing and shipping throughout the months of March through May 2020 in most of the country, and in some states continuing in some capacity through the summer of 2021. However, in most western countries, and specifically here in North America, the pandemic-driven supply chain disruption was, for the most part, surprisingly short-lived. The major supermarket food chains executed emergency replenishment plans that leveraged alternative manufacturing, warehousing, and shipping systems throughout the nation to keep doors open, stock on shelves, and shoppers safe.

Here in Texas, H-E-B Stores, one of the largest supermarket chains in North America, already had a prepared plan in case of calamitous situations like hurricanes, which had been well-tested with recent events from Hurricane Katrina in 2005 to 2017's Hurricane Harvey, tied with Katrina as the costliest hurricane in history.[23] Taking immediate action, H-E-B was able to keep its shoppers reasonably stocked and performed heroically in the process.

H-E-B Stores had built and tested their supply chain resilience strategy, ready to execute. Sensing the difficulty and communicating with retail chains all over the world, H-E-B prepared a full scale rollout of an emergency plan which included reducing store hours, increasing salaries of employees, and scrambled corporate executives to executing emergency purchase contracts with secondary suppliers, driving trucks, and working the warehouses. The consuming public, of which I am one, took advantage of the quick H-E-B turnaround to weather one of the most devastating economic and personal hardships our country has had to endure.[24]

Several retail chains and online e-commerce vendors had to respond in similar fashion. With manufacturing operations in total shutdown, states in total lockdown, and people fearing the worse, mercantile in the USA slowed, but quickly began recovering—a testament to the supply chain resiliency and sustainability that's been built over the past 100 years. Throughout all the danger, damage, unemployment, and political nonsense, the consumer maintained an air of resiliency of their own amidst a heavily taxing change to virtual work and family life. Turning to e-commerce even more than in previous years, the American consumer purchased over $860 billion in 2020 compared to $598 billion in 2019, a jump of more than 44%.[25]

Retailers had to adapt, and some could not. For instance, curbside pickup expanded considerably with consumers not wanting to leave the confines of their vehicles to shop and buy products they wanted and/or needed. According to Digital Commerce 360 and the US Department of Commerce, there was a huge expansion of stores offering curbside pickup options and systems. In 2019, only 6.9% of the top 500 Digital Commerce 360 retailers offered this service. By August 2020, 43.7% of those same stores now offered curbside pickup.[26] What this did for so many retailers teetering on the brink of the financial abyss was nothing short of survival.

While *survival* may have been an end result for many retailers, pleasing the consumer was quickly becoming top of mind. The Covid-19 pandemic has changed the way people look at almost everything in their lives, but for the merchants (brick-and-mortar as well as e-commerce), it represents a deviation, planned or unplanned, from the standards of operation which require changes in infrastructure as well as how the consumer is viewed.

Addressing the Consumer

This chapter defines the way a consumer acquires goods for themselves, their household, or their company. The term *consumer* is anyone who acts as a *buyer* of products and services and consumes, uses, or accesses the product or service. It usually applies to an individual, however, it can also apply to a *group* of individuals, as in a committee which is in place to decide about which office furniture or computer server system to acquire for their company, school, or organization.

There is a natural progression a person typically goes through to become a consumer. It begins with the feeling or desire for something to fulfil a particular need, and continues through the process of researching, deciding, buying, consuming (using), and deciding if they are satisfied with the end result, product, or service.

If you add to that the expansion of the well-worn process of sharing opinions of the good or service with someone else which social media has blessed us with, you now have a complete loop.

This is the *Consumer Chain.*

Of course, the variations on the term *consumer* and the resulting *consumption* of the good or service are voluminous across the Consumer Chain. The uniqueness of that process will depend upon the specific procurement requirement and use case. We will address those in some important examples within this chapter, however the focus of this book will concentrate on the individual as the consumer—the shopper.

Figure 4.1 The 13 Steps of the Consumer Chain

Now, think of the methods used by manufacturers and resellers to lure us in. Advertising, coupons, transit signs, outdoor billboards, program sponsorships, and even apparel are all media vehicles used by manufacturers/suppliers to get our attention.

The resellers depend on local advertising, direct mailers and preprinted inserts into the newspapers, and all manner of in-store promotional tactics like banners, stickers on the floor, shelf tags, displays at the ends of each aisle (endcaps), and the plethora of last-minute deals (impulse purchases) while you are standing in the checkout lanes. But of course, one of the most valuable and effective methods of promotion is price—the reduction of the standard price over a temporary period of time.

Every nickel of that money is paid for or funded by the manufacturer/supplier. As we said in earlier chapters, most of those funded promotions fail to attract enough shopper interest to offset the high cost of the promotions themselves.

Why?

To answer that question, we need to understand the individual *links* to the *Consumer Chain* and what can be done to impact each one.

Impacting the Links of the Consumer Chain

The level of sophistication now evident in the modern engagement of consumers is going to further tax the trade channel promotion paradigms because of the way CPG manufacturers typically manage their trade promotion programs and processes. So, trade spending levels we see today, which approach 30% of gross revenues for the largest consumer products companies, are likely to experience a new incremental increase, exponentially higher than the patterns of the past two or three decades. To understand the reasoning for this projection, we need to consider what the *Consumer Chain* is and how it impacts the typical buying process of the consumer.

We will dissect the components to gauge the way modern trade channel promotion funding, execution, and performance measurement paradigms must change to achieve success in the *Consumer Chain*. Leading consumer products companies already know this, and many are becoming adept at creating promotions which focus on triggering the consumer response for each of these links in the chain.

Identifying the Need

Identifying a Need

"I want..."

What	Why	When
...a Steak	Have not had one in a while	
T-Bone...	My favorite cut	
...for Dinner tonight	Nothing in the pantry	
...with a Baked Potato	Always compliments steak	
...with Butter	Of course	
...Cheese	Always	
...Chives	That's nice	Tonight!
...Bacon	Love the taste	
...Sour Cream	My usual	
...Lite Sour Cream	Need to reduce fat intake	
...and Asparagus	Need a steamed green veggie	
...with a bottle of Cabernet Sauvignon	My favorite wine	

Figure 4.2 The First Link in the Consumer Chain—Identify a Specific Need

Everything starts with a brain synapse firing in the direction of a desire, and a rapid-fire string of supporting data. I'm hungry. I'm hungry for a steak. I want a ribeye steak. I want it for dinner tonight. I want baked potatoes with that. I want butter, cheese, bacon, sour cream, and chives on that potato, and I would like fresh asparagus with it. Oh, and a great bottle of cabernet sauvignon would top off a *bon appétit*.

Most marketers will tell you this is where you create demand, and they would be right. Typically, consumer products companies will generate interest in the product through broad national and regional advertising campaigns to attract the attention of the consumer. Beer and alcoholic beverage companies are notorious for creating broadcast commercials and print ads to stimulate the senses and promote their beer, wine, whiskey or whatever as the only way to satisfy the craving they hope to incite.

A fundamental question, however, is how a retailer can do the same? They cannot afford ritzy commercials for specific products, so they must count on the manufacturer's ad campaigns to create and stimulate the *need* and *desire* for the products they sell and hope to leverage that consumer desire by providing a location where the need or desire can be satisfied in the form of a purchase. But does that strategy suffice today in a rapidly evolving digital marketplace?

Traditionally, the brick-and-mortar retailers did not concern themselves with the issue of creating and stimulating a *need* in the consumer's mind, but rather used their trade promotion funds to build displays, reduce pricing, and ensure sufficient stock of the product on the shelf when the consumer shops—assuming the consumer walks in already knowing what they want. Now however, with the intense competition of e-commerce, where the buyer can get the visual stimulation of a need or desire through a video or attractive visual, and then see the product, price, and descriptions right in front of their eyes, the retailers have to up their game to begin stimulating *need* as well.

But wait. Is it not true that manufacturers have been successful at creating demand through intensive research into what the consumer wants, where and how they shop, prices they will accept, packaging that attracts them, and clever advertising that stimulates desire for the product? How can all this creativity and scientific analysis still fail to generate tangible success in trade channel incentive promotions?

Because if the shopper has no feeling of *need* for the product or service, they simply will not be interested and will not buy. The typical trade promotion incentive, for the most part, is not as appealing as it could be. For instance, one of the actions retailers and manufacturers/suppliers count on is impulse buying. This is traditionally more effective inside the store than online because of the visual stimulation the shopper has as they move through the aisles of the store putting their selections in their carts.

Even though impulse purchases have reduced significantly, due primarily to the pandemic of 2020, there are ways to target specific links in the *Consumer Chain* to increase the chances of an impulse buy.

In August 2020 during the pandemic, *Field Agent* reported that shoppers purchased 38% *less* products on impulse than previous years' averages.[27] The majority of those respondents cited the pressures of unemployment and the need to save money as the primary reason. But think about how you felt walking into a store with rows and rows of empty shelves. Your keen senses were heightened, and you looked closer at the products that were left to get what you needed. Your brain was telling you your shopping list is now out the window, and you have to get creative for the next few meals—and what options exist for toilet paper substitutes. You began to think of what you truly need, and that stimulated far more unplanned buying than ever before.

Impulse buying is indicative of standard consumer behavior shopping in a physical retailer location. For that reason, the most important consideration both the retailer and the manufacturer/supplier should have is to optimize this visual advantage. This is exactly the type of tactical plan which can leverage the *Consumer Chain* to increase the size of the shopper's market basket by building promotions that stimulate *need*. There needs to be more alignment between the sophistication of consumer marketing and the instore impact of the trade channel promotions because what happens now is often unsynchronized promotional calendars that fail to capitalize on both national and local brand and product promotion strategy. All too often, this leads to confusion in the marketplace and worse—direct conflict in product promotion and price incentives. Shoppers do not spend much time instore trying to determine what the difference is— they simply walk away.

What is required is a more concentrated attempt by both the retailer and the manufacturer/supplier to *appeal* to the shopper—to create the promotional opportunity that aligns with their desires, needs, and wishes. The shopper needs to see alignment between what they see on TV at night and what is promoted on the shelf or online when they shop.

If there is one thing the Covid-19 pandemic showed us, it's if we do not *need* a product, we will not buy it. It is clear that trade channel promotions, especially instore displays, and low prices, can be designed to stimulate impulse purchases, but that depends upon randomness and the off-chance a shopper would come into eye contact with the product and just happened to decide to buy. We already have too many promotions that are based on "off-chance" and subsequently fail to generate the successful outcomes which were planned.

There have been so many books, articles, blogs, and speeches on the psychology of consumerism, and many on the best way to create demand by inciting desire for a particular product, beginning with curiosity, and ending with fulfillment (in our theme here, let's call it the decision to seek out and buy something). In the recognition of this first major link in the *Consumer Chain*, how can we improve our chances of successful trade promotion spending by creating *need*?

In his 1954 article in the *British Journal of Psychology*, Daniel Berlyne postulated that the aforementioned *curiosity* is broken down into two types: Diversive and Specific.[28] A *diversive* curiosity would be more informal or spontaneous but focused on an intellectual or physical uniqueness or experiential issue. On the other hand, a *specific* curiosity would apply to something more tangible—a particular product or service, for instance. This is more applicable to product marketing and a consumer's thoughts toward something he or she would need. In our case here, we would be talking about the *need* of a steak for dinner.

Berlyne went a bit further to show how curiosity is itself impacted through complexity, conflict, uncertainty, and novelty—all acting upon the initial complexity to produce a logical train of thinking.

In a consumer's daily life, the environment plays on the mind and categorizes experiences through these stimuli to create curiosity, which in turn creates interest and drives ongoing personal attention until either a satisfactory conclusion yields the desire to acquire, or simply fulfills an intellectual informational gap.

A critical component of his logic and theory is there is a "sweet spot," of sorts (my terms, not Berlyne's) which calibrates the level of curiosity and determines whether action is taken or not. While his explanation is a bit deeper than we need to go into here, essentially it means that the stimuli can be too high or too low—either of which will result in no action.

For a consumer product application, it would need to be tempered—fitting the individual comfort level of the curious person. For instance, the <u>cost</u> of the subject product of curiosity must be within a range of acceptability by a consumer. If too high or, sometimes too low, curiosity wanes and the consumer moves on.

Using Berlyne's hypothesis referring to a *specific curiosity*, then, the consumer either smiles with the satisfaction of knowing something about a product that was not previously known, or they *want one*. When the latter occurs, a *need* is created and defined, which begins the *Consumer Chain* reaction and continues through to a decision to continue to need and continue to buy.

Given that corporate marketing departments in a consumer product company are responsible for the initial generation of consumer desire or need, their role will be to research the consumer marketplace to understand what the consumer needs, and what motivates interest. Translating that research into strategic direction in the type and content of media used to reach the consuming public, we know the promotional event and advertising calendars will be tuned to strike at the right time and place, with the message designed to hopefully stimulate the demand for the product.

In fact, if you consider how much the average consumer products company spends on consumer marketing, it is about 11% of gross revenues.[29] However, the average spending on trade promotion is around 25%,[30] more than twice the cost of building the initial consumer interest and demand. Going by those statistics, then, shouldn't trade promotion spending at least *significantly contribute* to building that "need" in the consumer?

Yes, it should. But instead, trade promotions are, at least in theory, designed to appeal to a consumer who already knows what they need and want, and basically points them to a place where they can buy it and the price they will pay. So at least from the perspective of the manufacturer of the product, it seems quite unbalanced.

This is the source of lament of so many in the corporate marketing organizations who have seen their budgets drain over the last five decades in favor of funding trade channel promotions. But in this digital do-it-myself world we live in, the consumer is quite content with the lower prices which are subsidized by trade promotion funding.

Keeping the engines of mercantile running strong is the purpose for all channel incentive promotion programs, but there are some particularly good opportunities to support the *need* factor in the *Consumer Chain*. The amount of money spent in the Invisible Economy is great enough to impact and direct the action taken by the consumer once that need is identified.

Researching the Product

Product Research

"Which kind of steak?"

Question	Findings
What type of steak is best?	Ribeye, ¾", slightly marbled
Best way to cook it?	Grill over open flame, charcoal – not gas
How do I want it?	Medium Rare is best
How long will it take me (So I can plan)	3.5 Minutes per side – 7 minutes max
Price Range?	$8.00 - $10.00
Best type of marinating solution?	Teriyaki and garlic rub, plain salt and pepper

Figure 4.3 Second Link In the Consumer Chain—Product Research

Using our "need" example of wanting to eat steak for dinner, the next step a consumer typically takes is research. While it might not be as laborious an effort as researching new lawn mowers, cars, or washing machines, it is the natural follow-on questions which must be answered. Deciding now on what *kind* of steak, how thick, how to cook it, and how to flavor or marinate it, are all areas where the trade promotion and channel incentive funds kick in. This is also the point where marketing and sales promotions should naturally merge and align.

You buy your meat at the grocery store or a meat market. OK, in some cases maybe you have it delivered to your home; but what about those other questions that come after the need is identified? Makers of products like meat tenderizers, marinades, salt, pepper, and sauces all get to *accelerate* the need through the senses—how great would this teriyaki marinade taste with your next steak—*that* would be the content for a national advertisement, to be sure. However, most consumers already have a preference in most cases, so the chances of a 30-second commercial creating a *need* to buy a certain branded marinade sauce is rather slim. Instead, the most effective use of the money would be to appeal to the consumer's sense of taste for a particular marinade while they shop—perhaps a companion display for marinade or seasoning at the meat counter, for example.

Better yet, as you shop, there is a small booth next to the meat counter where a demonstrator is cooking steak and offering taste samples of a nice ribeye with a new marinade sauce. And, oh, by the way, it is on sale for 50% off! Take one, please (leveraging the sense of taste and contributing to the shopper's ***need*** to have their steak taste like THIS tonight)!

This combines two tactical types of promotional activities: the temporary price reduction (TPR), and the demonstration. The cost of signage and perhaps a display behind the demo booth will also come out of the trade promotion funds, to be sure. Leading retailers also know how to turn the quest for a steak into something more by combining the *needed* product with other products to stimulate the potential impulse purchase by placing and offering other "companion" products at the point of focus—in this case, the meat counter where the consumer shops for their steak.

Sure, this clearly adds to the shopper's experience, and can create the need factor which drives the impulse buy; but what it really does for the retailer is increase the *profit margin* by bringing products together that are not being promoted at a reduced price. For instance, you can bet that steak being cooked by the demonstrator will not be at a special reduced price, but the marinade will. In addition, there may be a small display of bottles of wine or tenderizer, neither of which will be discounted but both potentially dropped into the shopping basket.

So here again, we see the power of the trade promotion to not only fulfill a consumer's *need*, but to fulfill the retailer's *need* to generate higher revenue and profit. Most shoppers are smart enough to look for these "deals" as they do their product research. It is why the print ads feature attractive images of a nicely marbled ribeye steak with any number of specially-priced products included. Stimulating the senses in the research is the key, but the *pièce de résistance* is to have it right at the meat counter when the consumer picks up the steak.

The next time you get your newspaper, look online, or receive a direct mail piece from the supermarket, take a look at how the products appear in the ad. Notice the location and proximity of the peripheral products and note which ones are at special discount prices. Smart shoppers are doing this when they prepare and research their product lists. The consumer products companies and retail channel know this, which is why and how they leverage their funds to generate the highest amount of interest across multiple products that combine to build higher sales and profit margins.

Researching the Optimal Shopping Experience

Shopping Research

"Where should I shop for it?"

Question	Findings
Grocery Store	Good meat, and I can get the rest of my dinner groceries
Meat Market	Better meat, a bit more expensive, more driving (have to go to grocery to get other items)
Mass Merchandiser (Walmart)	Better prices, but less of a selection and not as fresh
Delivery?	Do I have the time? More expensive option and I don't get to pick the cut

Figure 4.4 *Where Do I Shop* Is Typically a Decision Made Early in the Consumer Chain

Historically, for most consumers, the *location* of the purchase of groceries may be a forgone conclusion—I shop at my local supermarket. Period.

But when grocery dry goods items began showing up on Amazon, as well as the expanding online presence of the retailer channel, things began to change. E-commerce tracking is only two decades old at this point; but with the pandemic-driven stay-at-home purchasing, the percentage of US sales on e-commerce versus brick-and-mortar retailers crossed the 20% figure for the first time ever, at 21.3%.[31]

Certainly, the Covid-19 pandemic created this extraordinary leap in the percent of sales for e-commerce, but it only serves to show that consumers have an even higher number of shopping options than ever before. Some of the sacred brick-and-mortar only products like fresh produce and meats seemed to be immune to the rush to become an e-commerce commodity standard. But even that has changed. With the purchase of Whole Foods Markets by Amazon in 2017, the idea of shopping online for meat and produce is no longer a non-starter for the consumer. Our example here, a prime ribeye steak can easily now be searched online, marbling and all, and ordered for delivery within 24 hours.

The brick-and-mortar retailers have had the leading edge when it comes to creativity with manufacturer-funded tactical promotional activities, and the ability to generate hard profit from the funds offered to them by the major consumer products companies. But e-commerce has stepped in and begun grabbing their own share of this money. The tactics have changed a bit as well, enabling the smart e-commerce players to use video, multi-frame images, and high resolution visuals to attract and appeal to the consumer. With two- and even one-day shipping, and the offering of fresh produce, meat, poultry and fish, the consumer now does all their grocery shopping online.

The brick-and-mortar retailers have not rolled over. Their own e-commerce has picked up steam, and they are now playing the same game as Amazon and Alibaba, leveraging their physical footprint to one-up their e-commerce competition by the offering of *BOPIS*, "Buy Online, Pick-up In Store" for those who still want to go inside the store, as well as "Curbside Delivery," discussed earlier in this chapter where the consumer drives up and has their grocery order put right into their car. This became a huge value during the pandemic, of course, but seems to remain immensely popular as the pandemic weakens, and people begin moving normally outside again.

Both brick-and-mortar and online retailers are fighting hard for every dollar of trade funding available to them, and then some. The growth in promotion funding we discussed back in Chapter 3 has been rather flat for the past several years, but now it seems like the pressure on the key account managers who have responsibility for planning and allocating funds are demanding increased spending levels and higher budget allocations. Manufacturers have a serious dilemma on their hands. Do we borrow more money from the corporate marketing budget to fund trade promotions, or do we raise wholesale prices to generate higher budgets? Both decisions are costly and there will be no help from the retailer community, whose margins are so low that trade promotion funding is the only way they can realistically grow profit.

The e-commerce juggernauts of Amazon and Alibaba have a much higher margin to deal with, but you can bet your bottom trade promotion dollar they will not give in and reduce their own demands. They already feel underserved in trade funds, so this will be a non-starter.

The bottom line for this link in the *Consumer Chain* is the consumer now has two major avenues to pursue to shop, and decisions to make about where and how they shop. The intensity of competition for the consumer's decision where to shop is both undependable and elusive.

Making the Decision to Purchase

Billions of dollars have been spent by both retail and consumer products companies to get the consumer to this point in the *Consumer Chain* journey. This, however, is where the green flag is waved, and the shopping process begins to take on the tangible value.

> **Decision to Purchase**

"Definitely buying the ribeye steak."

Consideration	Action Required
Prepackaged or special cut?	If no good pre-packaged cut, ask the butcher for a special cut
Alternative cut?	If no acceptable ribeye, how about a T-Bone?
Regular or natural?	Look at options in the meat case
Weight of each steak	6 – 8 ounces each, four cuts
Communicate the menu?	Notify the family members in advance

Figure 4.5 The Complex or Simple Decision to Purchase Is a Key Link in the Consumer Chain

In our example above, the consumer determines that ribeye steak is the preferred choice, but an alternative is chosen just in case the *right* ribeye is not available. Throughout the thought process here, the decision to purchase is honed finely into a series of micro-thoughts which support the original need. What kind of marbling or fat content can I get away with? What size steak do I want? Do I want to go with a standard or natural grain-fed beef option, or perhaps one of those fancy Japanese steaks, eh?

Smart retailers use this micro-thought process in their advertisements, and certainly at the point of purchase instore or online where the additional criteria can be easily accessible. This is where the retail trade promotion can be more effective, especially instore where the shopper is facing the product and able to see the options that drive the micro-thought.

For instance, have you shopped for a particular garment, an untucked shirt, perhaps, where the decision to purchase is made, but the color, size, style, or print, is displayed or available on the rack to finalize the purchase decision? Here, online shopping seems a lot easier because the consumer can decide size, then click through color combinations, short or long-sleeved styles, and so on to see what is available. Brick-and-mortar retailers have a tougher time of it because they must ensure case or rack space and make sure to stock all of the options—a higher risk in cost and margin sustainability.

Other purchase decision micro-thoughts include the expected scenarios resulting from the purchase. Again, using our steak example, the consumer will naturally want

43

to make sure everyone in the household will be good with it. If someone has a red meat issue, perhaps a great bone-in pork chop will be a great complementary purchase, for example. Again, leveraging the trade channel promotion content, especially around displays, demonstrations, or embedded consumer reviews, the retailer and the consumer products company can bring all the marketing and sales history data into one place to create a more effective and productive shopping experience.

Can you see how this type of micro-thought reinforcement can extend the value of the money spent on promotions? All too often, even the leading CPG and retail companies overlook this point in the *Consumer Chain* and miss valuable opportunities for upsell and increased margins.

How Will I Purchase?

This is the point in the process where the brick-and-mortar retailer can win or lose the sale. It is, of course, the same for an e-commerce vendor as well. But given the rise in the percentage of e-commerce versus brick-and-mortar retail purchases mentioned earlier, the brick-and-mortar retailer is on the defensive and has the most to lose.

| Decide Purchase Method |

"Definitely buying the steak at my grocery where I can pick up the other items."

Consideration	Action Required
Timing	When do I go? How much time do I have to shop?
Shopping list	Check the pantry and refrigerator, determine what I need to complete the menu
Does the car need gas	Stop at the gas station before going to the store
Parking	Get there early to park near entrance

Figure 4.6 Multiple Purchase Methods Compound the Thought Process for the Consumer

In just one decade, the percentage of sales through e-commerce nearly tripled, rising from 5.6% in 2009 to 15.8% in 2019.[31] The pandemic of 2020 clearly increased e-commerce sales significantly, but obviously, a Covid-19-driven statistic is an unfair measurement. Still, with the largest pool of money to spend, the brick-and-mortar retailers must be more aggressive if they have any hope to slow the increasing trend toward online purchasing. Indeed, they play the same game, as we mentioned earlier, but the importance here is to gain the eventual sale.

The consumer makes the decision of where to buy based on several factors, primarily convenience. Selection, consumer reviews, and price are all mentioned as top reasons for online purchase versus shopping in a store. Traditionally, retail grocery stores have had the advantage as consumers preferred shopping for their food, especially produce and meats, in the stores. However, we see that trend changing.

According to the Nielsen Connected Commerce Global Survey 2018, 30% of global respondents said they will increase their shopping online for FMCG products including fresh produce and meats.[32] We all know what happened in 2020 with the pandemic-driven increase in all forms of online sales, but this trend must alarm the brick-and-mortar retailers. And it does.

In North America alone, according to the 2018 Nielsen survey, only 4% of consumers shopped online for FMCG products, but 32% said they would increase that level. In Latin America, 11% shopped online and another 42% said they would increase FMCG shopping online. Those are flashing red lights the brick-and-mortar retailers are seeing right now. The only defense for a FMCG consumer products company is the old "If you can't beat 'em, join 'em" strategy, and to increase their own internal online infrastructure to grab their share of direct e-commerce. But that means a very precarious tightrope walk for the suppliers because most of their revenues and profit come from the brick-and-mortar, glass and steel of retail customers.

Right here is where one of the biggest failures occurs in trade channel promotion. Manufacturers, especially those with FMCG products, have sophisticated internal consumer marketing research analysts and technology. They know so much about the consumer and they leverage this intelligence in their national advertising, market positioning, events, and public relations. Unfortunately, most of these corporate marketing organizations do not have strong collaborative relationships with their own sales organization that spends two-thirds of the company's total marketing budget on trade promotions. This is due to the effect of seeing their marketing budgets reduce for the past five decades in favor of increased trade promotion budgeting and allocation, and the frustration with the resulting efforts to maintain the company's brand image and promotion.

As a result, too many of the corporate marketing and direct-to-consumer promotions are unaligned and even in conflict with the strategic product content, pricing, and positioning of the promotions run with their retail partners. It is, unfortunately, not uncommon to see a local store promoting a product with a different type of offer, such as a buy one, get one basis, at the same time the company is offering a national coupon with a buy one, get TWO offer. This leads to a confusing shopping experience for the consumer, and one that, more often than not, leads to either an option to use the coupon (for which the retailer gets nothing) or worse, a failure to buy the product at all.

Pull the Trigger

Make Purchase

"Get a special cut from the butcher."

Consideration	Action Required
Instore Timing	Buy the meat first to avoid the wait time at the counter
Sauces	Need Worcestershire Sauce – buy medium bottle
Trim the Fat	Reduce weight and cost – ask the butcher to trim extra fat off the steaks
Rest of Dinner Items	Buy the rest of the shopping list for dinner prep
Wine?	Check the red wine section and pick up a good bottle of cabernet sauvignon

Figure 4.7 The Physical Act of Purchase in the Consumer Chain

This is the moment of truth.

Every step the consumer has taken up to this point is in preparation, both physically and emotionally, to buy. Whether a simple point in the decision process or, as popular author and speaker, Russell Brunson might call it, the *Epiphany Bridge*,[33] the consumer arrives at the point where they make the purchase. It might be as simply done as taking the wrapped steak from the butcher and putting it into the shopping basket, or as complex as the half day at the auto dealership signing off on the reams of paperwork required to buy or lease a new car. Nonetheless, there is a nice feeling of satisfaction at that point.

Or perhaps it is a feeling of nervousness, dread, anticipation, or fear instead.

Either way, the deed is done. The die is cast, shall we say. What follows this step is the process of *consumption*, or that series of processes which give us the title of "consumer." This is the culmination and checkered flag, if you will, of the trillion dollars of promotional funding from the manufacturers which makes up the Invisible Economy of consumer products.

However, that said, with what we know of the new digital economy, social media, and the sheer magnificence of the power of the global consumer, one purchase does not make for the definition of *loyalty*, does it? The purchase has been made, but there is a long road to travel before this purchase creates and sustains a level of loyalty to this type of steak or any product purchased so that the next time a need is defined that this product satisfies, the consumer will buy it again. We will talk more of that in the next series of links in the *Consumer Chain*.

The opportunity for both the manufacturer/supplier and the channel partner (retailer, wholesaler, distributor, or reseller) is also what happens *peripherally* around the making of the purchase. As shown in Figure 4.7, there are ancillary decisions which can, and perhaps should, be made in connection with the purchase.

What happens when you sit down with the business manager of the dealership when you buy a car? You will be asked to think about extended warranties, loan forgiveness insurance, tire options, service packages, and maybe even life insurance to pay off the loan in case something dreadful happens to you. This is perhaps one of the worst examples of the downside of the point of purchase, but something we face in almost every instance of making the purchase.

Back to our example of the planned steak dinner—think of what *else* would make sense for the consumer to think about when putting the wrapped steak into their basket. Remember that the consumer often plans ahead and thinks about these decisions when writing the shopping list. Adding wine, perhaps a new marinade, or the flashing memory of being almost out of Worcestershire sauce, are common examples of the ancillary decision.

The butcher grabs the steak you selected in the meat case, and you wait for him to wrap it. But he holds it up and asks if you want him to cut the strip of fat around the edge for you. Hey, wait, that is a good idea! Not only does it save you from doing it when you get home, but it reduces the weight of the steak on the scale and saves you money. Although some progressive retail chains are beginning to add these types of services, most butchers will not do that. But this particular butcher is smart enough to know that you will now appreciate this service and will remember it when you want another cut of meat.

It takes a very smart retail organization to make this work. This is not what promotional funding pays for, to be sure, but in the end, it is what constitutes an excellent customer experience. And this is what *sustains* the shopper's loyalty.

Now, what the funding can and does pay for is the promotion of ancillary products that might trigger those decisions. For instance, if we are going to grill the steak, we have a deal on grilling tools in our hardware section. We have a nice wine selection with some great discounts on vintages of cabernet sauvignon to suggest, or if you buy the ribeye steak from the meat counter, we will give you a bag of fingerling potatoes and a pre-made Greek salad to go with it.

The most successful promotions typically feature these kinds of peripheral deals. When promotional planning is done within the context of this type of thinking, the money goes further, and the revenues and margins are typically higher.

We will discuss the planning in a later chapter but know that the entire focus of technology and process consultants today is on the ability to optimize these promotions by extending the successful execution and being more efficient with the money.

So, think of the point of purchase as not just the one single act of physically and emotionally buying something, but instead, adding value to the lifestyle and happiness of the consumer. That is the ultimate goal of the Invisible Economy of consumer engagement.

Transfer of Ownership

> **Secure Possession**

"Scan and go."

Consideration	Action Required
Reduce time shopping	Self-checkout
Secure wine and steak	Double bag to avoid breaks and spills
Avoid missing items	Check bags to ensure all items purchased in bags
Return home	Non-stop return drive home
Satisfaction Level	Tentative if a first-time purchase, otherwise good

Figure 4.8 Secure Possession—Physically Receiving the Product

I am a musician. One of the great thrills of my life is strapping on a newly purchased guitar for the first time. I played it already in the music store, of course, but nothing is like having it in your final possession.

Now that might be a bit of an over dramatization, but essentially this link in the *Consumer Chain* is the culminating act of the physical purchase—you take possession. Whether it is walking out of the store with the product in a bag, receiving it on your porch from an online purchase, or opening the bottle after it drops through the slot in a vending machine, the result is the same: you now have what you need in your possession.

Buyer's remorse aside, there is a level of satisfaction that you have accomplished a goal. There are so many different views and theories on the psychology of the buyer after a purchase that there is no need to spend the ink here for such a doctoral thesis. But one of my favorite works around the satisfaction of need that drives the purchase of a good or service is Richard Oliver's 2010 book, *Satisfaction: A Behavioral Perspective on the Consumer.*[34]

One of the many excellent points he makes is a simply stated formula which establishes the measurement of satisfaction as the ratio between the buyer's understanding or *expectation* of the product quality and the actual *experienced* quality of the product. Naturally, our perception of how well we did purchasing and consuming a product depends on the product, true.

Thus begins the consumer's journey toward the assessment of value and the early decisions of loyalty to a product. Also, this is a point in the consumer engagement by both the retailer and their manufacturer/supplier where, in my opinion, neither understands how to effectively move forward.

Is the promotion process over?

Did we do our job?

Did we spend the money well?

Have we pleased the consumer?

Do we care?

The "take home" measurement in a grocery store is the beep you hear when the product is passed over the laser scanner at checkout. That beep is a big deal. It should be a *gong*—something akin to Big Ben striking the hour, because it is the microsecond every bit of data is captured about the sale of the product. This data is collectively called "Point of Sale" or "POS" data and is arduously reviewed, analyzed, and calculated to provide both the retailer and the manufacturer with the results of the promotion.

While this information is carefully studied to determine the success or failure of the promotion, it is also used to decrement and measure existing instore inventory and report revenue and margins. The retailer will use the information in their corporate frequency and loyalty programs to track the consumer's shopping history and maintain demographic data as well.

But what about product satisfaction?

Generally, the only true method of gauging the ultimate consumer satisfaction is through this loyalty data (i.e., how often does the consumer return to shop and do they continue to purchase *that* product?). But there is no reaching out to the consumer directly, except for the occasional survey, and that will generally be about the store shopping experience, not a specific product. The manufacturer is even further removed from the "satisfaction" element because, since they do not get loyalty and credit card purchase data, they do not know the consumer as the store does.

Again, judging the level of satisfaction, then can only be through high-level indirect evaluation, social media, or complaints. We will get more into this later.

But for now, know that the personal satisfaction in the securing of the product and taking it home, consuming it and having an opinion of the quality or performance is going to remain elusive to both retailer and manufacturer/supplier.

The Product Experience

So, you have unwrapped, marinated, and prepared your steak. Fire up the grill, cook the potatoes and make the salad, we're having this fine cut of ribeye steak!

You make several decisions along the way to the actual consumption of the steak, don't you? How long do I cook it? Differs by family member, does it not? How much marinade do I use, how much salt, pepper, rub, or tenderizer? All those questions come to mind and must be answered before you plate your juicy, perfectly cooked steak.

> **Consume/Use Product**

"Cook and enjoy."

Consideration	Action Required
Refreshment during cooking	Open the wine and pour!
Timing	Prepare other dinner dishes first
Grill	Start grill and monitor heat levels
Cooking	3 ½ minutes per side, 7 minutes, done!
Fine dinner	Enjoy the steak and side dishes

Figure 4.9 Product Consumption and Use Is the Pinnacle Act of the Consumer Chain

Your research as a consumer is key here. For our steak example, the chances of your having a ribeye for the very first time in your life are probably extremely low, so you may be greatly confident in your choice of purchase. On the other hand, opening the box of a new Wi-Fi router with voluminous instructions for set up that you did not expect may, in that second, cause you to rethink your purchase. The blouse you bought does not look as good in your light versus the overlit department store, or the super cool truck you just drove home for the first time does not fit in your garage. You still have some work to do, but so far, you are still good with your purchase decision.

This is the area controlled by the manufacturer when it comes to a durable product, and the retailer if you are bringing home what looked like a great head of green leaf lettuce but now appears to have a less-than-fresh core. Product quality, the packaging, and initial setup has to be simple or at least well-defined. All this falls under product quality, so it is easy now to see how it all relates and how this ocean of money spent on product promotions and consumer marketing can all be for naught if the product is difficult to deal with when taking it out of the package.

The emotions of this moment are on highest alert. The slightest nod, scrunched up nose, widened or closed eyes, or level of difficulty slicing a piece of meat will be carefully observed and noted. As the purchaser of the steak, you become the hero or the goat, hopefully the former, not the latter.

The Verdict

Nothing compares to that first bite. Nothing compares to the first drive home out of the dealership in your new car. You can't beat plugging in that new video game and taking a shot at whatever monster or obstacle you face. It all adds up to the process of *consuming* the product you just purchased and brought home. The eyes of your family and satisfied groans of pleasure tell you that the steak is a winner… and so are you.

Or not.

Evaluate Product

"Great dinner."

Observation	Take-Away Opinion
Extremely good cut	Note size and marbling
Well seasoned	Teriyaki a good choice for marinade
Well cooked	Perfect medium rare quality – note the timing and heat
Spouse loved it	Duplicate at the next special dinner
Totally consumed	Everyone ate all of their steak – nothing left!

Figure 4.10 Product Evaluation in the Consumer Chain

This is the definition of *satisfaction* and the measurement ratio Richard Oliver spoke about in his book.[34] If the product meets your expectations, you are satisfied. If not, you are not. And this begins the next section of the *Consumer Chain*, and the most critical new issue facing the consumer products industry players. What happens next along the chain must become the new focus of the Invisible Economy: the sustainability of the consumer's loyalty and continued purchases.

Internally, the sales and marketing people at the consumer products manufacturer may be oblivious to this unless they are the people in charge of customer service or complaints. Products made and assembled overseas are particularly at risk without a comprehensive alignment between the product research and development, marketing, and sales leadership. There are often far too many "Chinese walls" between departments, but here, at this point in the *Consumer Chain*, it matters a great deal how well the corporate value chain comes together and considers what the consumer deals with when they buy the product.

If the product is not of a high quality or simplicity, no amount of trade channel promotion or corporate marketing money will make it right. The lesson of this link is that all the internal value chain forces must come together to focus on the consumer's satisfaction from beginning to end of the *Consumer Chain*.

Thumbs Up or Down?

Validate Decision to Buy

"Excellent cut, great taste – worth the extra cost."

Observation	Validation
Expensive cut	Worth paying the extra cost and having the butcher cut and trim special
Less fat	Healthy way to get red meat fix
Happy my grocery store had the cut	Less expensive than a meat market and just as good

Figure 4.11 The "Moment of Truth" – Did I Make the Right Decision?

You may not operate a prime steak house every night, but tonight, you have. Your family hasn't rendered their judgement, but you already have. The moment you tasted your own steak you knew—this was the right thing to buy. And it was worth the money.

This is the confirmation every consumer needs. It validates their decision to buy, and virtually guarantees that the next time the family (or you) wants steak, you will revisit the butcher and ask them to get you the same cut and trim it the same way. The sense of satisfaction you now feel is a lingering memory, just as it would have had you not been happy with the result.

It is funny how those things happen, is it not? As consumers, we want that experience, and more and more of the consuming public are becoming very picky and highly intelligent when it comes to their preferences. Say 'thank you' to social media for making us all smarter consumers. But at the same time, the variables change in a heartbeat, creating so many conditions that contribute to the overall study of consumer trends and buying profiles.

For consumer products manufacturers, this is also what makes it difficult to project promotional success, for instance, because the exact same circumstances that generated a super successful promotion today may fall flat one year later with all the same conditions and tactics. The facts and figures that CPG companies use to forecast incremental sales volume lifts do not always tie back to the ebb and flow of consumer mindset patterns, pandemics, or politics. Therefore, the pressure felt by the software developers to write artificial intelligence and machine learning-based algorithms to project and predict behavior is higher every single day.

I may really love steak today, but next month I get diagnosed with hemochromatosis, so my red meat eating days are over! What AI algorithm can accommodate *that*? While this may be viewed as a clear outlier, the number of situations where the defined outliers are increasing are beginning to impact any chance of a consumer products supplier's ability to understand the true sentiments a consumer feels during or immediately after consumption. First impressions matter, do they not? The corporate marketing organization has the primary functional responsibility to determine consumer sentiment in general, and the level of product sentiment *decay* after consumption in particular.

Your excitement at the purchase point for your new virtual reality gaming system may immediately turn into frustrating anger and pain when you try it for the first time, and it does not work. The sentiment decay curve would be almost immediate. That data is difficult to collect unless you are tracking the customer service or tech support line activity from the customer complaint. But what percentage of consumers will *never* spend time to let you know how they feel? That is the missing link in this section of the *Consumer Chain.*

Show and Tell

Share Experience

"Check out my steak on Facebook!"

Communication Medium	Shared Posts
Facebook	"Was pleasantly surprised my butcher at the grocery was willing to make some special cuts in the back rather than buy pre-packaged product."
Instagram	"Check out my steak for tonight's meal – beautifully marbled and my store butcher even trimmed the fat!"
Store Website	Review: "Butcher did a terrific job of cutting four beautiful ribeyes for my family meal tonight. Saved me from having to go to the meat market. Great job!"
Neighborhood Chat Site	"Did you all know that you could ask for special cuts at the grocery meat counter? You may have to wait, but it was worth it!"

Figure 4.12 Sharing the Purchase and Consumption/Use Experience in the Consumer Chain

Have you ever read a consumer review that said, "Eh, it's, OK?"

No, you probably have not. That is because people who share their experiences do so with emotion—*I love it*, or *I hate it*! Rarely, except perhaps when polled and offered a middle-of-the-road response, will someone take the time to tell someone about their product experience. In today's hot social media world with the likes of Instagram, Facebook, or even YouTube, the savvy consumer is easily able to shout their feelings to the world in seconds.

This steak is great, so you take a picture of it plated with a nice side of asparagus and fingerling potatoes and upload it to Instagram with the quick comment about how great it was. Twitter even lets you talk about how the butcher made the cuts for you and how happy you are with the taste. You have just shared your product sentiment with the world.

And the smart retailer and supplier noticed it.

And they captured the data and are analyzing how they can duplicate the experience for you and every other potential shopper.

If they are smart enough to be called industry leaders, they will no doubt use this data to project and predict future product promotions with the hope to generate a higher return on their investment of all those billions of trade and channel promotion funds.

In the USA, 93.1% of Americans use some form of social media.[35] Globally, 3.78 billion people, roughly 48% of the population, post regularly to one form of social media or another.[36] There is no escaping social sentiment and there is no other better, more informed method of rapid access to consumer sentiment than through these various social media sources.

Using this data has become a much more challenging analytical effort than older forms of performance data to be sure. There is always the low percentage of untrustworthy responses, but like any statistical analyses, paying attention to the core responses gets the data consumer products manufacturers/suppliers and retailers need to determine how their product performs at consumption.

The cost of this data is another component of the *Invisible Economy*. The growth in social media marketing, and sentiment data analytics suppliers, is staggering and continues to rise. Consumer products companies are beginning to plug this intelligence into their more sophisticated artificial intelligence technology to reduce the time lag to gain precious consumer intelligence and, at the same time, dramatically accelerating the quality of data about the consumers' needs, buying habits, and eventual product sentiment.

What you feel in the first few minutes of consuming the product is key, and this is the gold which the consumer products companies and retailers are trying to get to. Their systems are immature for the most part, but the knowledge of the availability of this data, and the escalation of the issues to corporate C-level executive management, is happening in every company. So, expect the ocean of promotional funding making up the bulk of that Invisible Economy to rise in the next few years. The retailer and the supplier want to know what you think, how you feel and whether you will buy from them again.

The consumer is not only the king (and queen), but also the most powerful component in the entire value chain.

The Follow-Up

This link in the *Consumer Chain* is all about making sure a repeat performance of pleasure and happiness from the consumption or use of the product becomes "standard operating procedure" in the household. It is the action taken to formally record your experience with the purchase—revise or create a new menu card for the steak with the details that remind you what to do the next time you go shopping for a steak dinner.

Monitor Consumption

"Add a note to my recipe box under **Steak.***"*

Action	Value
Add a new recipe card in the STEAK section of your recipe box/files	Reminds you to ask the butcher to make a special cut when you want a special steak meal
Pay attention to timing to plan the next steak meal	Segregate the special occasions where a fancy steak is a must versus grilling a steak every now and then for the family that does not require a high-cost cut
Note the size and amount consumed at the meal	Enables a more efficient and less expensive size cut the next time

Figure 4.13 Making Critical Observations and Recording the Consumption / Use in the Consumer Chain

If your purchase was for a durables product like a video game console, new vacuum cleaner, 54" flat-screen TV, or a new electric chainsaw, it means making sure that you take care of it and treat it right. Your feeling of accomplishment for the purchase may not necessarily mean a euphoric state every time you use it, but at least it continues to provide validation and justification for the smart purchase you made.

Or not. And if not, then it works the other way in reverse. You rue the day you made the decision to buy it and you make mental and physical notes to never make the mistake again. You may return it for another model, get your money back, or just sit and stew in anger because you went beyond the 30-day return policy!

Either way, most consumer products companies would do themselves a great service if they follow up with every purchase, as many do, within a 30-day period of the original purchase. This costs money too, especially if the supplier or retailer decides to crank this data into their product research and development, marketing strategy, or product assortment plan. The more sophisticated consumer products companies are leveraging this data as further intelligence to help determine how best to portray the product, configure price, and if necessary, redesign the product for the next release.

The bottom line aspect of this specific link in the *Consumer Chain* is that, as with all of the information about your needs fulfillment, this critically important time and sentiment is a distinction between an average consumer products company or retailer, and an industry leader.

The Reprise

| Reorder/Replace Decision |

"Let's do it again the next time we have steak!"

Consideration	Action Plan
Worth the extra cost?	If so, take note of the next time you want steak and decide if the occasion warrants the cost
Always buy at the grocer meat counter?	Not always, continue to visit the butcher at the meat market as well in case of an exceptional deal
Bad decision	If the steak had proven not worthy of the cost, make the note in your recipe box for THAT as well. Go to the meat market for special cuts from now on
Cooking Process	Make a note in the recipe card or file of the size and cut of meat, and of the heat level and time for cooking a medium rare steak

Figure 4.14 The Final Step in the Consumer Chain

The last link in the *Consumer Chain* is what the retailer and the consumer products supplier hope for—the culminating act of repeating the purchase decision.

The need, firmly established, should now dictate the fulfillment because of the entire process the consumer goes through in the *Consumer Chain*. When the consumer has the need again, for either a steak or a new car, he/she will remember all the ups and downs, good and bad, and right or wrong connected with the previous decision. Here is where loyalty and trust are built.

As a broad measure, brand and product loyalty is more difficult to achieve in the digital mercantile world today. The 2020 pandemic played havoc with loyalty statistics, especially the first six months of the year when most states were in some sort of lockdown and supply chains were suppressed. Consumers were forced to buy brands which were available versus what they preferred; and of course, many of the classes of products were difficult to find or out of stock when the consumer did shop.

If we look at 2019, then we can see the trends in loyalty more clearly, and 2021 began to mirror those trends as the world began to emerge from the pandemic. Although loyalty has so many different categories of definition, 67.8% of the people say that their definition of *loyalty* is repeat purchasing, versus love for the brand (39.5%).[37]

More precisely, the largest group in that survey (37%) of consumers said their definition of loyalty is buying from the same company at least five or more times.[37] So, the emotional self-described state of loyalty seems to hinge more on frequency than pure love of the product after an initial consumption or use. Someone whose eyes go wide when they say, "This is my new favorite steak," is not as loyal as the one who says, "I buy this all the time, isn't it great?"

For the consumer products company, focus on establishing loyalty is certainly a primary strategic objective, but tactically it falls to the corporate marketing organization to build a promotional event and advertising plan that reaches the consumer to incite the demand, fuel the *need,* and continue pushing the qualities of the product to establish the desire to buy.

But it falls to the sales organization and the retailer to "close the deal," so to speak, with the purchase incentive—the trade promotion that dangles a discounted price, an instore display that attracts the shopper's attention, and the local advertising which hopefully extends the manufacturer's own corporate product or brand message.

The retailer, on the other hand, is more often the "face" of the product than the national advertising messages themselves, because it is the point of contact the consumer has with the product. In our steak example, you may not ever see national advertising of the product because it is purchased from the meat counter or meat market; but for any other packaged or durables product, the retailer has the best position to not only determine, but to drive a consumer's loyalty.

Most major retail chains have some sort of customer loyalty program where values are earned from purchases, and discounts offered on an exclusive basis for membership. Rewarding the consumer for purchasing in their store is clearly one of many winning strategies for creating an excellent customer experience—a motivator that 93% of consumers say drives their repurchase decisions.[38]

Sustaining the consumer's penchant to "buy again" takes a combination of all three forms of marketing and promotion, and it is extremely costly to do so. The *Consumer Chain* is not just the intellectual, emotional, and physical steps in the fulfillment of personal needs. It must also frame the primary purpose in the process of funding, planning, and execution of the entire scope of their strategic and tactical marketing and promotions.

In today's marketing, and especially trade channel promotion planning, this is the foundation for the failures which happen every day. This is what *should* drive the Invisible Economy of consumer goods, but it is unfortunately all too often left out of the largest line item in the entire corporate marketing budget—channel incentives and trade promotion. What company, no matter the size, can ignore the links of the *Consumer Chain* in configuring their consumer engagement strategy?

None of them.

CHAPTER 5

THE SHELL GAME

E very form of channel incentive devised and executed by manufacturers has its roots in the concept of leveraging the locality of the retailer to promote the critical information about how, where, and how much you will pay to purchase a product. In Chapter 3, you read how these programs evolved and how governmental regulatory intervention attempted to keep the programs fair and square.

Fairness, it seems, was defined as ensuring against a monopoly, which resulted in the inability of smaller manufacturers or retailers to compete on at least an equal and proportionate basis. In the United States, Canada, and throughout the European Union, there are certainly laws with a bit of teeth in them to protect smaller companies. However, as the business of mercantile rolls on, the actual *practices* do not always seem to be enforced. That is because most major corporations within the consumer products industry sectors have, over the years, refined their legal positions to provide satisfactory arguments for how they do business.

"We are well aware of Robinson-Patman," says the chief legal counsel for one of the world's top CPG manufacturers. "When our budgets are defined, they go through the scrutiny of equality and proportionality, both here in the United States, as we do in Canada and in the EU."

When asked directly about issues like "Every Day Low Pricing" offers for Walmart, for example, as opposed to the promotional budgeting for other retail accounts, he folded his arms, sat back, and said, "Any of our customers who want to opt out of trade promotion funding for EDLP deals can certainly be accommodated."

Armed with legal teams and precedent, most major CPG companies are confident that their practices are not only legal, but certainly fair in the schemes they present, and the program terms and conditions which drive the promotions. Smaller companies still struggle, but the main difference between how it was in the 1960s when a flurry of Robinson-Patman violations were prosecuted by the FTC, and today, is that the digital marketplace, e-commerce, and social media have done remarkable things to level the playing field.

"Look, we believe our products are ten times better than the big CPG competitors," said the CEO of a small but quickly growing snack foods company. "We have a killer e-commerce engine, a beautiful website, and the type of R&D and quality which makes our products better—and the consumer knows it." So do the retail accounts, it seems, because they have successfully displaced positions on the shelf that were formerly dominated by the global super CPGs they compete with. As a result, they find themselves rising up the category for most major retail accounts, and their investment in trade funds, although significantly less than their major competition, seems to be generating higher ROI than the average top 100 consumer goods company.

We will use this company's example later in this chapter. When it comes to the reality of the trade promotion planning and forecasting playing field today, anticompetitive actions still take place, unfortunately, although there has not been a major industry-shaking event like the 1968 Fred Meyer decision.[16] What we do see is the market environment, and certainly the consumer, seems more eager to buy the smaller company's brand, when the perception is quality, price, or availability, than they are for the big name brands across several categories. So, even the smaller consumer products companies are leveraging this popularity in their marketing and promotion planning to become more aggressive and willing to spend the money to move up in the category priority for the retailers. This competitive action compels the larger CPG suppliers to lay out more money, knowing cash is still a major advantage they have over their smaller competitors.

With the availability of more and frequent consumer data and powerful AI-driven analytics, the playing field begins to even out across all sizes of suppliers. Retailers, distributors, and indirect resellers all want and need the expanded intelligence to drive a more aggressive sales plan. All of this makes for a highly volatile promotion planning and execution environment which drives even higher investments in technology and process reengineering.

What's the Deal?

In the context of channel incentives and trade promotion, the "Deal" is defined as the agreement between two parties, the manufacturer/supplier, and the channel customer in this case. The deal consists of an amount of money or some other consideration (i.e., free goods, extended payment terms, shipping discounts, etc.) which is pledged in exchange for specific actions taken to market and promote said manufacturer's/supplier's goods and services to the consumer.

In today's consumer products marketplace, the manufacturer can sell its products through multiple channels of distribution. Selling through the retail, wholesale, or reseller channels of distribution is classified as a *Business-to-Business* (B2B) transaction. Selling products directly to the consumer via e-commerce online shopping channels is called *Business-to-Consumer* (B2C) transactions. In the former case, the structure of the deal is intended to produce a combination of offers made by the manufacturer/supplier to provide money for the expressed purpose of subsidizing the cost of promotion which the channel customer incurs marketing and promoting the product to the consumer.

Ostensibly, the manufacturer's/supplier's goal is to reach the consumer through a less expensive form of promotion than they would pay if they purchased media directly from the local newspapers, broadcast stations, cable operators, or other promotional media. But, in reality that is not the intention of the *deal*, at least for the manufacturer/supplier's sales representative. They have a forecast sales volume and revenue target to achieve. They are heads-down making sure this objective is reached. They go into the selling process with that goal in mind, and this process is called the *Sell-In*. Most formal dictionaries use this term as a shortened statement of selling product *into* the retailer for ultimate sale to the consumer/shopper.

The *Sell-In* is one half of the process of selling to the consumer. The other half is called *Sell-Out*, or the resulting sale to the consumer in the store or online. The rather unvarnished truth in modern consumer products is that the manufacturer/supplier's sales representative will be focused on the results or *Sell-Out* only when considering what it might do to his/her next order, not so much the quotient of success achieved by the retailer in the actual instore promotion.

I spoke with the buyer for the pasta category of a major retail grocery chain in the midwestern United States about this. "Don't get me wrong, I think [supplier's key account manager] is very nicely focused on the success of our promotions," he said. "But when I ask him about what he is seeing in his demand curve, and what he projects or believes the actual rate of *Sell-Out* will be, I hear crickets chirping." There are reasons for this we will touch on later in the book.

But the point here is that, for the traditional consumer products manufacturer's/ supplier's key account managers and sales representatives, getting the agreement on the *volume* and *price* is the ultimate goal of the *Deal*.

Now, let's go back to what we discussed in Chapter 3. The original intent of trade promotion, co-op advertising, or any other channel incentive is to provide financial support to the channel customer in promoting directly to the consuming public. Early on, from 1900 to 1970, there were significant controls in place to audit compliance that ensured the money spent by the retailers, resellers, wholesalers, and distributors was for the exact cost of the promotional media and nothing more. As the sales reps planned their forecasts, they made assumptions based on the historical costs paid to each account and used these numbers to support and incite the retailer to agree to the purchase order for the forecasted volume.

It was simple. If the co-op or trade promotion fund offered equaled 5% of net purchases, and the retailer agreed to a $100,000 order, the promotional fund was $5,000. The rep and the buyer understood that if any other offer was made, it was likely to result in a potential violation of Section 2 of the Robinson-Patman Act. There may have been some grumbling about the fact that 5% was too low to adequately support the level of promotion needed to sell all the volume *sold in*, but the deal stood.

When the fast moving consumer goods (FMCG) industry began seeing retailers suffer huge margin reductions, and manufacturers took 90 or more days to reimburse promotion claims, the entire process changed. Instead of submitting documented proof of performance claims and waiting on reimbursement, the retailers began deducting the cost of promotion directly off the merchandise payments to the manufacturer. In addition, the buyers were issued marching orders that essentially required any manufacturer/supplier who wanted on the shelves to pay for the cost of promotion *they* set, with no relationship to the actual cost of print space, broadcast time, or other variables for promotional media. With margins for actual product sales below 2%, the retailers recouped their margins through negotiated trade funds.

How did the retailers justify this new course of action? They knew the law. They had battalions of lawyers who could quote the Robinson-Patman Act and every European, British, Australian, and Latin American regulatory statute ten times over. Instead of butting heads with the law, they used it as justification. The "equal and proportionate" provisions of Section 2(d) and (e) of the Robinson-Patman Act were interpreted to represent a fair justification of their action by working with their manufacturers/ suppliers in showing that they are in a unique position as a major reseller competing in a consumer market. Their basis for the justification of the higher funding levels was the higher cost of doing business and the better value they brought to the consumer because of their buying power. Their ability to purchase far greater volumes of product from the manufacturer enabled them to reach economies of scale that, in turn, produced a much greater discount in pricing as well as a larger inventory to satisfy the consumer—exactly the argument that Fred Meyer Stores used in the late 1960s that forced the FTC to take action in the form of a formal set of rules called the "Guides for Advertising Allowances and Other Merchandising Payments and Services," ("Guides") referred to often as the Fred Meyer Guides that resulted from a landmark 1968 court battle with the FTC.

The FMCG manufacturers and suppliers were faced with either granting these mandates of their channel customers or losing the distribution. They opted for the former and could not afford the latter.

So, manufacturers began changing their settlement policies and procedures to accept the *deduction* as the primary way to transact trade promotion and co-op funds. They began to use the retailers' stated costs as the basis for allocating funds to tactical and strategic activities associated with the promotional events, without regard to the actual net cost less all discounts and rebates their media vendors charged. This was the process in place, growing and flourishing throughout the numerous legal challenges, adoption and updating of the "Guides" from the 1960s through the 1990s. Manufacturers and retailers, wholesalers and distributors began to structure their funding and payment policies and procedures to lean toward some semblance of *equality and proportionality.* Corporate legal teams reviewed the new regulations carefully, across the face of the planet, making sure there was a valid argument in place that proved compliance.

"We looked carefully at what we were doing back then," replied a corporate legal executive at a global CPG conglomerate. "Our position was simple—if another [retail] competitor wanted the same deal we had, they needed to achieve the same level of volume and sales performance for the suppliers that we did… simple as that." While it was not as simple as that, it did imply a foundation of logic that most major CPG/FMCG companies adopted and practiced in the process or allocation of funding and settlement of trade promotion spending. There has not been a major challenge since that time which was enough to significantly alter either Section 2(d) and (e) of the Robinson-Patman Act or the "Guides" for advertising and merchandising allowances.

The methodology of promotion planning had forever changed in FMCG. Across most of the other consumer products industry sectors, the formats for incentive program fund accrual, claim, and payment rules remained largely unchanged, to this day. Planning in those industries is similar in scope and intent—present a full program of offers and incentives that will trigger an approval to purchase a stated volume of product at a particular discount price. There may be some "over and above" funding that is provided, but this is typically based on a set target of revenue, volume, or market share achievement that would be offered equally and proportionately to any competing retailer making an equivalent commitment.

We will cover the specific issues of the multitier distribution channels later, but for now, let's concentrate on the consumer products manufacturer/supplier and the retailer.

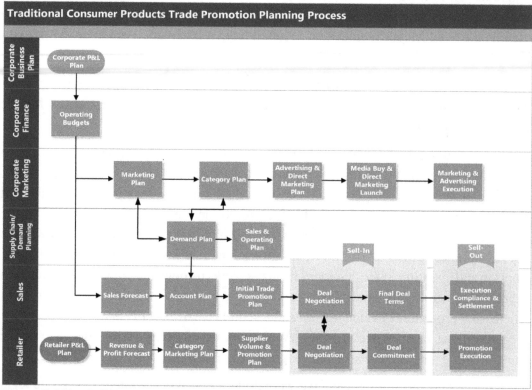

Figure 5.1 Basic Planning Process for Trade Promotions

Figure 5.1 is a very high level representation of the traditional deal cycle from the planning through the execution and settlement. Most actual trade promotion or channel incentive program management processes are certainly more complex than this, but the idea is to illustrate the basic flow of the "deal."

Note the two sets of steps labeled "Sell-In" and "Sell-Out." These are the initial agreement of the terms and conditions of the promotional deal, and the actual execution of the promotion in the store, respectively.

The "Deal" for a manufacturer's KAM or sales rep is the Sell-In. The planning and scoping of what the deal needs to be is a responsibility shared by both the retailer and the manufacturer. The retailer will have their own profit and loss plan that cascades down into a specific supplier promotion plan, but here in the *Sell-In* is where the manufacturer's sales representative focuses all his/her energy and is, most likely, the true measure of the overall value of the promotion *for him/her*. Although few, if any, real polls have taken place to measure this, just look at the compensation programs for field sales reps and key account managers. Traditionally, they are compensated on two primary metrics: (1) volume sold, and (2) profitability of the sale.

The retailer, on the other hand, has multiple objectives for the deal. To the category buyer, who is most often the primary negotiator for the deal with the manufacturer/ supplier, their energy and focus will be on achieving three goals: (1) generating the most operational profit margin, (2) satisfying the category and product assortment requirement, and (3) support for the tactical activities their marketing teams have provided that are designed to motivate the shopper to buy the product.

These goals and objectives are, at the end of the negotiation, supposedly mutually advantageous; however, most manufacturer sales reps and key account managers will tend to lean more toward their retailer counterparts as achieving more of the benefits. That is most likely because the strength of the retailer's position is often far greater than that of the supplier. And, as I implied earlier and throughout this book so far, that is how it has been much of the past 50 years.

The Sell-Out

The *Sell-Out* process of the trade promotion deal is the end game—the point at which the product is passed over the scanner at checkout and formally purchased by the consumer. Considering over a trillion dollars are spent globally on trade promotions, you would think that this is the ultimate goal. But it unfortunately is not.

While it IS a major metric for promotion performance measurement, the number of sales made is often secondary to both parties' goals. For the retailer, the actual sales figures signal promotion success. It validates the choice of timing, product or promotional product group, and tactical activities executed.

Over the years, it has come to justify the retailers' choices in a promotional planning process more than those of the manufacturer/supplier. That is primarily due to the proximity to and direct knowledge of the consumer/shopper versus the intelligence data provided by the manufacturer.

In fact, today's most vigorous discussions in consumer goods are around the accessibility of the *retailer's* data which includes not only point-of-sale (POS/scanner) data, but also loyalty card usage, credit card information, demographics, and instore shopping studies. This is golden data to the manufacturer/supplier because it is not something they can get otherwise. All the consumer research the manufacturer's marketing organization can provide is critically important overall, but regarding the planning of a successful trade channel promotion, not so much.

So, while the key account managers and sales reps are quick to point to their measure of success being the volume, revenue, and profit margin gained in the sell-in, they have not been in a particularly good position to ante up an equal share of sell-out support for the retailer as far as providing valuable intelligence about the sell-out.

Until now.

Technology, most notably in the form of artificial intelligence and advanced machine learning analytics has combined with a more aggressive sharing of POS and shopping data, has given the manufacturer the ability to aggregate data from all retailers to provide meaningful statistical direction for future promotional success.

This sharing of data, which we will get into much deeper in later chapters, has increased the visibility of consumer purchases instore and online on a more frequent basis (daily, in a growing number of cases) to provide a rapid response to, and analysis of, the results of the trade channel promotion.

As this intelligence becomes more widely available, it will begin to show how and why the structure and content of a promotion can be adjusted to produce higher sales. The higher level of collaboration between the retailer and the manufacturer has already seen marked improvement in the number of sales registered during or as a direct result of the promotion.

Basic Point-of-Sale Data Supplied to Manufacturers/Suppliers by Retailers

#	Point-of-Sale (POS) Data Description
1	Product SKU (unit) Identification
2	Product Price
3	Promotion Status (On promotion or not on promotion)
4	Number of units purchased
5	Date and time of purchase
6	Store location
7	Checkout Register Number
8	Type of payment
9	Credit and Loyalty card information (usually not shared by retailer with supplier)

Figure 5.2 Point-of-Sale Data

Where's the Pea?

So, the *Shell Game* is a game of illusion where, under one of three shells a pea is placed, and the shells are quickly moved around to attempt to make you lose sight of which one it is under. In the *Shell Game* of trade promotion planning, the pea is the *consumer*. The *Sell-In* deal certainly has a significant dual benefit for the retailer and the manufacturer/supplier; but then where is the consumer? The easy response is that the consumer is represented by the *value* of the discounted price of the product on the shelf and the fulfillment of the consumer's need (Remember the first link in the *Consumer Chain*?) for the product.

But if that is true, shouldn't every promotion produce the outcome desired—selling all the product the retailer purchased for the promotional event period? Why are trade promotions so prone to failure— unable to produce a positive return on investment of all those billions of dollars spent?

As we stated back in Chapter 2, Nielsen says as much as 71% of trade promotions fail to generate positive return.[4] That means a failure to incite consumers to shop and purchase the product on promotion, and a negative difference between the volume of product purchased by the retailer for the promotion and the volume of product sold. Yet in the 2018 Survey on Trade Promotion by Consumer Goods Technology, 27% of the respondents said that they achieved the objective set forth in the plan *better than 75% of the time*! Another 45% said that their promotions achieved the plan objectives between 50% and 75% of the time.[39]

27% of the respondents did not know.

And more than 71% of the survey respondents were in the manufacturer's *sales* organization.

So, you tell me, how is it that more than *one-fourth* of the sales forces surveyed (and these are major global consumer products corporations) do not even *know* the actual sales of the products on the promotions they planned and executed with their top accounts?

Remember that the original intent and purpose of trade and channel incentives promotions is to drive *consumers* into the stores specifically for the purpose of purchasing the manufacturer's products. In the shell game they are playing, do they even care about which shell has the pea?

Over and Above

In most countries, as we have established, there are specific regulatory statutes in place to protect small manufacturers and retailers from being discriminated against by the major corporations. These regulations and laws have, as the foundation of their purpose, the provisions of equality and proportionality embedded within the language of the statutes. If the planning process between the retailer and the manufacturer/supplier is based on whatever both feel is the right combination of money, product, timing, and tactics, where in this effort does the oversight and protections come into play when assigning money to fund the promotions?

As with so many words and phrases in our global languages today, the meaning can be interpreted in multiple ways. If a manufacturer offers Walmart $1 million in funding and $1,000 to a smaller retailer down the street selling the exact same product, it will all come down to a claim that the difference is *volume* of product purchased. Walmart buys six truckloads of product a year, and the retailer down the street buys one pallet of product a year. Therein lies the distinction that the industry will have you make, and the definition of equal and proportionate they will hang their hats on.

So far, the government (in the USA to be sure) accepts the equal and proportionate provision of the Robinson-Patman Act to allow for the "treatment" of funding to be tied to volume. It works. "If you look at our funding practices, you will see how we do, indeed, treat each of our retail customers with equal and proportional allocations," replied the corporate attorney for a breakfast packaged meat supplier. "Does it mean we have to give the same amount of money? Of course not. But it does mean that we offer equal consideration to each of our customers when we are planning and allocating trade funds."

In virtually all the durables industries offering channel incentive funding, the amount of the funds accrued is a fixed figure, or a published range of figures, representing a percentage of the net sales of product. A 3% co-op allowance is earned across the entire customer base. If you purchase six truckloads or one pallet a year, you still earn 3% of every dollar paid. That is the textbook definition of equal and proportionate funding. This is how a traditional co-op advertising program works.

Of course, there are other funds that are typically offered "over and above" the published co-op or trade promotion accrual rate, but again, those are typically either based on a fixed amount and/or performance requirement which the customer has to earn. This is also how a typical co-op advertising or market development fund (MDF) program works to offer equal and proportionately higher amounts of funding to larger customers who are truly capable of exponential sales volume and market share for the manufacturer's/supplier's products.

However, in the FMCG/CPG sector of consumer products, the *Invisible Economy* is just that—the trade funds allocated across the channel customer landscape are neither published nor formulated through a fixed accrual rate. They are, instead, *allocated* based on a budget available to each sales organization that cascades down to each key account manager and sales representative.

Let us go back to the planning process. In today's modern trade channel promotion planning within the consumer packaged goods industry, the retailer has the upper hand. The key account managers and sales reps who are responsible for developing an initial promotion plan comprised of a suggested timeframe, specific products, and tactical activity recommendations, will allocate an amount of money they believe to be satisfactory and sufficient. The retailer will often override this plan with the plan they have created, and there the negotiation begins.

"I would say that my initial plan is accepted and approved by my account about 10% of the time," said one key account manager. "Invariably, my allocated money will not be enough and if my [tactical activities] are not what the retailer wants, we go with his."

There is logic here. As I discussed earlier, the retailer is closer to the consumer. They have far more information about who they are, how they shop, and what will satisfy their demands, than the manufacturer. But that said, the manufacturer has enormous caches of intelligence about the consumer and about how their products perform across the entire global landscape—something the retailer will not know and will definitely *want* to know. So, there is a trade-off of sorts, but at the end of the day, the amount of money that is committed and approved is not going to be equal and proportionate to every other trade promotion deal agreed to. It just cannot be.

Expanding the Game

In the early days of this FMCG-based promotion planning process, there were many complaints from competitive retailers, and certainly many from smaller manufacturers, who would never be able to afford the level of funding offered by the majors. But after more than 50 years of this practice in FMCG, it has become an accepted norm.

Over the last 50 years, the United States Congress has changed parties many times, and there have been six Republican and five Democrat presidents, and the only real changes in the regulatory environment have been a couple of updates to the Federal Trade Commission *Guides for Advertising Allowances and Other Merchandising Payments and Services.* There are few, if any notable challenges or case law that has made a change in the way the *Invisible Economy* of trade channel promotion is managed.

The traditional shell game consists of three shells and one pea. Today's shell game of trade channel promotion planning has expanded into multiple shells and multiple peas. Online shopping, and the advent of one-day or same day delivery, has created an even more challenging objective for retailers and manufacturers/suppliers. Considering the accepted objectives of volume and revenue for the manufacturer and profitability and demand fulfillment for the retailer, there is virtually no chance of major change in the near term.

Innovation in advanced prescriptive and predictive analytics, infusion of and alignment with consumer direct marketing, and near real-time POS data acquisition will no doubt enable more effective planning, better insight into consumer demand, and higher returns on the trade spending investment. For the FMCG industry sector, it validates and justifies the practice of one-on-one allocation of funding, and pinpoint planning of promotions to achieve everyone's objectives.

The retail landscape is also evolving, not just brick-and-mortar, but online. People are moving across the landscape and bringing with them the practices, policies, and procedures they are most familiar with. Executives are moving from retailer to CPG, from online e-commerce vendor, to run revenue growth management at major consumer electronics vendors, and mass merchandiser executives are running startup salty snack manufacturers. Throughout the entire landscape of consumer products, the knowledge, domain expertise, and practice philosophies of aggressive executives are evolving the marketplace.

I interviewed a 30-year veteran of Walmart® who was now the CMO of a company dominating the sport drink category. She hired executives from Apple to manage her customer service operation, an executive from Coca-Cola to manage their category marketing, and was instrumental in bringing in a former Procter & Gamble executive to build their revenue growth management organization (which, by the way, now included the ownership of their trade channel promotion). Across the entire corporate infrastructure, they changed how they went to market, and adopted numerous practices of other companies not even in their category, to create fresh and innovative offerings to their customers.

"We were strong in almost every major category and category captains with virtually all of our major accounts," she said. "But we needed to grow our brand and expand the category in areas we were not used to." She had the task from her CEO to grow the brand to a level that most would have simply said could not be achieved. Leveraging her employee base and executive team, she sought out domain expertise across different areas and created plans to move into new markets.

"We dominated sports and were the go-to sports drink for Hollywood and Broadway, but we had to become innovative and uncomfortable—penetrating a new market and growing it. We selected a couple of industries where our product would provide relief, and one of them was the construction industry. We took it by storm, promoting in construction magazines, attending trade shows, and pushing our product as the right drink to satisfy and refresh on the job."

The program and promotion were a huge success. With a direct marketing program that features everything from t-shirts with the brand logo, to hardhat decals and lunch boxes, the visuals were smart. But also, the co-op advertising funding was split into a fixed accrual base for smaller contractors and a MDF offering that provided additional funding for more rigorous promotional campaigns. The co-op funding could be used for a large array of media and tactical activities and was reimbursed at 100% of cost of promotional tactics. The MDF program had three tiers of funding that offered larger companies the ability to cover their higher costs of marketing and promotion. The MDF funding would be based on a collaboratively planned promotion, just as with a typical FMCG retailer or distributor.

Similar efforts were offered across industries like industrial equipment, manufacturing, lawn and garden services, HVAC, and automotive aftermarket. The bottom line is that the *bottom line* was significantly increased with incremental volume and revenue created where no previous sales were made outside of a consumer's personal decision to buy and drink their products.

The critical take-away here is that the process of planning and the collaborative efforts that may not be totally "equal and proportionate" are, however, representative of the reality in channel incentives and trade promotion. That *reality*, by the way, is arguably difficult to adhere to as a regulatory requirement of equality totally and strictly. Kroger, Walmart, Costco, and Best Buy are always going to demand and receive incentives to drive the huge volumes they can and will deliver. The smaller independent retailers and distributors will not be promoting as often and cannot commit to the sales volumes required for the larger promotional funding.

In many ways, the shell game played is a necessary part of ensuring that the manufacturer meets their revenue forecasts, and the retailer delivers the traffic in their stores, or on their ecommerce sites, to generate the volume of sales and an overall satisfactory shopping experience demanded by the consumer.

So, in the business of consumer products trade and channel promotion, the pea is under all three shells.

CHAPTER 6

THE BATTLE FOR HEARTS AND MINDS (AND SHELF, BASKET, AND PANTRY)

Most people equate the phrase "winning the hearts and minds" with the American strategy during the Vietnam war; and that is certainly reflective of statements made by the military and the Johnson administration of the time. But the first to use the phrase "hearts and minds" was British general Sir Gerald Templer in February 1952, during what was called the *Malayan Emergency,* where a major tactical emphasis was on the support and caring of the Malayan people against the communist insurgents' threats and hostile actions against the populace.[40]

Although born out of military strategy, the winning of "hearts and minds" is also a strategic objective in consumer marketing and the primary focus in creating demand for any good or service. Everybody understands the basic intent and goals of national advertising and consumer direct marketing, and most people realize it is a very costly activity. But as we have shown in previous chapters, the portion of a consumer products company's total marketing budget that supports the winning of those hearts and minds of the consumer is only about one-third of that total marketing budget.

So, how does a smart modern consumer products company leverage the other two-thirds share of the overall budget represented by trade channel promotion to do the same thing?

This IS the *Invisible Economy*. In Chapter 5, we talked about how the goals and objectives of a consumer products company's key account managers and sales reps seem to focus more on getting the initial buy-in than on the results of the actual promotion they configure to incite the buyer to purchase high volumes of products. What hearts and minds are being won with the *Invisible Economy*? This is certainly the question for most companies today; but the target and the intent of trade promotion must change to more of a consumer engagement focus.

Tactical Failure

According to the American Heritage Dictionary, one of the main definitions of *Economy* is a "Careful, thrifty management of resources, such as money, materials, or labor."[41]

The more than one trillion dollars of trade channel promotion spending globally represents more than 27% of the gross revenues of consumer products companies.[42] In fact, according to the Promotion Optimization Institute's 2019 report on the *State of the Industry* for trade promotion, almost 40% of the consumer products companies polled spent more than 20% of their gross revenues, and more than 14% actually fell into the highest category spending more than 27% of their gross revenues on trade promotion. This is not the entire marketing budget, rather only that portion spent on trade promotion.

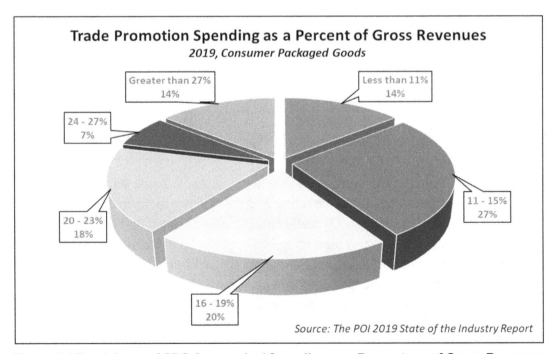

Figure 6.1 Breakdown of CPG Companies' Spending as a Percentage of Gross Revenues

Given that Nielsen says more than 70% of this money fails to generate positive breakeven, does this meet the American Heritage Dictionary definition of "careful, thrifty management of resources?"

No, it absolutely does not.

In Chapter 5, we explored the methods and policies of both retailers and manufacturers/suppliers in the process of planning trade promotions and what specific goals and objectives are sought in the results of trade promotions. We told you that, for both sides of this negotiation, the consumer was often NOT the primary target, and for the manufacturer/supplier, generally not even in the equation of the definition of success. We also told you that, for the retailer, the tactics—those promotional activities that comprise each promotion—are determined by their marketing and merchandising organization based on time-tested use.

For the manufacturer/supplier, the decision to recommend specific types of tactics when presenting a promotional plan to a retail buyer is usually based on a previous similar promotion which produced strong return on investment. In today's modern marketing technology, perhaps the largest segment of technology spending is analytics, and especially the more sophisticated artificial-intelligence-based modeling and predictive tools. Over the past two decades, consumer products manufacturers have spent billions of dollars annually shoring up their hardware and "big data" software platforms to accommodate the high speeds and heavy volumes of today's marketing intelligence requirements.

However, based on the results of the 2020 *Retail and Consumer Goods Analytics Study* conducted jointly by *Consumer Goods Technology* and *Retailer Information Systems* magazines, emphasis on predicting higher ROI on trade promotions is taking a back seat to more traditional forms of reporting of after-the-fact results and post promotion analytics.[43]

Business Function	Basic Departmental Analytics (Ad Hoc Reporting of Information)	Basic enterprise Reporting (After-the-Fact Information Reporting)	Basic Analytics (After-the-Fact Trends and Analysis)	Investigative Analytics (Correlation/Causal Analysis, Investigational Techniques)	Predictive Analytics (Predictive Modeling, Optimization Algorithms)
Assortment Planning	11%	11%	52%	22%	4%
Space Planning	27%	19%	31%	15%	8%
Pricing & Promotions	8%	23%	31%	31%	8%
Promotional Effectiveness	11%	30%	26%	30%	4%
Marketing Spend	7%	41%	26%	26%	0%

Source: CGT & RIS "Retail and Consumer Goods Analytics Study 2020

Figure 6.2 Level of Capability and Innovation in Advanced Analytics Across RGM Functions

Clearly, the Covid-19 pandemic has created an extremely high emphasis on product assortment, space planning and execution, and the need to focus on the movement of products through the supply chain. 2020, as a year to evaluate ongoing promotional success, may end up being a wash; but even so, the low response rate to predictive planning as a significant focus and direction of marketing technology spending is telling a tale of status quo rather than rapid movement toward better predictive planning.

That said, what does it say about the ability of both the retailer (and wholesaler, distributor, or reseller) and the manufacturer/supplier to up their tactical activity planning games, translating after-the-fact results of promotions into more effective predictive ROI? Not much, I assure you.

We will dive deeper into the area of promotion planning data and analytics in a later chapter; however, what Figure 6.2 depicts is a realistic status of *thinking* among the revenue growth management (RGM) executives today who have been charged with the responsibility to increase the effectiveness of promotions across all marketing sectors, and to do that, they must understand what makes the promotions successful.

This is critical because today, it is really not working.

Even considering the glowing results stated in the CGT/RIS study[43] by the CEOs and CMOs of many of the world's great consumer products companies, many believe that the report card on how well the key account managers and manufacturers' sales reps performed sports a pretty low grade.

For even those more aggressive and progressive CPG companies that have more sophisticated AI and machine learning technology, there are still significantly high failure rates of promotions in the stores and online. While we can easily point to the pandemic of 2020 as a primary causal factor for low promotional success, a return to normalcy in 2021 and 2022 will not find the results that much better unless there is significant focus and improvement in the tactical planning capability—being able to discern which promotional activities have the highest response rates, and why.

The "why" is the thing. It means being able to understand what happens to the consumer when they experience a promotional tactical activity. How does a particular tactical activity impact each link in the *Consumer Chain,* and how can the key account managers and reps, buyers, and merchandisers optimize the use of these tactical activities in each promotion?

The Consumer Chain represents a fluid step-by-step process of thought and action, from the point of realizing a need, to the point of fulfillment for each consumer. At points along the way, the manufacturer and the retailer need to come together in lockstep to provide the right incentive to keep their products front and center in the consumer's ongoing thinking and actions.

Super clean-up guru Marie Kondo created a methodology of organizing and "tidying up" known as The KonMari Method™[44] where you would move through a process of six steps with a particular item ending with the key question, "Does it spark joy?"

In her methodology, she talks about physically holding an item in your hand and sensing a feeling of joy or something less. If you feel joy from it, keep it. If not, ditch it!

As a consumer, you know that there are certain "feelings" or sensory perceptions which help you determine if something "sparks joy" enough to move to the next level in the *Consumer Chain* toward an eventual purchase, and even more, a wildly excited opportunity to share your joy (or disappointment) with someone about it and of course, to buy it again. This is the same thing as Marie Kondo's methodology, isn't it? If you are researching a product, whether sitting in front of your computer, or picking through the apple bin to pick the right Honeycrisp apple, there are observations and immediate analyses your brain makes to decide to keep it or keep looking.

I recently decided I wanted a chainsaw. And yes, I am from Texas, so it is a mandatory product for your workshop! But my dilemma was whether to go with a traditional gas-powered unit or purchase one of the electric chainsaws. I looked over the more common brands at my local home improvement big box store starting with the gas-powered ones I was more familiar with. Simple. Mix the oil and gas (it was a two-cycle engine that required it) and pull the rope to start. How hard is that? Run it until you finish, or it runs out of gas, right?

Then I looked at the electric ones. Sleek, powerful, much cleaner and a little lighter. But they took battery packs.

Really expensive battery packs that had to be charged. And you had to buy the charger and battery separately unless you found a combination set. They were much more expensive and, of course, batteries ran down, don't they? So, at about $60 per battery, the recommendation was to buy at least one other, perhaps two, to be sure you can complete the job.

Neither sparked joy in me. Not until I saw an ad from one of the local stores that offered a free charger, about a $75 value, did I return to the idea of an electric saw. Now the deal looked better, and I decided to go with the electric version.

Free goods. Buy one, get one. Buy one, get one at half price. All of these are tactics which are commonly used in promotions and are designed to "spark joy" in the consumer, hopefully making the purchase decision easier to make. The corporate marketing organizations do considerable analysis and research on what sparks joy among the consumers, but for the lion's share of the budget, trade promotion spending, are these tactics working?

Evidence is mounting that they do not. As consumers, we go through endless thinking processes about what we want, how much we want to pay, and where to go to purchase it. The mindset we have is simple. We need it, so we go find and buy it.

We know we can check a newspaper ad, look for coupons, and hopefully see the product on sale at a discounted price when we shop. The question for the consumer products companies is which tactic does the trick? If a combination of tactics, which ones work to get us to pull the trigger on the purchase?

Trade Channel Promotion Tactics

In the FMCG and CPG industries, trade channel promotions are comprised of one or more distinct tactics or promotional activities. Some companies call them "Promotion Mechanics," to refer to the methods used to attract the shopper.

For most companies, there are four primary categories within which these tactics fall:

1. **Temporary Price Reductions (TPR)** – Any form of price discounting including reductions in price per unit, buy one-get one free (BOGO), or some variation of free or discounted goods with purchase of the first.

2. **Displays** – Multiple forms of physical product promotion ranging from Instore-developed stacks of products with signage (as an example, an end-cap display at the end of an aisle), signs and videos, and kiosks to special free standing shelf units that are pre-shipped by the supplier (often referred to as "Shippers" where the portable shelving is shipped fully stocked with product for immediate setup).

3. **Advertisements** – Any form of advertising on media including newspaper, broadcast, direct mail, instore flyers, door-hangers, or on cart ads (affixed to video or sign boards on the shopping cart itself).

4. **Demonstrations** – Often called "Product Sampling," involve people in small booths or at tables cooking or sharing single serving samples of food or beverages with shoppers as they walk through the store.

PRIMARY TRADE PROMOTION TACTICS
All Consumer Products

Tactic Type (Category)	Tactic Name	
Temporary Price Reduction (TPR)	Percentage Discount (Off Regular Price)	Free Goods with Purchase
	Buy One Get One Free (BOGO)	Multiple Product Purchase Offers
	Flat Amount Off Price	Price Rebate (with Claim/Reimbursement)
Display	On Shelf	Gondola
	End Cap Front	Freezer/Cold Case
	End Cap Rear	Free-Standing/Shipper
	In-Aisle	Front Entrance/Lobby
	Floor	Shelf Video
	Checkout	Kiosk
Advertising	Newspaper	Permanent Signage
	Pre-printed Insert (Local)	On-Vehicle
	Free-Standing Insert (National/Regional)	Instore Carts-Print
	Broadcast	Movie Theater
	Social Media	Hang Banners
	Commercial Outdoor	Window Signage
Demonstrations (Product Sampling)	Instore Demonstrations	"Vendor Days"
	Free Samples	External Demonstrations (Events)
Coupons	Free-Standing Inserts	Instant Coupons
	Direct Mail	POS-Generated

Figure 6.3 Primary Tactical Activities for Trade Channel Promotion Planning and Execution

Figure 6.3 gives you a well-rounded view of the various primary tactics used in FMCG and throughout trade channel promotions across the entire consumer products industry.

Within the FMCG sectors, virtually all trade promotions are comprised of one, two, or all three of these primary tactical activities. By far and away, the most common of these will be a temporary price reduction (TPR). According to the latest data from a survey conducted among 294 consumer products manufacturers, 64%[45] of all trade promotions included some sort of temporary price reduction (TPR) as part of the offer.[5]

It would be easy to say that the popularity of the TPR as a promotional tactic is because both the manufacturer and the retailer believe that price is the main driver in the shopper's decision to buy when in the store, but I beg to differ. It is not so much the driver of the shopper's decision to buy as it is the retail buyer's decision to purchase the product from the manufacturer/supplier.

Remember what we talked about in Chapter 5. The "Shell Game" of promotion planning is predicated on revenue and profit margin—especially for the retailer. After all, the retailer needs the promotion to be successful, sure; but they need to sustain margin and profitability to survive. The manufacturer/supplier needs to push the volume at a reasonable profit margin to meet forecast.

Make no mistake about it, the price in the promotional tactical plan has more to do with the incentive to make the deal than it does an incentive to attract the consumer. It always has been, and you should be somewhat happy to hear that, because in the end, the beneficiary is us, the consumer, is it not?

This is not so much an indictment of the players making the deal (the retail buyer and the key account manager) as it is of the process itself. On top of that, it is unfair to label the "TPR" as only a tactic to generate the incentive to do the deal, because the competition in the shelf is intense and if the pricing is not attractive, the impact is felt at the checkout register in fewer sales, to be sure.

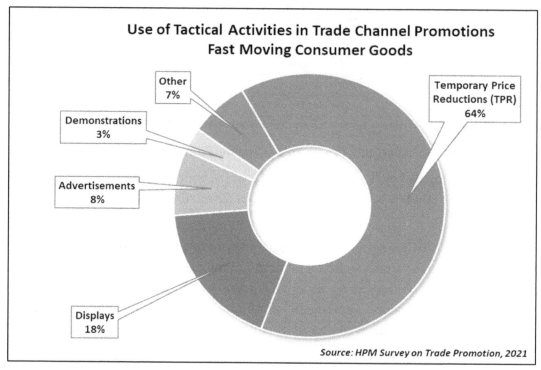

Figure 6.4 Average Usage of Primary Tactical Promotion Activities in CPG

Demonstrations are growing as a tactical vehicle to generate shopper interest. Supermarket chains are building extensive instore cooking areas where a demonstrator is cooking and sharing dishes, sauces and other food items with the shoppers gathering around. The growth of online and television food programs such as the Food Network™, the Cooking Channel™, and thousands of online cooking and recipe sites is creating strong interest in food preparation and meal planning; and these demonstrations are drawing crowds and selling products.

The *Coupon* is expanding into a multifaceted, multisourced promotional tactic. Most of us know the coupon as a hard-copy printed document that contains a promotional offer of some price reduction or other advantage providing we purchase the product.

Coupons are used by both the manufacturer and the retailer to incite the consumer to buy the product(s) promoted. Manufacturer coupons are typically distributed through *Free-Standing Inserts* that can most often be found in your Sunday newspaper when you open it up and all the inserts fall on the floor.

Seriously though, the "FSI" as the medium is most widely known as a printed piece that you get as a separate publication in the newspaper; but it can also be distributed through the mail, dropped on your front porch, or now on your mobile phone, and online in the form of a "click and print" document. There is an entire industry around the creation, distribution, fulfillment, and redemption of these promotional vehicles, and historically, the returns have been less than stellar.

According to Coupons.com CEO Steven Boal in an investor call in February 2020, the free-standing insert coupon business has a very precarious future. His concern was based on a projected 20% reduction of his company's printed FSI coupon customer forecast, and a fear that it would lead to a downward spiral in printed FSI coupons overall. "One of the things that happens when you start to change the dynamics of a vehicle like that is that others who are left in that vehicle are left sitting in a nonperforming asset," Boal said of FSIs. "So, they're sitting with the dollar value of coupons in a product that isn't being utilized anymore, because the aggregate value of that product has gone down. And so that sort of speeds up the process a little bit."[46]

The prediction may be a bit premature, on the other hand, because FSI stalwart, Valassis/Vericast, had projected a 24% increase in FSI coupon inserts for 2020, going to 47 weeks versus 38 weeks for 2019.[46] According to Kantar, 2019 FSI coupon activity fell 12.4%[46] while digital coupons were up 8.5% that same year. So, Boal's predictions may be accurate after all.

Paper coupons from FSIs are still popular, even in the pandemic-driven environment of 2020, with more millennials using paper coupons from the retailers themselves, collected instore while shopping, at a rate of 84% versus coupons direct mailed or in FSIs at a rate of 82%, and click and print coupons at 74%.[47]

In fact, according to Valassis/Vericast, nearly 47% of consumers actually have at least one coupon app on their mobile phones, and based on research by Invesp, 68% of consumers believe that digital coupons contribute to higher product and brand loyalty.[48]

Tracking retail-offered coupons is extremely difficult because the nature of the coupon is a price reduction offer, therefore part of the TPR tactic used. Clearly engaging the consumer with a coupon is not only a powerful incentive, but maybe more widely used as a tactical medium than even displays or ad features. So, for trade promotion management executives, perhaps there should be a new *mechanic* or tactical activity designated purely as a *coupon,* and perhaps a subordinate hierarchical relationship to the general category of TPRs.

This is exemplary of the importance of data quality in promotion planning. Today, the historical data definitions for promotion tactics are broadly vague and misleading. The reason is that each of these subcategories of tactical activities has unique qualities and specific values that contribute to the success of a promotion. Measuring them at this level is critical, because otherwise, as we have seen often in the analysis of the *Invisible Economy,* the trust and precision of analysis of performance is lacking and decisions are being made on erroneous assumptions. As promotional planning becomes more sophisticated with the use of higher quality advanced AI-driven predictive analytics, having this definition breakdown will clearly increase the quality and accuracy, hence *trust* in the forecasts of promotion ROI.

ADDITIONAL CHANNEL INCENTIVE TRADE PROMOTION TACTICS
All Consumer Products

Tactic Type (Category)	Tactic Name
Commercial Activities	Professional Services
	Equipment
	Training/Education
Search Engine Optimization/Management (SEO/SEM)	Optimization Tools/Tech
	Talent
	Maintenance/ Management
Warranty	Warranty Offering and Management Costs
Literature	Product Literature
Vehicle	Purchase Assistance for Required Vehicles
Financing	Subsidizing Financing Interest/Fees
Digital Development	Websites, Social Media Sites, Online Payment Setup

Figure 6.5 An Example of Common Tactical Activities Used by CPG Companies

For co-operative advertising programs and supporting funds offered over and above accrued allowances such as MDF, business development funding (BDF,) or similar channel incentive promotion offers, manufacturers, resellers, distributors, and wholesalers all rely upon more relevant tactical activities and media than you find in typical FMCG promotions. The major consumer products sectors of fashion, hardware/DIY, automotive aftermarket, consumer electronics, over-the-counter pharmaceuticals, personal care, and health and beauty aids all leverage very practical support incentive tactics that not only drive consumer/shopper incentives, but also business-to-business (B2B) incentives to support direct and indirect-purchasing resellers, wholesalers/distributors, and value-added resellers.

As mentioned previously, most of these programs require strict adherence and compliance with detailed documentation of cost and proof of performance before payment is made. And in many cases, especially with more non-media commercial tactical activities, pre-approval would be required.

Plugging a Decades-Old Gap

"Consumer Engagement" is a term finding its way into the primary lexicon of consumer products strategic and tactical planning and execution. It is about how the company engages and interacts with the consumer from the point of creating demand through the purchase and consumption or use of the product.

A consumer products company *engages* the consumer through four primary channels. These channels are:

- **Corporate Marketing** – Advertising, consumer research, promotional events, coupons, rebates, and sponsorships.

- **Customer Service** – Customer call centers, hotlines, online chatbots, and other direct communications with consumers who have purchased, consumed and/or used the product(s).

- **Retail/Wholesale Channels** – Leveraging the channels to offer consumer promotions in retail, wholesale, or multitier reseller channels of distribution.

- **Logistics and Shipping** – Shipping and delivering product directly to the consumer when purchased online through the company's e-commerce websites.

Those channels are controlled by different organizations inside the company, and alarmingly, all four operate somewhat independently of each other. Nowhere is this truer than between the corporate marketing and sales organizations. Historically, these two groups have rarely, if at all, communicated, much less collaborate to ensure an aligned promotional message to the consumer between the corporate advertising, events, and direct-to-consumer marketing and trade promotions.

The sales organization owns two-thirds of the total corporate marketing budget in the form of trade channel promotion funding. Corporate marketing owns the other one-third and uses it to conduct research, buy and execute media advertising campaigns, develop corporate messaging and positioning, and manage the paper and digital couponing campaigns and promotions. In most companies, the customer service organization is operationally part of the corporate marketing group. The supply chain management organization owns sales and operations planning, logistics, transportation, warehousing, and demand planning. There is typically alignment between sales (key account managers and sales reps) and demand planners because the sales forecast is dependent upon the projected consumer demand models.

In the summer of 2019, a major CPG company, a category leader, ran into a buzzsaw of negative consumer sentiment, and a furious major account, when two competing offers for the same products hit the marketplace. A $147,000 trade promotion was planned and executed for six days with one of the top two customer accounts that included a TPR, display and advertising that provided for a "Buy Three of a specific size package in any one of five different flavors and pay $1.89 per unit"—a full $1.00 per unit price discount.

All the analytics and predictions from the manufacturer's trade promotion optimization engine projected a 344% ROI based on similar successes in similar deals, timeframes, tactics, and product groups. Two days into the trade promotion, the corporate marketing organization dropped a national coupon in a FSI that offered a "Buy Two Units (of the same exact SKUs and choice of flavors) and receive a discounted price of $1.44 per unit, a savings of $1.45 per unit.

The retailer saw that the huge volumes purchased by the shoppers tracked by the checkout scanners for the first day, completely disappeared on the second and third days of the promotion pointing to a disastrous failure in the trade promotion. The promotion was immediately stopped. The consumers seemed either very confused or preferred to buy only two units of the product instead of loading their pantry with three, as the trade promotion required.

Had corporate marketing not dropped the coupon, it appeared that the promotion was headed for a successful outcome, and the large volume buy by the retailer would have ended up in a successful deal for the key account manager. Instead, the KAM had to provide another $55,000 *with no supporting sales volume* to subsidize a further price drop to move the excess inventory on hand to clear the retailer's shelves before any new deal would be possible.

The marketing coupon drop also suffered because losing the support of one of the largest supermarket chains in the USA impacted projected redemption rates. The shoppers were confused, and in cases where the retailer could not accept overlapping promotions on the same product group in the same time frame, neither discount was offered, negating both promotions.

The sales team and the KAM had no idea of any impending coupon drop by corporate marketing because they did not have visibility to the corporate marketing calendar, nor did they have any collaborative communications with their colleagues in marketing. Likewise, the marketing team had no knowledge of any impending trade promotion and did not have access to the trade promotion calendar.

Sadly, this is a common problem, and it is surprising that this continues to be an issue today with the sophistication of technology we have at our disposal.

The Ground Game

To reach and engage the consumer requires significant money, as we have been saying throughout this book. For FMCG companies, and other high volume consumer durables manufacturers, this means that a great deal more effort must go into what it takes to not only get the attention of the consumer, but to actually drive them through the *Consumer Chain* and incite a fierce loyalty to the brand and product portfolio.

Continuing the analogy of war, a winning strategy is one that requires the efficient use and optimization of all assets. Back to the American Heritage Dictionary definition of *economy*, this means marshalling the entire scope of human, technical, and intellectual capital into one singular focus that, across the entire landscape of the marketplace engages every consumer consistently and continually. It means sustaining this effort throughout the entire process and maintaining accurate and detailed intelligence that enables smart decisions, wise predictions, and high return on investment.

It means not only ensuring that corporate marketing and sales work together, but also in concert with channel partners as well, to form a triumvirate of power that can meet the consumer's needs and demands at every link in the *Consumer Chain*. This is difficult for the modern consumer products manufacturer because it requires a total departure from the operational standards that define the policies and procedures of corporate marketing and sales organizations.

The corporate marketing organization knows the consumer better than any other group in the company, including the entire sales organization. From the CMO on down, every thread of action taken is designed to seek out and understand what the consumer needs and how to create a high enough demand to incite action that ends in a purchase. But that is not all. A good marketing team can also tell you what it takes to sustain loyalty, define the product lifecycle, improve future products that are hopefully one step ahead of the consumer's needs, and of course, how to create the right message of quality and price that stimulates consumer action.

The corporate marketing team has partnerships with leading advertising agencies, public relations firms, production houses, digital technology superstars, and social media sentiment analysis vendors. They have access to terabytes of consumer data and employ super smart marketing gurus who know how to translate all that data into actionable direction.

They also typically control the customer service organization, so there are direct consumer interactions that they can infuse into their messaging and positioning as well as helping to define how the product should be changed, upgraded, or dropped.

The sales team knows the channel. They are retail, wholesale, and reseller distribution experts and know what it takes to drive the product volume. They can read the reports, they understand the ebb and flow of the consumption, and they keep a keen eye on the movement of product. They are the field commanders. They are on the front lines of the fight and their weapons are demand plans, product knowledge, channel relationships, and trade promotion, co-op advertising and market development funds.

But they are *not* marketing experts. Yet they have full and complete control of more than two-thirds of the company's financial resources that are designated as *marketing funds* with the full and complete intention of driving the consumer to the stores, e-commerce sites, and distribution counters to buy the company's products. They feed the channels of distribution. who are the final point in the purchase cycle, with billions of dollars in funds and, along with their channel customers, are the final decision makers about where and how that money is spent.

The marketing organization knows the consumer from all the intelligence they gather, and the insights created by very smart people who are paid to translate the intelligence into successful messaging and positioning. But it is the retailer who knows the consumer *personally*. They have credit card data. They have walking and traffic patterns in their store. They watch every purchase and know more about what products are selected at the moment of purchase decision than anyone on earth. They have demographic data on every neighborhood they serve with a store location. They know how to create visuals that stimulate the shopper to buy, and they know how to create a great shopping experience for the consumer.

The retailers are the ground troops. They _are_ the front line. No consumer products company is successful without their total commitment.

For the consumer engagement process to be successful, all three of these organizations need to be in synchronous alignment in strategy, timing, tactics, and intelligence. All three teams need to work together, collaborate, and plan effectively to ensure successful campaigns for the hearts and minds of the consumer.

But that is not happening today.

Oh sure, there are innovative organizations and companies trying at new ways of working together, and that is worth the applause. For the most part, however, the marketing and sales organizations do not engage with each other. They do not collaborate on promotional calendars and they rarely, if ever, work together to determine the right combination of tactics, timing, and products to meet the corporate revenue forecasts.

"We are aware of the trade promotions we run, and for the most part, they are successful," explains the CMO of an over-the-counter pharmaceutical giant. "We regularly provide consumer reports to the sales organization and have regular calls with the demand planners [statistical analysts responsible for the creation of the sales baselines], but frankly, we still see some pretty large pockets of misalignment and outright ignorance of our brand messaging and positioning in the trade promotions that are run."

When I talked to the executive vice president of sales for that same company, I heard something a bit different.

"Well, yes, of course we do see the reports on consumer intelligence from [marketing], and we strive to ensure that the messaging is always accurate. We work with our accounts to make sure that any signage, displays or other visuals have consistency," he said. "But at the end of the day, [marketing] has no role in the sell-in negotiations other than maybe how we plan the demand curve and generate the incremental volume we need to meet forecast. That's on us."

But then I asked about tactics.

"We look back at what worked," he said. "The combination of [tactics] we used in previous promotions and the results guide our KAMs in the planning stage. Of course, you have to weigh the impact of current versus the historical period; but overall, it generally works well."

I asked, "Do you consult the corporate marketing promotional event calendars when you plan promotions?"

He replied, "Not always. Sure, we keep whatever national advertising campaigns in mind, and we do try to make sure we are not overlapping promotions with another account in the same market, but generally we keep to our trade calendars as the primary guide."

In other words, no, there is no real collaboration with marketing on an ongoing process.

All the elements that comprise a successful consumer engagement campaign are there. The ability to create demand, the capability to translate and respond to that demand, the historical evidence required to prescribe a promotion that delivers on the forecast and generates high ROI, and the instore intelligence to drive the shopper to the product purchase, are all present within the combined forces of corporate marketing, sales, and the channel retailer.

Together in an aligned and synchronized campaign, both the manufacturer/ supplier and their retail channel customer can win the battle for the hearts and minds, as well as the shopping cart, the pantry, and the sustainable loyalty. The data exists. The technology exists. But the process and the infrastructural policies and procedures are hurdles that continue to seem very difficult to overcome.

RGM to the Rescue

Revenue Growth Management (RGM) could be the way out of this mess.

Historically, revenue growth management has been largely dedicated to price management and, over the past few decades, product assortment optimization. Recently, however, consumer products companies of all sizes have begun elevating RGM to incorporate more critical pieces of the consumer engagement and revenue generation process like demand planning, retail execution and now, trade channel promotion management and execution.

As more companies expand the RGM practice, they also elevate the organization leadership, giving it strength to make critical decisions that directly impact the entire company's top and bottom lines on a faster pace and with more accuracy than before. RGM leadership is joining the C-suite with positions of Chief Revenue Officer. Companies like Unilever, PepsiCo, Kimberly-Clark, and Mondelez are establishing global RGM organizational infrastructure, and beginning to take advantage of data, technology, and new ways of working together to begin synchronizing and aligning the corporate processes and organizations.

New studies being done on expanded RGM practices are showing the quantitative value as well.[49]

Business Improvement with Revenue Growth Management	Survey Response
Returns of 2% to 5% on annual trade spending	24%
Returns of 6% to 10% on annual trade spending	9%
Elimination of poorly performing promotions	44%
Improved forecasting	33%
Process improvements	51%
Improved go-to-market strategies	18%
Greater visibility of business opportunities and risks	44%
Improved relationships with retail customers	20%

Source: Promotion Optimization Institute, "State of the Industry Report, 2021"

Figure 6.6 Improvement in Critical RGM Metrics Is Driving CPG Companies to Expand and Innovate Key Functions

With more strategic focus on RGM, trade promotion is becoming the target of upgraded technology, increased data acquisition, and functional integration across the entire value chain. Many of the largest FMCG and consumer products companies used pandemic-stained 2020 to build and/or integrate technology platforms to accommodate an expanded RGM function.

Figure 6.7 is an example of a real RGM initiative for a global consumer products company with revenues in excess of $8 billion across more than 75 countries.

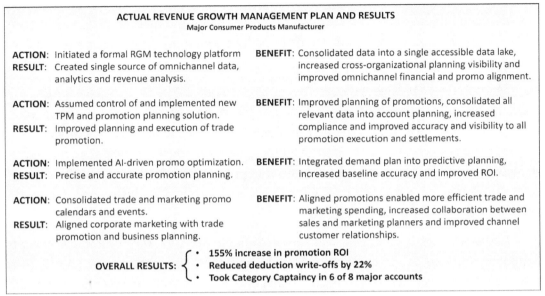

Figure 6.7 The Experiences of an Actual Global CPG Category Leader During Late 2019 and through 2020

This initiative took more than 13 months to complete, but many of the results you see in this chart were realized within a few months. The value to the company and to its channel partners are rather obvious, however there is another value to the *consumer* as well. The lesson learned from the example before about the coupon and trade promotion virtually cancelling each other out is that there is always the threat of negative impact on the consumer. That impact is confusion. When consumers are confused, they make bad decisions, or worse, *no decision*. They walk away.

Flags of Truce

The animosity between sales and marketing organizations has a long history. As we noted in previous chapters, when trade promotion spending grew exponentially during the past 100 years, the corporate marketing budgets tilted toward the sales organization to fund that growth. Both organizations had their views, with marketing feeling like they knew more about the consumer than sales, hence they should be the ones to own any and all promotions. Sales, on the other hand, pointed to the fact that, without this money, there was no way to meet forecast and generate the revenue requirement demanded by the company.

The argument has continued through generations of CMOs and CSOs and is still evident today.

To add salt to the wound, with the intensity and growth of digital media and e-commerce, brick-and-mortar retailers felt the pain of losing sales and had to up their own games to attract the consumer. This meant more demand for funds, which mandated higher annual trade spending budgets. The communications and collaboration barrier that has been building between consumer products sales and marketing departments is still very much in place, but there seems to be light emerging from the end of the dark tunnel.

More trade gatherings today are beginning to address the issue of consumer marketing and trade promotion collaboration. There are numerous case studies given during these meetings from consumer products companies relating their stories, and examples of how they have improved the quality of consumer engagement and reduced consumer confusion due to conflicting promotions. A "flag of truce" of sorts seems to be waving across the FMCG and consumer products industry, and that is absolutely a great thing to see happening.

Based on what I have seen over the past couple of years, the corporate C-suite is beginning to put more gas into the RGM tanks and giving them far more authority over virtually all actions that drive consumer engagement, sales volume, revenue, and profit. And it only makes sense, does it not?

My friend Bill is a longtime executive in the corporate marketing world with stints at some of the most famous and largest CPG companies on the planet, as well as serving as a senior executive advisor and consultant in the area of consumer marketing in the food and beverage sectors. He has been around for enough years to have been part of the riff between marketing and sales and is an experienced budget warrior. Here is what he has to say about the way things are going today:

"Sales reps have their job, and it is a tough one, I'll grant you that. They are in the trenches with the account teams and their very livelihood hinges on them being able to beat the forecast against reduced budgets and lacking technology. I totally get the angst they feel. But, I don't blame them for my loss of budget over the years, and I realize that the account pushes them to spend more money, usually far more than they allocated. Instead, I blame the system that we have. I have tried several times to work within this system to collaborate with the key account [team] but the timing never works. We have to buy media months and sometimes years in advance, and we have to create the messaging and themes far earlier than the KAMs are ready to begin their promotion planning. As a result, even though they may see our calendar and understand the campaigns we are planning, their customers push their own category plan, and often that is where the conflict lies."

Bill went on to remind me that in his organizational background and experience, the revenue growth management operation dealt primarily with pricing, and since corporate marketing messaging and positioning rarely, if ever, had price as a component, they never had any real working relationship with them.

Another colleague of mine, Amanda, has been a successful sales executive for one of the world's premier beverage makers. She began as a territory sales rep and worked her way up to CSO over the course of 15 years. Like Bill, she had to work within a prism of intensity that basically drove her to use any financial means she could to generate the volume, revenue and margin required. Working with the marketing organization was always painful for her, and she had to endure countless meetings with the COO and CFO acting as referees between her marketing counterparts, who often demanded that her budget be cut back to redirect funds toward corporate advertising, e-commerce, or even customer service initiatives. Here is what Amanda had to say:

> "I am not now and never have been a marketer, and I have to object to anyone who says I have to be. I have one job, and that was to deliver the volume—sometimes JUST volume, irrespective of revenue and margin. I believe I had very good intelligence from [our syndicated provider] that told me which promotional tactics worked better than others, and I plugged those into my promotion plans. My trade promotion data was not always accurate, but in the end, I always managed to hit and most of the time exceed forecast. Marketing had their jobs, and I have always been impressed with their knowledge of the consumer; but that is what they have to do. My job is to make sure my account scored with solid promotional ROI, sometimes even at the expense of my own profitability; but that's the job. That is what I had to do, and that costs much more than running national TV ads. I love our media messaging and creativity; but I have to follow the directives of my buyer and his merchandising teams. My planning is done every year, but every day one of my KAMs has a new event or promotional opportunity, and if I don't grab it, [my competitors] will. I can't plan the way marketing does, and the timing is nowhere near the same, so one of us would have to be out of synch and it can't be me!"

Now, however, leading consumer products companies are beginning to bend the old calendars to blend promotion planning into a single time frame across the sales and marketing landscapes. E-commerce and online promotions are now becoming part of the overall roadmap planning in early stages, with the sales executives sitting in and being part of the initial discussions of themes, messaging, positioning and timing. Category, brand, and product planning is being forged into single time frames that are beginning to bring all the consumer engagement teams together, including customer service, logistics and retail execution (e.g., field merchandising and compliance audits). Each of these organizations contribute to the generation of revenue, and certainly impact all aspects of consumer engagement. Therefore, it is smart for any manufacturer of consumer products of any kind to create a consolidated planning routine which establishes a single, aligned, and synchronized promotion calendar.

The retailer plays a key role in this as well. The effort to convert shoppers to loyal customers is the responsibility of all three entities: corporate marketing, sales, and the channel (e.g., retailer, distributor, wholesaler, reseller, and so on). There are three phases of consumer engagement, and each individual organization is responsible for their part of it:

- **Demand Creation** – Realizing a need, creating a product to fulfill that need, building the story of how this product satisfies the need, and executing advertising and marketing to deliver the institutional brand and product message.

- **Establishing the Channel of Distribution** – Furthering the brand and product message to support the channel resellers' ability to promote that message and positioning to the local customer base it serves and move the inventory to the store fronts.

- **The Shopping Experience** – Promoting the location, availability, price, and incentives for the consumer to acquire the product.

This is not just a partnership, but a team event. A *relay race* if you will.

THE CONSUMER ENGAGEMENT RELAY
The Collaborative Process for Efficient Consumer Engagement

Figure 6.8 The Three Main Players and Processes in a Typical Trade Promotion

In a modern, successful consumer engagement, it takes more than just the right tactic, timing, product, and price. Each organization in the value chain must function as a single team, handing off the figurative *baton* at each point where the other executes its specific role. You can plug in brick-and-mortar retail, e-commerce, and online sellers, and even wholesale distributors into this model, but the goal is to win—to create a loyal customer from what has become a very fickle society of consumers.

The RGM team is not waving a flag of truce, but more appropriately, a rallying flag of union. Paradigms must change, and change management is the order of the day, because to make this work, we must change people like my colleagues Bill, and Amanda did.

When you consider the incredible data available to each of these organizations, you can easily understand how a consolidated strategy can not only attract the consumer to consider the product as the right answer to satisfy their need, but also point them in the direction of the right place where they can buy it at the right price and the right incentive.

This new paradigm of collaborative partnerships can change both the consumer and the channel customer. It wins the hearts and minds of the consumer and fills the shelves with the manufacturer's/supplier's products. It can incite the consumer/shopper to pick up the product and drop it into their shopping cart or basket, buy it, use it, and tell everyone how happy they are about it.

That's not only winning the hearts and minds, but it converts a sometimes picky shopper into a loyal customer.

That is worth the paradigm change.

CHAPTER 7

Digital DEFCON 1

DEFCON 1 is the highest military alert status and the most critical defense condition. It means you are about to go to war. As with most military campaigns, there are multiple battle fronts. In the case of consumer products manufacturers and suppliers, the two major "fronts" would be the brick-and-mortar retailers, and the online e-commerce vendors (including, of course, the manufacturer's/supplier's own e-commerce channel).

Those brick-and-mortar retailers, by the way, have been in DEFCON 1 since the first consumer placed an order over the internet. For consumer products manufacturers, DEFCON 1 applies to the conditions caused by having to address two separate fronts in the new digital world: transforming their internal systems and infrastructure to accommodate digital technology; and the ongoing cultivation of their growing omnichannel distribution partners who are, themselves, evolving their own digital strategies.

Manufacturers of consumer products have historically sold their products through distribution channels of wholesalers, retailers, and value-added resellers. These are the aforementioned brick-and-mortar storefronts and physical service counters that consumers walk into and up to in search of items to purchase. With the advent of e-commerce, the channels of distribution are now divided between physical and online entities. Today's manufacturers/suppliers must walk a mercantile tightrope to not only satisfy their traditional brick-and-mortar and e-commerce channel customers, but their own internal online shopping revenue sources as well.

Digitally Transforming the Invisible Economy

"Digital transformation" is the phrase we hear a lot these days. Simply put, it means it is one of the highest focus areas for the business community today.

For consumer products companies everywhere, it is an extremely important business initiative. "Digital Transformation" refers to the changes in business that are taking place to modernize and upgrade existing processes and technologies that leverage advanced digital tools such as social media, cloud operating systems, mobile devices, and advanced entertainment and visualization products. It means reengineering systems to move from older on-premises and analog-based products and tools to achieve faster, more accurate and easier-to-use functionality which delivers higher revenues and profitability. It results in achieving higher efficiencies and effectiveness across the entire business.

It is simple to envision moving from analog to digital in the way we communicate, for instance, using sophisticated mobile technology capable of individually more computing power than the first computer on board the Apollo spacecrafts. When we address digital transformation in a typical consumer products company, the vision of what that means spans the entirety of doing business across all industries and lines of business. The most common examples of digital transformation include some of the following:

- **Supply Chain Management** – Implementing real-time visibility to the entire supply chain, from production to the store shelf, using advanced analytics, mobile communications, and enhanced data.

- **Demand Planning** – Leveraging near real-time point-of-sales data (POS) and advanced analytics to determine actual incremental volumes and revenues to establish more realistic, trusted and dynamic forecasts of expected performance baselines.

- **Warehousing and Logistics** – Using real-time digital tracking sensors, drones, smart inventory, and integrated procurement. It includes route tracking, real-time shipping status, and carrier management.

- **Customer Relationship Management (CRM)** – Sales force automation, advanced lead generation tracking and analysis, real-time customer interactions and metrics for loyalty and retention, and using digital media and communications to increase personalization.

- **Manufacturing** – Adding digital sensor technology, equipment monitoring, and artificial intelligence to predict failure rates, schedule maintenance, and provide analyses and ongoing recommendations for maximum efficiency of the process and equipment. It also means connecting key inputs like materials procurement, tracking and tracing of raw materials, and environmental health and safety of the workforce.

So, for trade channel promotion and channel marketing as a whole, what does "Digital Transformation" mean, exactly?

Across the landscape of trade and channel promotion, let's take the primary functions:

- Funding and Budget Allocation

- Promotion Planning

- Execution and Compliance

- Promotion Settlement and Closing

- Post-Promotion Analysis

The maze of steps and functions in a typical process map for each of these individual functions is rather large. Certainly, not every individual action and function can be covered here; but for the purposes of demonstrating what *Digital Transformation* might mean for the mainstream activities of trade channel promotion, consider these to be a solid representation.

Funding and Budget Allocation

Current Analog/Manual Process

- **Sales Reports from Enterprise Resource Planning (ERP) (Flat File Uploads)**
- **Sales Reports from Distributors (Hard Copies)**
- **Proof of Purchase Claims (Hard Copies for Rebates)**

Digital Transformation of Process

- **Real-time auto-population of sales data from ERP**
- **Direct uploads of indirect sales data to TPM systems**
- **Auto-calculation of accrued funds, allocations and accounting**
- **Digital device entry and settlement of rebates, and special incentive payments**

Figure 7.1 Digital Transformation Road Map for Funding and Budget Allocation

In most consumer products companies, the first action taken is to determine how the promotional funding will be determined. In traditional consumer products channel incentive programs, the standard is to designate a percentage of the net cost of product purchases by the channel customer, at a price that is the net of all discounts and rebates. These rates of accrual are generally calculated against purchases that are made within a given timeframe. Funds accrued are available on a timed basis which is usually annual or could be on a rolling basis of a given number of months (i.e., money earned during a rolling six-month cycle but lost if not used).

97

These funds are calculated by extracting the net revenues from the company's ERP systems and calculated through manual spreadsheet calculations or processed through a separate transactional system which produces a final fund amount. For indirect buying channel customers who purchase their products through wholesalers or distributors, the process is a bit more complex. The wholesalers and distributors will generally manage those funds and, when appropriate, inform the consumer products company via special reports showing the volume of products shipped, but without reference to a price to protect the pass-through markup pricing. In many industry sectors, the manufacturer limited or no visibility to the "end reseller" due to the contractual agreements with the wholesaler or distributor.

For CPG or FMCG companies, funding is based on several potential factors, but the money is generally allocated based on each customer's ability to generate the individual sales forecast of the key account manager or sales rep. There may or may not be a "base rate of funding accrual," or at least not one that is published or made known to the channel reseller, distributor or wholesaler.

However, generating the revenues and making them visible to the planners of promotions is a mission critical function. So, the source of sales data, whether it comes from the corporate ERP systems, or externally via the wholesale/distribution channels, is important in the determination of promotion performance and ROI.

Companies today will all have some form or brand of ERP system that contains the contracts and reports revenue data from which the allowances are eventually calculated and budgeted. The wholesale/distribution revenues are often flat file, or even spreadsheet reports, leading to potential errors and confusion in trying to identify the net amount of funding required for a promotional campaign.

In the future, as is noted in Figure 7.1, even with the advancement of ERP systems, the extensive use of spreadsheets, and other manual reports to calculate and maintain trade promotion, co-op and market development funding is responsible for millions of dollars of errors and miscalculated funds across all consumer product sectors. This problem is not limited to consumer products, as it is also causing financial and service issues for high tech, insurance and financial services, consumer telecom, automotive, and commercial and consumer software. These and other consumer products companies will manage these calculations and fund accounting issues internally through spreadsheets and/or home-grown technology, use trade promotion management (TPM) systems from a variety of different vendors or even employ outsource service firms with technology to manage these functions.

The level of sophistication for fund management is far lower than it should be after so many years of innovative trade promotion management solutions on the market. The wild swings in variations and exceptions in funding governance and practices create myriad nightmare scenarios for even the most powerful TPM systems to address and solve.

I recently worked with one of the hardware industry's most prominent brands to assist them and their new trade promotion management software vendor with the implementation of a sophisticated trade promotion and co-op advertising fund. Once we sat down with the trade marketing and sales finance team to set up the designs for the funding and accounting processes, it became clear that most promotions were so uniquely planned and executed that the basic business rules and program policies didn't apply—the "exception" seemed to be the rule.

Like most companies, they had a basic trade promotion fund accrual rate that was to be applied to every sales dollar generated. But the deeper we dived, the more complicated and confusing the policies became. All funds accrued on an annual basis except for certain products that had earning cycles within the year. Some of the funding earned in those cycles were to be added to the total available money the retailer had, but *not all of them*. Several separate funding rules applied to those funds which prevented them from being added into the overall fund, or, worse, from being paid out at the same rates of reimbursement (which was 100%). These funds could only be used on certain tactical activities and media; but even within those, you could not use all the funds available in the account, but instead only 50% at any one time.

Reimbursement for promotions were requested by submitting a claim with documentation of proof of performance compliance; but in most of those claims, the media and tactical activities were often used in the same campaign, which meant the TPM system had to make multiple determinations of how much money to pay based on the complex rules.

We attempted to have them change their policies, because not only was it confusing to the new TPM vendor and the retail channel customers, but also to the people internally who had different interpretations of the rules.

If anything screamed for artificial-intelligence-driven functionality, this situation did.

Looking at Figure 7.1, digital transformation here would clearly be the ability to end the human involvement in these complex calculations and maintenance of funding. Aside from the value of changing the rules and governance, AI-driven solutions would also kick in to ensure claims were paid accurately, and that funding was accurately debited from the balances in each fund.

Regarding indirect fund management through the wholesalers and distributors, clearly this is another area where, instead of massive manual and/or late reports of reseller funding, the systems could be integrated and enable real-time transactional visibility. It would also enable the wholesalers and distributors to have more control and, at the same time, provide their manufacturer/suppliers with better overall performance intelligence and ROI on the trade channel spending.

Our digital communications today are very sophisticated, so we are seeing the emergence of direct entry of purchases to establish the funding basis for rebates and other similar financial incentives where pools of money are set aside to cover the cost of rebate submission and redemption. This will become more of a common practice as direct-to-consumer marketing and promotions increase at the levels we are seeing indications of now.

The Invisible Economy IS the money, so managing the funding must be more of a priority than it has been. You will begin to see more tech-savvy consumer products companies move the fund accrual process up in the priority for digital transformation, with more of an emphasis on AI-driven calculations to provide faster, more accurate funding data to those like promotion planners, customers, and settlement teams who all need to understand the balance of available money on a real-time basis.

Promotion Planning

Current Analog/Manual Process	Digital Transformation of Process
• Excel Spreadsheet Reviews of Past Promotions • Syndicated reports of POS and Consumption • Selected direct POS data (Walmart, Target, Carrefour, Tesco, etc.) • Manual "trail and error" configuration of promotional content • Meetings with retail buyer, marketing and merchandising teams (Sell-In) • Manual addition of committed promotion to trade calendar (spreadsheet)	• Expanded, harmonized, cleansed and aligned data • AI-based predictive, prescriptive configuration of promotions with user-directed metrics and criteria for success • Collaboration platform between sales, marketing and retailer for real-time planning and approvals of promotions • Integration of social media sentiment analytics, consumer research and customer service data in near real-time • User-configured dashboards and reporting with real-time access

Figure 7.2 Digital Transformation Road Map for Promotion Planning

Of all the component processes that make up trade channel promotion management and execution, the planning of promotions is the most critical. Today, unfortunately, it is also one of the most seriously flawed and fractured of them all as well.

Tough statement?

Sure, perhaps, but regrettably true.

Promotion planning is also the one major process which will benefit the most from what digital transformation can do for a consumer products company, no matter what category or sector of the industry they represent. Already we see many presentations in CPG conferences and webinars where case histories and success stories are told relating to how a particular brand improved their trade promotion ROI because of better data, more advanced technology, or an overhaul of their program terms and conditions. Some of those stories are amazing indeed, but we are a long way from the goals and objectives this industry needs to achieve to make a positive dent in the improvement of ROI—and it all stems from the process of promotion planning.

As I am brought in to assist a company in the effort to improve promotion effectiveness, it always amazes me to see the inefficiencies within the process they use to not only plan promotions, but to evaluate performance and determine what makes a successful promotion. Almost every company, no matter whether they are a multibillion dollar global consumer juggernaut, or an emerging single-category manufacturer, works through a maze of spreadsheets and all-too-often limited performance reporting tools to manage the bulk of the process of planning new promotions.

As Current Analog/Manual Process shows in Figure 7.2, the lack of real intelligent insights, that drive which direction a promotion should take, is costly. Virtually every company depends upon the syndicated data providers such as Nielsen and Information Resources Inc. (IRI) to deliver the right intelligence to configure the right combination of timing, tactics, products, and costs that delivers a high return on their next promotion. These two firms, as well as others like them, deliver a combination of point-of-sale (POS) data and promotional results that help promotion planners to understand what has happened in past promotions that may assist them in determining what to do in the next one.

This data is important, to be sure. The quality of reporting on POS and consumption is clearly the most effective intelligence the planners have—but is it enough?

History and current statistics say probably not.

As inefficient as the manual processes are now, most key account managers feel like the ability to truly optimize a promotion eludes them, even with all of this current available data.

"I don't know, I can't really feel comfortable about the information I get these days," says the key account manager for a leading global cereal and breakfast foods manufacturer. "I depend on [syndicated provider]'s data, to be sure, but it is always late and I know it is a sampling of markets that gets me nervous about extending the insights they give me to my account's entire market."

Latency is one of the big problems, but although most of the syndicated providers have improved on their timing of reporting, it is still considered "looking into the rear-view mirror." So, it would require the promotion planners to depend upon other tools to help them assemble the right combination of insights that drive an effective *predictable* outcome for the promotion.

"There are so many variables," our KAM says. "Even if I get direct POS data from the retailer, I still have a problem looking back on previous promotions to determine whether the combination of tactics would still work, or if I need to make changes." He also pointed out that, for him, the timing is a crucial factor. But while he knows there may be differences in the marketplace from one period or year to another, it may be all he has to go on, so he is likely to repeat a previously successful promotion to the letter.

"I've been burned too many times on that, but I don't know what else to do," he laments. He is referring to a common problem in promotion planning where too many decisions are made to repeat a promotion that was successful before, only to see it fail when repeated in exactly the same terms and timing. "For me," he continues, "I would want to see the company spend more money on a true promotion optimization solution that would take all of the information we have to manually process and deliver a smarter promotion."

Looking at the other current promotion planning processes for most companies, the level of effort is significant. Multiple meetings with the trade marketing organization, with demand planning, with supply and operations planning (S&OP), finance, and of course, the customer (e.g., buyer, category managers, marketing, and merchandising teams) take time and energy with often fruitless results. Our KAM continues: "You have to do this. It seems that we are not selling, but of course we are. Each of us has to drive toward that final sales negotiation, and promotions are a critical piece of it. I just wish I could press a button have a promotion produced that has a better chance for success."

Bingo.

That is probably the best definition of a successful digital transformation of trade channel promotion planning, isn't it?

The good news is that we have the technology to do just that.

Looking at what constitutes digital transformation for promotion planning, note that data is one of the most important components of the solution to what our KAM and thousands like him want. The absence of truly relevant data has created a huge gap in the ability for even the most sophisticated of CPG companies to plan, project, and consistently deliver high ROI on promotions. There is absolutely no excuse for why this is the case because the data exists.

If you consider the so-called digitization of promotion planning, you must be ready to devote the time, technology, and talent to get the data into one place, then clean, harmonize and align it so that it is not only accurate, but trustworthy. Right now, for too many good companies, that is not the case in trade promotion planning.

Let's go back to the numbers. According to the statistics we have already stated, nearly three-quarters of all trade promotions fail to generate a positive return. Return, as a definition, is to sell more volume than is sold to the retailer. Other metrics of success are involved, of course—but here are the top solutions to making sure promotions have the best chance of success:

- **Data** - The data is clean, harmonized, aligned and trustworthy. Without good data, you cannot have faith in the outcomes.

- **Optimization** – Another "buzzword" or phrase, *promotion optimization* means there is a powerful AI and machine-learning-driven set of algorithms that improve with continued scenario analysis and deliver the most optimum combination of tactics, timing, promoted product groups, and cost—for both the manufacturer/supplier and the retailer.

- **Inventory Tracking** – Out-of-stock conditions rank among the top reasons for promotion failure. According to the *Journal of Consumer Research*, 15% of advertised products are out-of-stock at some point during the promotion.[50] Receiving POS data directly from the retailer means seeing yesterday's data and gives both the manufacturer/supplier and the retailer the visibility to reorder immediately when a promotion seems to be going south.

- **Marketing Alignment** – One of the recent focus areas these days is on the longstanding failure of communication between sales and marketing where corporate marketing, advertising, and national couponing promotions are in conflict with, or at least non-supportive of, the trade promotions. Little if any data exists on the extent of this. However, we know that too many conflicts occur and all you have to do is line up both promotional calendars to see the lack of alignment on timing.

The digital transformation of promotion planning should include upgrading systems and processes to support the improvement of all the above sources of promotional failure. This will mean advanced analytics capable of leveraging all the data into smart, predictive scenarios that deliver optimized promotion content and near real-time tracking of inventory in the supply chain and in-store.

There are some strong products in the marketplace today that utilize advanced AI-driven optimization and decision tools. They do offer predictive analytics and are the first generation of products built for trade promotion management to focus on more than just backward-looking analysis of performance. Several trade promotion vendors commonly promote an advanced optimization tool set, and some do; however, in general, as it stands today, there are very few options for real AI-based promotion optimization solutions.

The good news is that the technology is advancing, and the options are growing—but until the data becomes more available, and the platforms used become more capable of managing the data, this problem will continue to plague the consumer products promotion planning processes.

One of the most important transformations, digital or otherwise, is the need to create a formal collaboration *process* and *platform* between the sales organization, which is responsible for planning all trade promotion, and the corporate marketing organization, which controls the consumer engagement on a national and global scale with advertising media, rebates, coupon marketing, and e-commerce. The essence of an omnichannel strategy is to blend, align and coordinate everything that the consumer sees and experiences, which of course must include the retail execution of trade and channel promotions.

In a true digital environment, there would be an integration of pure consumer data including any consumer preference and demand research, customer service or call center input (to measure effectiveness of messages, positioning, product performance and so on), free-standing regional and national coupon redemption data, as well as instant and checkout coupons.

Critical to today's consumer engagement strategy is the inclusion of social media analysis, tracking and shopping data. The power and reach of social media are no longer limited to entertainment and shopping. These days, every social media platform is deep into politics, sports, and religion to the point where any CPG company, retailer, or wholesale distributor ignoring them does so at their peril. Privacy laws aside, these social media juggernauts command the attention of anyone who can read, write, or open a browser, and that applies to every single *consumer*.

The key account managers who are responsible for trade promotion planning with brick-and-mortar retailers rarely, if ever, see or take advantage of shopping data from the e-commerce channels. This includes data from their own company's online purchase performance history as well.

So, why is that? How can promotion planners justify NOT having online product promotion and purchasing data to help feed the intelligence and insights that drive more successful promotions?

We are talking about ignoring a major channel of distribution with its own tactics, timing, promoted product groups, costs and subsequent results. With billions of dollars at stake, it would seem every piece of data should be leveraged to optimize future promotional plans; yet even the most sophisticated trade promotion planning systems often fail to include this data in their source data.

Digital transformation of promotion planning cannot be considered complete until the data from all available channels are included within the same database as historical trade promotions, POS data, consumer marketing performance results, and demand planning baselines. The consumer is an omnichannel shopper, and to ensure the highest assurance that a promotion plan will achieve its best outcome, the modern optimization engines used to project results must consider the performance data from every one of those channels.

Status quo is not an option when we are talking about *The Invisible Economy of Consumer Engagement*.

Execution and Compliance

Current Analog/Manual Process	*Digital Transformation of Process*
• Manual scheduling of field merchandise rep visits • On-site manual capture of visit data into handheld tool • Upload data to corporate database • Limited access to current trade promotion plans • Limited access to past trade promotion data • Post visit report development	• Advanced trip scheduling generated by promotion planning and compliance requirements • Near real-time access by field reps of trade promotion plans, historical performance and consumer marketing calendars • Auto upload of data upon entry into handheld devices with real-time visibility across the company

Figure 7.3 Digital Transformation Road Map for Execution and Compliance

When a promotion executes, it is typically an instore event of anywhere from 5 days to two weeks. Within this period, the retailer should execute the tactics promoting the specific product(s) across all the locations agreed to. Some retail trade promotions are limited to certain regions, markets, or locations; but while the retailer has an obligation to execute the promotion as planned, actual compliance is a major problem in the consumer products industries.

Nielsen has reported that the average rate of compliance among retailers executing trade promotions is 30%[51]—an alarming statistic and clearly one of the main reasons for the high failure rates for trade promotions.

Once a promotion is run, the current manual or analog process often deployed to verify compliance is through the process of actual on-site store visits by merchandising representatives who are often independently contracted by either the manufacturer/ supplier or one of its brokerage partners. Their job is to visit a certain store location, chosen by a standard sampling methodology or by direct instruction from their manager, to perform activities associated with the verification of compliance of several contractual requirements.

These include, but are not limited to activities required to report the following information:

- **Shelf stock** – Verify the products are on the shelf in the right position and with sufficient quantities.

- **Backroom Inventory** – Checking the storage rooms in the rear of the store to determine what total inventory is on hand.

- **Promoted Price** – Check the price on each product on the shelf to ensure the price is accurately represented according to the contract, or that any promotional pricing is in place and accurate.

- **Displays** – Ensure all displays are in place and positioned in accordance with the promotion agreement and that they are not altered or damaged.

- **Competitive Product(s)** – Review and note the location of specific competitor products to ensure they are not occupying contracted positions of the company's product(s).

- **Advertising Media** – Check to ensure that any instore ad materials, flyers, coupons, or other assets are available in sufficient quantities, and replenish if necessary.

- **Education and Training** – Bring store manager and associates up to date on latest product and marketing programs with presentation materials.

- **Reorder Notifications** – Notify sales or shipping of any required reorders based on low stock levels

- **General Store Condition** – Report the cleanliness, order, and general quality of the store environment.

The field merchandising reps will capture and note all observations and communicate immediate needs and compliance audit details to corporate trade marketing, sales reps, and key account managers. This is typically done with handheld devices and mobile phones. But digital transformation here applies primarily to the ability to connect and align promotion plans with store visit scheduling and specifically to enable special instructions for actions needing to be taken when the rep is in the store.

The problems with the manual and analog functionality today are that the critical information captured in the store visit is often latent, and in many cases, must be manually emailed or called in to trade marketing and sales. Legacy software is limited in its ability to capture all the data necessary, especially about key aspects of promotional tactics like price, location of displays, and so on. Photography taken in the store is helpful, but again, it has to be uploaded or manually texted or emailed to the appropriate handler at the corporate headquarters.

In the digital world, the ideal situation for the merchandising reps would be to have real-time visibility to all reports and promotional performance data; but the older legacy systems do not support that capability. Immediate access to promotion history, past POS data, or even previous promotional performance reporting is critical, especially when being on-site inside the store.

The use of advanced tablets and mobile devices will improve efficiency and overall effectiveness and will give the reps the ability to provide real-time communications. The quality and capabilities of Retail Execution software, that is continually being improved for cloud-based platforms and real time communications, will be a necessary component of digital transformation. I am seeing more coverage of retail execution than I've seen in my professional history, and it is precisely because compliance is such a major focus, both financially, and from the perspectives of sales and marketing.

Promotion Settlement and Closing

Current Analog/Manual Process

- Manual processing of claims
- A/R-manual communication of deductions
- Manual deduction research
- Limited access to plans and historical data
- Manual duplication avoidance verification

Digital Transformation of Process

- Claim entry portals direct access by channel customers and immediate visibility across the company
- Automated deduction tracking within A/R systems delivering real-time visibility to full deduction data
- Automated deduction matching and duplication avoidance
- Immediate settlement and financial closing of deductions and payments

Figure 7.4 Digital Transformation Road Map for Promotion Settlement and Closing

Have you hand-written any checks lately?

Probably not too many.

Financial transactions today are largely accomplished through automated direct deposits, online payment portals, mobile applications, and EFT transactions. When I had MEDIANET, we had more than 60 client bank accounts and we generated thousands of checks each month reimbursing retailers, wholesalers, distributors, value-added resellers, and food service companies for their co-op advertising and trade promotion claims. We were the official paymaster for our clients and managed hundreds of millions of dollars every year in promotional payments.

Many companies, especially those in the fashion, consumer durables, and consumer telecom industries still make accounts payable transactions, but they are typically done through direct deposits. CPG companies process the vast majority of their settlements via deductions, as we have already covered; but even those, for the most part, involve heavily manual research and verification activities before the deduction is declared cleared and closed.

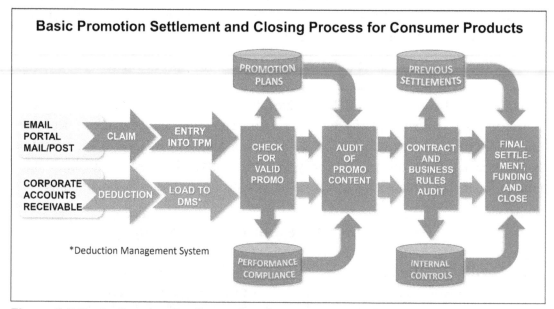

Figure 7.5 Basic Process for Promotion Settlement of Claims (A/P Transactions) and Deductions (A/R Transactions)

Figure 7.5 is a very broad and basic rendition of the standard settlement and closing process for trade promotions. The two primary types of transactions are claims and deductions. Claims, which are received through the mail, email, an entry portal, or even hand-delivered by the KAM or sales rep in some cases, are processed through an accounts payable (A/P) process with deductions being received by accounts receivable (A/R) and passed down to the deduction management team and settled as an acceptance of the deducted amount through A/R.

The major points of audit and control include the following areas of concentration:

- Is the deduction or claim valid (e.g., eligible under the contract, timing, product, or customer status)?

- Is there a plan recorded that links to one or more tactical activities being claimed or deducted?

- Are the tactical activities eligible under the terms of the programs or contracts?

- Are the costs in line with the plan or valid against known costs of the specific tactical activity?

- Does the promotional content meet corporate governance and business rules?

- Is a tactical activity of the deduction or claim a duplication of a previously paid claim or deduction?

- Are there sufficient funds earned or allocated to the submitting channel customer to pay or approve the deducted amount(s)?

Currently, for most consumer products companies, the management of settlements is well-established and one of the more standard processes in all of trade promotion. However, that does not say it cannot be complicated, and it often is, especially if funding rules, tactical usage, and other corporate governance is complex and voluminous. It may be seen as one of the last processes that would benefit from digital transformation. But, in the modern arena of trade channel promotion, we are learning that this is becoming more of a problem when upgrading systems and technologies—especially when it comes to the practice of settlement of deductions.

The process is virtually always manual, even with some of the most sophisticated spreadsheets you've ever seen. A/R receives the payments from the customers and notes where deductions are taken to determine what they are for. Many of them are for known issues like early pay discounts, shipping penalties, and contractual discounts; but most are undefined. A/R clerks send those deductions straight down to the deduction management team. For A/P transactions, claims for reimbursement are usually either hard copies mailed through the postal system or scanned documents attached to emails. Even where the TPM systems capture and display the details of the claims, the next steps are virtually all manually done.

In the CPG/FMCG sectors of consumer products, the deductions received must be researched manually, often resulting in hours of looking into promotion plans to see if the deduction is one or more of the tactical activities planned. Promotion plans are often less detailed than they should be, which means a lot of judgements have to be made by the deduction team members, and there is no guarantee that there will be a clean match.

Retailers can't often deduct promotional activities in *exactly* the same grouping that the promotion plan depicts. Advertising media costs come into the retailer marketing organization that has separate validation and processing of payments. Those line items may be deducted independently of, for instance, the money subsidizing the cost of a promotional discount. Displays are often deducted as agreed for each location in the retailer's market areas.

But as we saw before, with such a low level of compliance (30% says Nielsen), that will require an audit for sure. Finally, costs for demonstrators, promotional shippers (stand-alone displays preloaded with product) and other tactics can all be different from the promotion plan.

Current analog and manual processes to search for duplicates are one of the other pains associated with promotion settlement. Claim processing auditors and deduction team members have limited access to historical data and past settlement records. I do see areas of improvement, even within manual or analog processes and systems, but we have such a long way to go before we score a triumph in digital transformation.

As the consumer products company prepares for upgrading the trade promotion management (TPM) system, settlement becomes a major point of concern and focus. Over the years, I have been on several process mapping projects where we hold workshops with the key stakeholders who are responsible for various functional aspects of the settlement and fund accounting processes. These have been some of the most contentious sessions of all the process design thinking or journey mapping workshops because, frankly, it's about the money.

While many of the business management and key stakeholders are eager and excited to make changes in existing systems and processes, it seems almost a version of "Custer's Last Stand," where those who have toiled in the sales finance areas most commonly charged with trade promotion settlements are fighting for their survival. You will never hear the phrase "That's the way we have always done it," more than inside these workshops. The frustrating thing for systems integrators, TPM vendors and consultants is that this phrase always seems to be followed by another old phrase, "And for us, it works!"

So, regardless of the pushback that is more common than not, digitally transforming the well-worn processes of trade promotion settlement, co-op advertising audit and payment, and rebate processing is worth the "forest of thorns" we have to fight through to get it done. Remember, this is the heartbeat of the Invisible Economy – where the money leaves the bank account of the manufacturer/supplier and ends up in one owned by the retailer, wholesaler, distributor, or reseller. It must be accurate—to the penny accurate!

All of this is where digital reengineering comes in to play.

In one of my previous client's TPM implementation projects, a sophisticated settlement portal was created to provide an easier way for channel customers of all types—retailers, distributors, indirect resellers, and food service companies—to submit claims and deductions. This was tested for two quarters across the entire customer hierarchy and now enables a rapid, painless, and accurate procedure to open the settlement process.

The portal is designed to not only enable secure upload of claims with multilevel detail for tactical activities, but also contains the specific contractual terms for each customer account. When the customer logs on, the system recognizes the customer and opens the portal to allow either manually inputting claims that preloads the A/P transaction register and enables more detailed view of the tactics, timing, costs, and products promoted, or automatically populates the fields through an embedded business rule or previous update of the claimed data.

This eliminates two early steps in the process that cause major headaches for the claim processing auditors.

For deductions, there is a simple interface created with the invoice management systems that breaks down the individual promotional tactics and costs that align with the future deductions to be taken. This enables an automated capture of prededucted charges that will be formally deducted from future invoices and sets up the deduction management team with an expected pipeline of future deductions, and more importantly, establishes the details in advance for the deduction that is coming. So far, the system has reduced the time to process deductions from an average of 38 minutes per deduction to less than two minutes.

The advanced prededuction also sets up an alignment and initial check of past deductions to ensure no other charges have been deducted or claimed, eliminating almost 82% of all duplicate claims and deductions in the year prior and making it extremely hard for post audit deductions to be taken. The deduction tracking systems enable a virtual 360-degree view of the promotion from the time the plan is finalized until the final settlement and closing. More importantly, it enables a more accurate and predictive accounting of funding the eventual deduction, drastically reducing the write-offs caused by unidentified deductions and lowering the instances of chargeback, where the customer is re-invoiced for the deduction that is claimed to be unauthorized and unapproved.

With more efficient integration between key systems like warehouse management and logistics, advanced in-store retail execution tools, and even sophisticated sensor technology in the retailer shelves and displays, the human element can certainly be reduced. The Internet-of-things (IoT) is technology that directly communicates display status, inventory receipt and even pricing data, can be used to drive the future sensing and communication of data at high speeds and in near or real-time, enabling almost immediate validation of compliance, alignment with POS scan data, online and social media advertising, and rapid settlement transactions.

We will cover more about the IoT in a later section within this chapter.

As with the client example above, there are several areas where innovations around digital technologies can make a huge difference in how things are done. Digital transformation of promotion settlement takes what is one of the most frustrating, and yet extremely important functions in all of a company's business processes, from a manual, antiquated, and error-prone activity to a faster, more accurate, and trustworthy way of transacting the $1 trillion dollars of trade spending globally.

Post-Promotion Analysis

Current Analog/Manual Process	Digital Transformation of Process
• Manual spreadsheet-based research and calculation • Limited historical data due to limited data capture • Time consuming and limited customized reporting • Limited or no access to corporate marketing data	• Expanded data sources from retailers and distributors with near real-time accessibility and metrics • Integrated near real-time results across all promotion tactics and media • Real-time visibility into social media sentiment analyses and responses • Conversion consumption data for future predictive and prescriptive planning • Integration of and visibility to trade promotion and consumer marketing results for future alignment

Figure 7.6 Digital Transformation Road Map for Post-Promotion Analysis

Last, but certainly not least, is the digital transformation of analytics.

I once gave a presentation to a group of consumer products executives in sales, marketing, finance, and IT at one of the trade promotion industry events. My topic was "Trade Promotion Technology in the 21st Century." A bit cliché, I admit. But I began my topic by asking what software company had the largest TPM practice in the world?

Answers were spread out – SAP, Oracle, CAS, Exceedra, Vistex, Kantar, and so on. But none of them were right. The answer?

Microsoft.

After the laughter subsided, I asked how many, by a show of hands, managed the largest part of the trade promotion planning, funding, and accounting on Excel® spreadsheets?

Virtually every hand in the place went up. And the laughter returned with greater intensity.

Excel® is a great product, there is absolutely no doubt. And in my time working with hundreds of companies across the landscape of consumer products, I can tell you that there were some magical things done with spreadsheets. But in today's channel promotion and consumer engagement environment, the need to have real-time analysis of performance, and the conversion of data into actionable intelligence, demands something different.

Being in this business for almost five decades now, I am pleased to see that the C-suite is finally waking up to the critical importance of trade promotion, co-op advertising and all forms of channel funding. For so long, TPM was seen as a "necessary evil" and given very few resources, especially IT and marketing.

At MEDIANET, we produced some of the most advanced analytics around channel incentives marketing and trade promotion in existence at the time and were way ahead of anyone else in the scope and depth of coverage we produced for manufacturers like Frito-Lay, Sealy, Intel, IBM, Hanes, Black & Decker, Hewlett-Packard, and Zenith. We pioneered financial analytics for trade promotion, and even built the first viable promotion optimization engine used to leverage historical trade promotion performance data to generate prescriptive recommendations for future promotions. With all that data and intelligence, our clients always struggled getting the higher executives' attention—they simply did not read the reports we sent them.

My, how times have changed.

Now, trade promotion—and especially the concentration on analytics—is one of the top three focus areas when it comes to digital transformation. Did someone wake up?

You bet they did, and I would say "it's about time," but frankly, we're way late to that party. At least now it can be certainly said that the alarm clock has gone off, and the top corporate executives are waking up to the need to control the second largest line item in their corporate financials and begin to spend money on analytics.

AI and Machine Learning (ML) technology has skyrocketed in the past five years. In 2017, according to Gartner, only 4% of organizations had deployed AI within production systems. That figure expanded to 14% in 2018 but seemed to stall in 2019 with only 5% growth.[52] The year 2020, as we all know, is an anomaly with the pandemic; but it stirred up the need big time to have a smarter intelligence base and the ability to predict performance rapidly and accurately.

New technologies and advances in databases—with data lakes, lake houses, graph analytics, augmented analytics, and persistent memory servers—are driving more companies to invest in improving analytics, and no better place to start is with trade promotion.

Companies like IBM, SAS, Oracle, SAP, and Microsoft are all expanding offerings in AI and ML, and as I indicated above, the top consulting firms are already deep into the strategic development of their own products to provide AI and ML tools. Cloud data platforms like Google and Amazon are growing and expanding their commercial applications. By 2025, according to IDC, global data will grow by 61% to more than 175 zettabytes with 30% of that data being consumed in real-time.[53]

That plays nicely to the ears of key account managers and sales reps who have the responsibility for planning trade promotions, and corporate financial and operations executives who need to know what revenue generation is going on and what they need to do about it.

Real-time is no longer a dream, but a reality and a requirement.

Are we there yet?

No, unfortunately we are not.

What I continue to see is a lack of accurate and trustworthy data, time-consuming spreadsheet analyses, costly customized reporting, and significant latency in performance analysis. E-commerce vendors like Amazon and Alibaba have the advantage of immediate data on shopping and purchase data, but all CPG companies suffer from a lack of precision and trust in both their predictive and post-performance analyses.

There is a significant limitation to historical trade promotion performance and plan data. This is due to limited data capture from legacy TPM systems, or the lack of a TPM system in the first place (spreadsheets again).

All this AI and ML capability is nothing without the depth and breadth of data required to make the algorithms work. One of the most serious issues is the lack of access to corporate consumer marketing intelligence by the promotion planners. We will address this issue in more detail later, but the takeaway here is that ignoring trade promotion and channel incentives management systems has caught up with the average consumer products company, and a lot of work must be done to rebuild the data infrastructure before effective modern analytics tools can do the job they are implemented to do.

So, digital transformation in trade promotion analytics must start from the ground up. The good news is that the corporate C-suite seems ready and willing to invest. In a recent survey of 1,877 CIOs from 74 countries and across all industries, Gartner indicated that 58% said they will increase spending on business intelligence and data in 2021.[54]

Figure 7.6 shows what digital transformation looks like for data and analytics in trade promotion.

A must for all consumer products companies will be to expand the data sources. This will mean moving to more frequent data ingestion from retailers and distributors as well as expanding the data captured from existing trade promotions.

For instance, today, most TPM systems will have a single field for tactical activities (e.g., temporary price reductions, displays, ads, etc.). With the level of sophistication expected from AI and ML algorithms, the "fuel" for these calculations has to be detailed enough to allow for deep distinctions in the data.

A temporary price reduction is a tactic present in most trade promotions. Most TPM systems, and certainly, manually created spreadsheets, do not provide any details beyond the acronym, "TPR." However, if you do not describe the type of TPR, there is a wealth of data you cannot capture and allow the promotion optimization engine to learn. Take another look at Figure 6.3 in the previous chapter for "TPR" and see the variations of price reductions that can take place—each unique in their impact to the shopper and, therefore, critical for providing the right level of granularity to the AI engine to generate the machine learning and optimize the value of the future output.

Let's look at two individual promotions for a CPG company that ran in the same week one year apart. The CPG company is one of the largest multinational grocery products companies in the world with advanced TPM and analytics technology. At the time the second promotion was being planned, there was a trade promotion optimization tool being used to assist the key account manager in planning promotions (TPO—providing advanced analysis of historical trade promotions by preconfiguring promotions and projecting or predicting the best future outcome). Promotion 1 you see in Figure 7.7 was a joint decision between the retail buyer and the KAM. Promotion 2 was, likewise, an agreement between the two parties as well.

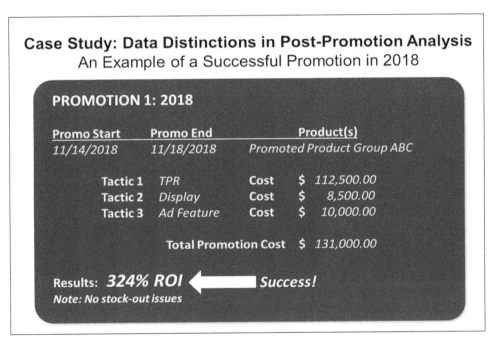

Figure 7.7 Case Study of a Highly Successful Promotion

The results from Promotion 1 in Figure 7.7 were a solid 324% ROI, which was calculated against the initial sell-in volume and pricing compared to the total sales volume during the promotion. The promotion was scheduled to run beginning on Wednesday, November 14, 2018, and conclude Sunday, November 17. There were no issues with stock outages and no unusual events or other environmental, political, or weather-related causal factors.

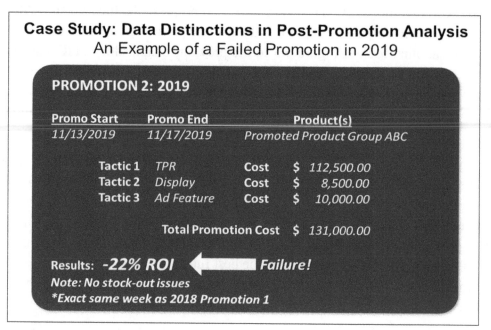

Figure 7.8 Case Study of a Failed Promotion

One year later, the KAM and the buyer decided to duplicate the success of the first promotion. The new promotion, shown in Figure 7.8, was scheduled to run in the same exact week period in 2019 with the same tactics, except for how the price discount would apply. In the first promotion (Figure 7.7), the "TPR" was a "Buy One, Get One Free" or "BOGO" promotion. The second one, however, was changed because the retailer had an abundance of existing inventory in addition to the 140,000 new units purchased, and wanted to simply discount the price of each item—a tactic the KAM and buyer both felt would move the new product and clear existing inventory. So, a $.50 off price reduction was granted on a product that retail priced at $3.24 each. The new promoted retail price was $2.74. Both the buyer and the KAM believed that this marginal discount would be as popular as the BOGO in the previous year.

It wasn't.

The failure rate was disastrous, both for the retailer, who was now looking at a huge inventory backlog of product that the discounted price failed to move and the manufacturer, who was forced to cough up another $50,000 to cover an extension of the program to hopefully offset the cost of the failure. Even with the discounted sell-in price, the retailer, and the manufacturer both had negative margins, so along with the incremental loss of volume, the financial impact was felt as well.

The trade promotion optimization tool predicted a success rate of more than 184%, by the way.

Why?

Because all the AI-driven algorithms had to work with was limited historical data. The historical data only included the tactic identification, "TPR," which was the only hard data the TPO could have used in the calculation of the prediction. Some TPM vendors are expanding the total number of tactics to include these distinctions, and that is fine; but if there is no hierarchical structure for tactics, you lose the ability to generate more effective post promotion analyses on tactic type which helps to refine the planning process and enables a more compelling story for the KAMs and sales reps when in negotiations with their buyers and retail/distributor counterparts. The important moral of the story here is to ensure that the data is granular enough to maximize the value of the sophisticated TPO tools that are now being implemented globally for prescribed trade promotion planning.

Gartner's prediction of 30% of the total global data being consumed on a real-time basis is clearly applicable to analyzing the Invisible Economy. The sensitivity of promotions now, especially in the wake of the Covid-19 pandemic, is higher than ever, mandating more attention be paid to what is going on inside the stores and online shopping sites. Promotions can go south quickly, and as of now, the only thing a KAM or sales rep can do is see what happened *after* the promotion ended—in some cases, weeks afterward. That is unacceptable.

Moving the data from the source to the company's database, data lake, and cloud, demands a shift in the paradigm of syndicated data provision and long cleansing and harmonization timeframes. Moving to receive critical POS data directly from the retailer is one very important objective. It not only gets you yesterday's data today, but you get 100% of the locations and market coverage, not some sampling methodology that has been obsoleted in today's analytics environment.

The process known as Retail Execution (REX) is another major area where digital transformation is changing the success of trade promotion for the better. A recent survey was done of more than 300 field merchandiser representatives charged with the responsibility to go to the stores and carry out the activities and audits before, during and after promotions. The number one problem noted in the survey was a failure to have a display in place when and where the promotional plan and agreement required it.[55] The second highest incident noted was the wrong price—an extremely problematic finding given that price is the number one driver of purchases in the stores.

Integrating the retail execution data (e.g., store visit and compliance audit information) in real or near real-time provides critical visibility to what is happening on the front lines. That data, especially the level of compliance with pricing and display assets, is a major contributing causal factor for future predictive and prescribed trade promotions. Imagine how effective being able to get updates on location-level compliance would be. With an ongoing live tally of results from individual location data on missing or mispositioned displays, incorrect pricing, out-of-stock conditions or competitor deals, the retailer headquarters team can be alerted, and action taken before the promotion becomes a failure.

With the emphasis on consumer engagement and the ability to manage all aspects of the Consumer Chain, being able to see the performance results from corporate marketing events and promotions, advertising, and coupon redemptions would dramatically improve a consumer products company's overall goals and objectives. When trade promotion is linked and aligned with the national and regional events and promotion calendars, the ability to predict an effective and profitable promotion increases exponentially.

This is a topic we will go into more depth on later; but the failure of CPG companies to align trade promotions and market development funding incentives to corporate advertising and marketing is preserving an inefficient and dangerous practice. This is one of the main reasons for promotion failure, and one of the most frustrating problems for retailers. One of the primary dependencies they have on their suppliers is being able to know and take advantage of brand promotions and advertising campaigns. The difference between the success and failure of a promotion can be related to missed opportunities to align the retail promotions with national advertising and marketing campaigns.

The incentive to share data, insights, and collaborate in promotion planning between sales and marketing also benefits corporate marketing as well. Knowing how the consumers are shopping in the store and the scheduling of major account trade promotions can become a powerful driver of future advertising media scheduling, content, and postperformance key performance indicators.

In the first front of the consumer products industry's campaign for winning the consumer engagement, digital transformation is a mandate for every component process in trade channel promotion management and execution. With my clients, I counsel and advise them to put trade promotion at the top of the priorities list for digital transformation initiatives because there is no other line item in the company's financials except for cost of goods that ranks higher in the eyes of the company's board and shareholders. It should also be so with the decision makers and stakeholders across the entire landscape of business processes.

Emergence of the Omnichannel

The second digital front for consumer products manufacturers/suppliers in the consumer engagement campaign is selling through the e-commerce channel. Ever since British inventor, Michael Aldrich hooked up a modified domestic television to a transaction processing computer over a telephone line, e-commerce has become the second largest channel of distribution in the world.[56]

Grabbing sizable chunks of brick-and-mortar retailer share of sales annually, the United States Census Bureau reports that, through the first quarter, 2021, e-commerce sales represented 13.6% of all retail sales.[57] While this number was obviously fueled from the pandemic lockdowns of 2020, there is no doubt that traditional retailers are in a battle for their very survival. With that being said, brick-and-mortar retail still represents the lion's share of consumer products manufacturer/supplier sales, as well. Selling through both channels, the consumer products companies have to balance their own company e-commerce sites with their external e-commerce channel partners and manage strong ongoing relationships.

Social media plays an accelerating role in influence and marketing power with the consumer. All consumer products manufacturers must accommodate and participate in the social media if they want to keep their brands and products relevant and meet sales forecasts.

In a recent survey on e-commerce, 45% of shoppers polled said that the first place they go for product research (referred to as a "touchpoint") is a social media post or advertisement.[58] That same survey indicated that two-thirds of the shoppers' pre-shop touchpoints were online instead of going into a store, seeing an offline ad, or getting a recommendation from someone. Also in that survey, it was noted that online shopping increased 22% over the previous year, most likely due to the Covid-19 lockdowns; but still, the increased percentage of overall shopping via e-commerce is steadily growing year-over-year.

An Immovable Object vs. an Unstoppable Force

The venerable old supply chain between manufacturers and their physical retail, wholesale outlets, and distribution centers has been perfected and enhanced for generations. We now have a very solid and well-tested way to get products from the factory floor to the pantry of the consumer. The brick-and-mortar still commands the lion's share of shopper activity; but since the entrance of Amazon in 1995, the entire Consumer Chain has evolved.

Amazon is a new definition of "huge."

Amazon is a new definition of "fast."

Amazon is a new definition for "shopping."

Progressive Grocer magazine puts Amazon in the number 2 position in their 2020 PG 100 top food and consumables retailers in North America behind Walmart.[57] That's a faster acceleration from zero than a Tesla Roadster.

Amazon alone had revenues of more than $220 billion in 2020, and that is excluding the natural foods grocery juggernaut, Whole Foods Market®, which Amazon acquired in 2017. This puts Amazon ahead of Kroger, Costco, Walgreens, CVS, Sam's

Club, Albertsons, Target and Ahold Delhaize, and Loblaw's in North America, and Metro, Tesco, and Carrefour internationally.

Huge.

Although Amazon does not dominate in every retail category, overall, it is estimated that it will surpass 40% of all e-commerce business in 2021.[59] Computer and consumer electronics is the largest category being purchased on Amazon, with apparel close behind. In fact, the only retail category where Amazon does not have at least 25% of the US retail sales is automotive aftermarket.

Each of those categories spend significant amounts of trade channel promotion, co-op advertising and market development funds, however the largest percentage of trade spend compared to gross revenues is the FMCG categories. This has not traditionally been a major category for e-commerce in general, but for Amazon, it is the fastest growing category with a 78.5% increase in 2020 over 2019. Of course, the pandemic lockdowns impacted that number significantly, however even in pre-pandemic metrics, food and beverage, as a category, increased almost 23%.[59]

Amazon, as with any e-commerce retailer has unique methods and opportunities to present and promote products. Each product has far more information within the same eye-space than a brick-and-mortar retailer can provide, even with a full end-cap display with signage and product information. We already know that CPG manufacturers/suppliers spend upwards of 27% to 30% of their gross revenues on trade promotion; but what are the numbers for promotional spending with Amazon or any other e-commerce retailer?

At this point in time, the percentage of the budget allocated to trade promotion for e-commerce channels is lower than the brick-and-mortar retail channels. Using Amazon, the 800-pound gorilla in e-commerce, McKinsey research shows that promotion funding in 2020 was 8.9% of the margin versus 11.3% for brick-and-mortar retail channels.[60] However, the cost of trade promotion will no doubt change, and the problems associated with generating ROI in e-commerce are becoming a key issue in a consumer products company's effort to effectively measure and optimize promotions.

McKinsey also points out that the higher margin cost of on-site advertising (9.2%) and shipping (9.3%) are higher than their brick-and-mortar channel counterparts at 5.7% and 7.3% respectively. This means that the premiums consumer products companies pay to Amazon and other e-commerce retailers for positioning on the "digital shelf" are higher than more traditional display and shelf space costs.

Order management and shipping are becoming issues as well due to the mixed pallets, reduced shipment sizes, and stringent packaging requirements for rapid shipping to consumers. Amazon, as with Alibaba and other major e-commerce platforms, has sophisticated and complex order management systems that configure the right order mix for online shopping, but may play havoc with more traditional warehousing and shipping processes and systems.

In fact, Amazon has a "CRaP" list, which is an acronym for "Can't Realize a Profit," that includes bulky or heavy products like bags of flour, and jars and cans of sauce and pickles, for example that are sold both in-store and online. Even the e-commerce pricing policies have difficulty reconciling a combination of discounts and promotability that simply makes no sense financially.

Having your products end up on the *CRaP* list is not something you want to show in your corporate financials at the end of the year.

While consumer durables, electronics, fashion, and personal care lead the e-commerce categories, grocery has been relatively low on the scale—until now. Twenty-four percent of consumers indicated that they would buy groceries online on Amazon's "Prime Day" promotion in 2021, a significant jump over the previous year.[61] Of course, the pandemic drove a large share of that; but the statistics continue to point to a significant rise in grocery product purchasing online over the next ten years, with an estimated 70% growth spurt.

Grocery retail chains and mass merchandisers are burning the midnight oil to blend their physical in-store strategy with how best to serve their shopper customers through online e-commerce as well. They see the numbers and they know they are in for a long and hard fight to maintain share. As a consumer, you probably feel, as most do, that shopping online for certain things such as meats, poultry, fish and produce, and alcoholic beverages makes no sense, and you would be among a very large audience.

Would you order your cod for fish tacos online today?

If You Can't Beat 'Em, Join 'Em—A Challenging Détente

For the consumer goods manufacturer and supplier, there is no choice—you must go where the consumer is. Don't get me wrong here, you can still create innovative campaigns and products that stimulate the "Need" element of the Consumer Chain. But as we have seen in so many surveys and research reports, the new generation of shoppers are tough to convert.

When it comes to trade promotion, the brick-and-mortar retailers have the deepest domain expertise to generate shopper interest and incite a sale. Traditional advertising has fallen off considerably over the past five or six years as both e-commerce and brick-and-mortar retailers continue to sink more and more money into digital media. The problem is that digital promotion has not had the success factor that traditional trade promotion has had (despite the 70+% failure rates of trade promotion as we have documented previously).

Shopper marketing spending has doubled, and digital marketing has tripled in the past five years.[62]

The big problem is the difficulty in measurement of incremental profitability and ROI for promotions in the digital realm, and that causes sales, marketing, and finance executives to pause in their zeal to spend more on digital e-commerce promotions.

Loyalty is one of the most difficult commodities to claim now, because the Millennial, Gens X, Y and Z, and even Baby Boomers have adopted the mobile device and tightened the demand curve to now, now, now. The percentages still favor purchasing in a store, but the exponential growth of e-commerce means that the consumer will generally shop online first (and usually Amazon, quite frankly) to make the product decision before they decide *where* to buy it, and that means a likely reduction in store traffic.

If the numbers stated above (70% increase in grocery shopping in the next decade) are accurate, your favorite supermarket will have to make some major changes to keep you motivated to jump in your car and drive to the store. But don't count out the supermarket chains just yet. They have done a nice job of playing the e-commerce card.

Brick-and-mortar retailers know that they have a seasoned supply chain and a healthy cadre of customers loyal to their store brand. Along with the incredible investments into beautiful and spacious new stores, test cooking islands and booths, and easy self-checkout lanes, they have also embraced e-commerce.

Even before the horrors of 2020 and the pandemic lockdowns, retailers were beginning to offer services like "Buy Online and Pickup In-store," and door-to-door delivery. Here in Texas, the dominant retailer is H-E-B Stores which has successfully weathered the pandemic run on inventory and was able to rapidly replenish critical supplies within a few weeks of the start of the lockdowns. Their story, as we told earlier in the book, has become the model for survival in the supermarket business and a guide to achieving supply chain resilience.

H-E-B has had a huge e-commerce channel presence with a growing revenue generation and an impressive site that rivals Amazon and top e-commerce retailers. Today, H-E-B has a new delivery service called "Favor" which promises 2-hour delivery, dedicated one-on-one service and no membership or subscription fees. Favor teams shop and deliver throughout the local area and are beginning to capture the hearts, minds, and digital wallets.

They even deliver beer, wine, meat, fish, poultry and produce as well as full gourmet meals prepackaged and ready to put into the oven.

Other retail chains are beginning to provide similar services connected with their e-commerce sales sites, providing the consumers with a "buy and pick-up" as well as "home delivery" in very short time windows. This is the way the brick-and-mortar retailers will stay competitive in the next several years and may be very difficult for Amazon or Alibaba to duplicate. It is an innovative way to maintain channel dominance, and promotional ads and merchandising is pushing this hard to every generation of consumer.

Tesco stores, in the UK are experimenting with "Virtual Shopping Walls" (VSW) where a consumer can walk up to a large screen with products on a shelf resembling the inside of a pantry or refrigerator, and order groceries to be delivered to their home up to three weeks in advance. These "Virtual Shopping Walls" are being deployed in major transportation hubs such as Tesco's VSW in London's Gatwick Airport.

Imagine you are heading over the pond to the states, and you've cleaned out your refrigerator to avoid spoilage during your stay and want to make sure you have a good cold drink, ice cream, meat, milk and produce to be delivered within hours when you get home. E-commerce is the engine that makes this possible; and given the innovations we are seeing in the market among the major supermarket and big box retail chains, such as Amazon acquiring Whole Foods Market® to add fresh produce and meats to their delivery capacity, and building clerkless "Amazon Go" stores nationally, no doubt we will see even more change coming.

How does this impact the Invisible Economy?

The rise in ordering grocery products online will also result in higher trade promotion expenses. Today, most of the money used to pay for the growing cost of online product promotion comes from either the advertising media budget or the slotting and "pay-to-play" costs. Corporate marketers know that the values returned from e-commerce are significant and often higher than more expensive national advertising. Digital couponing is being supported at the expense of more traditional paper coupons as well, but even those budgets are not going to be enough to fund the next decade of e-commerce promotion.

"I've seen the cost of trade promotion flatten over the past decade," says the CFO of a health and beauty aids company. "Our product categories are one of the highest in demand online, so naturally, we had to be there in force with deals the consumers want."

She said that her company was one of the top advertisers in e-commerce, but that she had to "rob Peter to pay Paul" to come up with funding which is about to dry up.

"I've cut my national ad budget in half, and we have suffered in the process, so I can't have my CMO continue to go that direction next year," she continued. "We currently spend about 22% of our gross revenue in trade [promotion] across all channels, and our projection is that we are going to have to bump that by at least two to three points." She also said that she has pulled funds from her newspaper inserted coupon budget and had her KAMs renegotiate slotting[6] agreements with top accounts to divert funding to both their accounts' e-commerce sites and Amazon as well.

She is right that the annual increase in trade promotion funding has flattened. Margins are so low, and both the manufacturer/supplier and the retailer can ill-afford the luxury of years gone by adding one to two percentage points to the trade funds annually. The money just is not there without raising prices.

However, the good news is that internal systems and processes are improving at both the supplier and the retailer side which is most likely where the new money will come. As e-commerce grows, and consumers continue to expand their purchases online, more traditional tactics like media advertising and couponing will no doubt take more hits.

The challenge of this *Détente* makes for great blogs and articles (and books), but the gloves are off, and we are in the middle rounds of this fight. E-commerce players are well-aware of the advantages and disadvantages each side of the channel has in this business, but the one winner in all of this is going to be the consumer.

Internet-of-(All)-Things

If you have been outside of the news or have not yet heard this phrase, the "Internet of Things" or "IoT" for short, then here is my favorite definition of what we are talking about:

> *"The Internet of Things (IoT) is a system of interrelated computing devices, mechanical and digital machines, objects, animals or people that are provided with unique identifiers and the ability to transfer data over a network without requiring human-to-human or human-to-computer interaction."[63]*

This definition is provided by Calem McClelland, head of operations for *IoT for All.*

Connected to our mobile devices, IoT enables us to control everything we own, and some things we don't. You can set your home temperature, trigger your alarm, yell at a porch pirate attempting to steal your Amazon delivery, start your morning coffee, and even start your car in the cold parking lot of the airport as you taxi into the gate. The sensors and communication devices that are adapted to virtually anything enables us to see, hear, command, and control the devices.

Sensors implanted in your heart monitor, report, and alert both patient and doctor when an event takes place that needs attention. Sensors injected into the bloodstream can detect clogs and report flow status, cellular issues or even video arterial walls.

In the CPG supply chain, sensors on product packaging can track and report locations and ensure shipping efficiencies.

IoT also works wonders in the manufacturing environment, with sensors that can monitor, sense, and alert when conditions are problematic or dangerous, as well as automatically adjust and control the equipment without human intervention. In the supply chain, sensors on product packaging can track and report locations and ensure shipping efficiencies.

Already in consumer goods industries, IoT is heavily used in warehousing, inventory management, shipping, and an incredibly important area of safety with the tracking and tracing of products with dangerous bacteria or other materials that would cause problems if consumed.

How does IoT figure into the efficiency and effectiveness of promotions? How does IoT help with the planning and execution of promotions? How can IoT illuminate the heretofore Invisible Economy?

Let's take two of the largest contributors to promotion failure—Out-of-Stock conditions during promotions and promotion compliance.

With IoT sensors on the product and packaging, the tracking and reporting of location would be easily recorded. Traditional problems of missed shipments, inaccurate order fulfillment, and lost pallets in the warehouse would be immediately eliminated. In the retail location, the shelf sensors would detect the number of individual items (called Stock Keeping Units or "SKUs") on the shelf at any time with alerts to the stocking team when inventory on the shelf needs replenishment. If the store has a run on the product, and the inventory begins to drop, sensors in the stockroom can connect and communicate with the order management system to immediately submit an order to ship products to that specific location to replenish stock.

The sensors communicate all this status to the central inventory management and supply chain systems, which then communicates with both the buyer and the key account managers, as well as the individual location store managers, making everyone aware that a promotion is underway, and the product inventory is in danger of hitting on-shelf threshold minimums.

This could not only reduce, but potentially eliminate any out-of-stock condition which, as we have shown, is one of the highest contributors to failed promotions.

Compliance is another area where IoT can ensure promotion success. Today, it takes a virtual army of merchandise field reps visiting a sampling of stores to conduct on-site validation of promotion compliance, including checking prices, ensuring displays are in place, and advertising assets are executed.

Sensors in the displays can be triggered when the store manager and stocking teams open the box and erect the display. Location beams throughout the store can transmit the exact locations within the store where the display is positioned.

Pricing systems are loaded with the accurate selling prices and those can be set to communicate with the shelf tags showing the price per SKU to ensure discount pricing is accurate and in place.

All this data can be collected for every store, every market, and across the country, without a single human action taking place. Compliance would be automatic, with the data transmitted directly to the trade promotion management team at the manufacturer's headquarters, and automatically updated when the deduction or claim is received or filed. Even before settlement, the IoT sensors could even generate the payments or automatically deduct the funds agreed for the promotion without having to create a deduction transaction or claim.

Experiments are now being conducted with "smart pantry" products in home construction and home improvement. Shelves come with embedded sensors that can detect size, quantity, and number of products. Future IoT applications will enable pantry shelf sensors as well as refrigerator and freezer sensors to directly communicate with the product sensors to determine how much of a jar of jelly or a bottle of milk remains, automatically generating a shopping list, or even better, a purchase transaction with your favorite store or online site.

This is not science fiction. It is happening, and you are no doubt already in possession of multiple IoT devices and sensors in your life. If you own a smart watch, it's on your wrist.

Think about it.

Digital transformation is more than just a buzzword. It is a new way of working and living. Consumer product manufacturers are already moving toward these innovative technologies, implementing them as quickly as corporate resources can allow. The technology is with us already, and testing is being done on a global basis.

Soon enough, the *Invisible Economy* will become very visible.

CHAPTER 8

REAL-TIME TELEMETRY IN THE 4ᵀᴴ DIMENSION

The word, *telemetry* made its way into the consumer lexicon during the early space age, when rockets launched satellites and astronauts for the first time, and we heard the phrase, "on board telemetry" to refer to what was going on with the spacecraft. The word itself, however, has been around since the age of steam power in the early 19th century when inventors like James Watt used something called *telemeters* to track pressure inside the boilers, displayed by a guage.[64]

Even after more than 100 years, the telemetry used to measure the *Invisible Economy* is, frankly, sadly immature. You would think that consumer products companies spending up to 30% of their gross revenues on trade channel promotion would have had a highly sophisticated technology making sure that all this money was producing high rates of return.

But the reality is that most companies, even some of the most powerful CPG brands in the world, have lagged in their ability to adequately measure the real-time value and effectiveness of all this money.

Consumer products manufacturers, retailers, wholesalers, and distributors are beginning to invest heavily into the new real-time telemetry. Analytics is becoming a hot topic among the key executives responsible for all this money—finance, sales, marketing, IT, operations, and revenue growth management leading the way. As advanced analytics technology becomes more prolific and affordable, the good news is almost every consumer products company seems to have one or more initiatives underway to create a viable telemetric environment across all phases and lines of business.

Never before has data become more critical than it is in today's modern trade promotion management and execution. All too often we hear the buzzwords of analytics and how "Big Data" initiatives of the past two decades are beginning to pay off.

But are they?

Right now, one of the prevalent topics of conversation among the industry stalwarts of analytics and data science is, well, *data.*

It must be clean and harmonized, and today that is a challenge. There has never been a lack of data, just a lack of good data. Data integrity and trustworthiness is paramount to success in all the dimensions of consumer goods analytics. If you don't have this, you don't have good data. If you don't have good data, it matters not what level of technology you have—you will have inaccurate and unreliable results.

Even before John Wanamaker, the famous American retail magnate, complained that he knew half of his advertising was successful, but did not know which half, the question of data value has been a constant problem for the consumer products industries. Throughout the past four decades, at least, managing data has been at the forefront of IT priorities.

Since Douglas Laney's breakthrough business book, "Infonomics," the pressure has been on all company executives to measure, report, and justify the expense of acquiring and maintaining the data required to perform every function, and run the company's processes to achieve financial and market success.

Millions of dollars a year in the United States are burned on bad data. In addition, industry analysts point to data ignorance as a primary problem, with up to a quarter of the industry having no idea what errors they do have in their data. More than three-quarters of business executives believe they lose significant revenue due to bad data.

But the problem does not solely rest with bad data. The lack of understanding heavily siloed data and analytics infrastructures, and the lack of collaboration and communication across internal business organizations, cause more grievous problems yet.

Beyond the "Big Data" Initiatives

The pressure of performance on a global scale has seen numerous waves of change in the IT organization, running just behind the even quicker pace of technology advancements. In the early 2000s, the term "Big Data" came into being to represent the new priority of making sure the company could manage the extreme volumes of data coming in from the factory, warehouse and logistics, transportation, financial accounting, order management, procurement, inventory, vendors, point-of-sale, and syndicated data streaming live, in many cases, into huge databases.

Wrestling with these big data projects meant determining the best course of action to take in procuring, implementing, and maintaining huge databases and data lakes, and the equally huge tasks of partitioning, distributing, and analyzing all that data. The metrics and standards were not yet totally universal with few experienced references, and seemingly no end in sight in the ongoing cost to meet the exponentially increasing volumes of new data sources. It was no surprise to see tier one, and many large tier two consumer goods companies spending between $10 and $100 million dollars to build a technology infrastructure to handle the future intelligence requirements of modern consumer packaged goods.

Primary, among the myriad tasks the chief information officer (CIO) and chief technology officer (CTO) took on, was the cost justification for this spending. For companies that were losing market share, not an uncommon situation for even the largest CPG companies, standing before the CEO and board of directors to explain the plan for intelligence and data to management became tantamount to a life or death decision for the company. Yet these decisions had to be and were made with careers on the line.

If then, there is a central figure in the critical task of monetizing data, it is the CIO. But while the CIO is the steward of data purity and integrity, it is the business leader who is now the go-to authority for WHAT data is required and HOW it will be used to execute the specific actions of his/her and everyone else's measurement of business processes and outcomes.

Creating the Corporate Infrastructure—The CDO

For most CPG companies, the past two decades have produced a scrambling of resources to build and operate large databases, ingest terabytes, petabytes and zetabytes of data, implement advanced analytical tools, and create governance around it all. However, the pace of business has often, and even now usually, forced a less than controlled process to achieve those goals. In the past, the responsibility for this effort has fallen on the IT organization, but the renewed focus on analytics and data has begun, for many companies, to create a specific function to effectively deal with these initiatives.

The senior corporate executive position known as the "Chief Data Officer" (not to be confused with the rising position of "Chief Digital Officer") owes its very origins to the need for a company to assign an executive at the highest corporate rank who oversees the management of data in the expansion of analytics across the entire business landscape. Today, CDOs are working closely with the CIOs and, together, are largely responsible for how a company generates intelligence and drives insightful decision-making.

Given the fast pace of today's consumer goods marketplace, that role is more challenging than ever. Often frustrated or worse, ignorant of the corporate IT vision and strategy, business organization leaders have built independent silos of data and analytics they feel they need to run their departments, creating a patchwork of decision processes often unaligned and dangerously inconsistent with other business organizations, corporate strategy, or even the marketplace. The resounding outcry among CDOs, CIOs and CTOs now is for this practice to end, with a higher priority focus on bringing all data back into one single repository. And it all begins and ends with making sure that the data is of the highest quality and trust across the entire business enterprise.

The Metrics of Data Initiatives

What this brings to the forefront is the critical importance of having a set of metrics that can be measured both in advance of, and upon completion of, a major data management or, if you prefer, data overhaul initiative. It is more than justification; it is a quantitative approach that can become a standard against which any company and every project can be measured. Today, there are many different metrics, especially across and specific to individual business operating units. However, it is NOT an apples-to-oranges comparison, and I have always believed companies need to do all they can to determine value propositions for any size or complexity of data initiatives.

Being able to pin a particular objective or goal attainment to a specific data metric is extremely hard to do. In the example depicted in Figure 8.1, ensuring quality and trusted data certainly leads to the final desired goal of corporate stock value. However, at each level of functional process performance in between, the variables are significantly impacting the overall metric. In other words, you may already have the highest quality, most trustworthy data available, but any system or function impacted could leverage that data incorrectly, or inappropriately, or fail to even use the data, resulting in errors, omissions, inaccurate calculations, or other failures which skews the data and impacts the ultimate results accordingly.

TRADE PROMOTION PERFORMANCE
Hierarchy of Measurements

LEVELS OF MEASUREMENT

- Company Stock Value — GOAL
- Profitabiity
- Revenues
- Market Share
- Consumer Engagement
- Retailer Sales (POS)
- Promotion Success
- Promotion Execution
- Promotion Plan
- Optimized Insights
- Quality/Trusted Data

Figure 8.1 Hierarchy of Measurements for Data Delivering Corporate Stock Value

So, before we can do any back-patting for successful data quality transformation, we have to ensure that the entire infrastructure of applications and process measurements also accommodate the data metrics and are measurable. Using the example in Figure 8.1, trade promotion, we have seen for decades the efforts of consumer products manufacturers who have struggled with attempting to eliminate the awful historical record of efficiency and effectiveness in trade promotion planning, execution, and performance achievement. Implementing new TPM systems, layering on analytics tools, and reengineering retail execution have done little to improve the results of key performance indicators (KPIs) we associate with trade promotion—promotion ROI achievement, shelf stock conditions, compliance failures, settlement errors and so on.

We discussed examples of using a "TPR" acronym to apply to all forms of temporary price reductions in promotion planning, and how that lack of granularity makes all the difference in determining the causal factor of a successful promotion. That is a very good example of how trade spending fails.

If a data transformation project does not include a deep review of capabilities across all systems, solutions, and applications that use the data, there is a higher risk of failure and certainly an outcome that will not earn the implementation team kudos by the CEO and CFO. This example is indicative of how and why data ROI metrics are difficult to measure and especially how important it is to ensure that operating systems that leverage this data are fully vetted for their own capabilities of data management, including sufficient granularity in data capture to assure effective tracking and measurement.

Strengthening the "Spokes"

As with any wheel, the strength and durability depend on the spokes. If the effort to improve the quality and trustworthiness of the data hub, the value of the entire operation (the "wheel," in this case supported by the individual functional processes) depends upon not only ensuring the integrity of data itself, but how it is used and aligned across the entire set of enterprise "spokes." Moreover, the ultimate value of the data use cases will depend upon each other's sharing of and/or collaboration between each functional process spoke as is depicted in Figure 8.2.

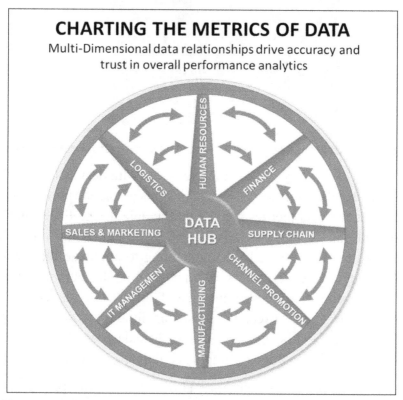

Figure 8.2 Charting Data Metrics within a Consumer Products Company

With siloed data and analytics, especially managed independently of each other, consumer products companies continue the age-old quest for the "one version of the truth," only to fail and ultimately limit the company's ability to be as successful as it could be. This is the trouble with today's "big data" analytics.

132

Up to this point, the purchasing of data and associated analytical tools has been primarily the responsibility of each business unit, creating so many variations of the same metrics, for instance, that there is often no way to get to that "single version of the truth." With so much money at stake here, and so few corporate mandates to consolidate analytical tools and standards, no wonder we have problems reconciling the ROI of trade promotion, co-op advertising and market development funded performance.

The bigger the company, it seems, the bigger the problem.

In Figure 8.1, I illustrate how the data infuses each level of a functional process with intelligence and insights to drive optimum performance incrementally and up through each tier toward contribution to the corporate success. Figure 8.2 shows the measurements vary with functionality, however, and each individual area of functionality impacts performance both vertically through the individual functional "spokes," and horizontally across functional processes to ensure smooth, consistent, and aligned performance.

Most CIOs are completely aware of the problems that arise from siloed databases and analytical tools; but they are often at the mercy of the business leadership across each of these internal operating organizations—many of whom are applauded for their independent "entrepreneurial" thinking and action. Further discovery and examination of issues, problems, and concerns around data quality and unified infrastructure uncover common causal factors:

- **Lack of sufficient governance to data access and usage** – Without well-defined rules for data access governance, operating business units are often free to ignore the data in the hub and build their own data sets, even though in many situations, the independent data is often more effective, accurate and useful. Still, it renders the primary corporate data hubs ineffective and severely unaligned. It also often builds unfortunate animosity between the business units and IT.

- **Independent data sourcing and maintenance** – Business leadership often conducts their own data selection initiatives that fail to unify and consolidate with other operating units or the primary IT data hub. With the justification of needing specific data to execute their respective functions (i.e., social media access, shopper traffic, consumer survey data, etc.) the business unit leadership often acts on their own without conferring with other business leads that could take advantage of the same data, or the IT organization responsible for housing all data in the hub.

- **Failure to acquire the right data** – Due to these siloed operating units, where communications and collaboration are rare or nonexistent, business leaders can easily be ignorant of data availability that could

mean the difference between success or failure, thereby running their
business using less than adequate avenues of insight and intelligence.
A good example of this is where companies often fail to leverage
the customer call center and/or technical support to provide a more
effective future product design, or to provide direction for future
promotional campaigns.

Modern initiatives to improve the quality of data differ from the "Big Data" initiatives of the past two decades in two significant ways.

First, as opposed to the former "Big Data" projects that were focused primarily on the hardware and software to manage the data, a modern data project focuses more on the *quality* of the data itself. Emphasis is on accuracy, trust, and usability. This is not to say the former big data projects did not address these issues, but more appropriately, less time was expended on the quality and purpose of the data than the massive efforts to build the database technology—whether in the cloud or on-premises.

Second, there is a growing focus on corporate infrastructure through and around which the data moves and is applied to running the business. This is where the metrics of the hub and spoke are applied, and the results are measured against the cost of the overall initiative. In Figure 8.2, consider that each of the spokes present their own individual issues, problems, and concerns when it comes to evaluating the existing and planned infrastructure required to execute any business process and function.

If we are honest with ourselves, we are most likely only scratching the surface of building a future set of cross-organizational metrics that would consistently use the data to optimize performance, whether it is ensuring a happy and informed employee universe in HR or producing consistently high ROI for channel promotions. Knowing WHY, HOW and WHEN to leverage the data is the right way to continue building high output and success.

The Data Value Vector

A vector is defined in two ways: (a) a line or element of a direction, and (b) the act of forcing an object toward a defined point. Measuring data ROI is both a defined direction or vector toward achievement of a specific objective, goal or destination, and the action that positions the right data elements to deliver insights and intelligence required to achieve those objectives and goals which define success.

Returning to the wheel in Figure 8.2, the process of determining the vector we need to lay in as a course of action requires a thorough examination of each of the functions across and within each of the "spokes" so that both the vertical and horizontal use cases are compared and factored into the definition of the roles and provisions of intelligence each data element has.

I know that sounds like a mouthful but think about what I just said.

For instance, if the supply chain management team wants to ensure that the baseline used to drive the sales forecast and subsequent promotion plans is both accurate and aligned with what the retailer is reporting in daily POS, the two functions will be required to use the same data element. Right?

In far too many cases across most consumer products companies, demand planners typically leverage syndicated data providers' POS data which does not represent each individual store location. This data is often averaged across selected markets, resulting in good, but not 100% accurate data—a business practice we will discuss in more detail later in this chapter.

This is the "level playing field" that is unfortunately the venue for virtually all consumer products companies. Yet there is a growing trend to include eventual promotion POS results as a component of the key account manager's or sales rep's compensation, which now adds more of an emphasis on results of actual promotions rather than simply sell-in achievement. Therefore, the success of the promotions in-store is now beginning to be watched closely and challenged by the sales managers in a far more aggressive manner. Aside from the new emphasis on promotion success, the POS data received from syndicated data providers can be weeks latent, restricting the ability to react quickly to consumer activities, store conditions, or social sentiment.

An audit of data use and organizational business requirements should include, at least, the following five questions:

1. Are you using the same data to determine the same business questions?

2. Is that data commonly available to each operating business unit?

3. What is the impact across operating units to decisions and results that have mutual ties or potential to support or counter ultimate results?

4. What barriers are in place that restrict mutual usage of the same data elements?

5. What metrics are in place to ensure an aligned result across business organizations?

The most effective way to answer these questions will be to bring the leaders and key stakeholders in the business groups to a formal journey mapping, or design thinking workshop, that is not afraid to dig deep into the operating technologies, work habits, functional processes, team mindsets and other variables of operations. These sessions should also be phased to enable inter-team groups first, with the selection of representatives (perhaps the team lead and representatives from the core unit), then convene a broader group workshop with the leads and their representatives from allied business operations.

This will ensure smooth, comfortable, and safe environments with the strategic and tactical intentions driving the larger group behavior and domain knowledge dynamics toward a unified and aligned vision and mission.

Any current Design Thinking or Journey Mapping format will be sufficient for this process. However, experience teaches that there is no way a critical discovery audit, and analysis of data quality and use case application, for modern consumer products data can be done in a short period of time or even one extended workshop. The history of siloed databases, analytics, and ideologies within the multiple business organizations of a typical consumer products company are as varied as there are separate organizations.

The effort has to be executed in three ways:

1. Understand the data availability and usage requirements.

2. Define the requirements, sources, and use models of data that will drive the achievement of objectives.

3. Create the matrix of metrics and measurements that directly relate to the value of the data.

To cover the breadth and depth of the company's infrastructure, there will be a need for multiple workshops with a single goal of producing a plan with a set of metrics that enables bottom-up measurement of data usage and results while, at the same time, enabling efficient top-down direction that impacts execution for any one or more operating units. This allows sufficient input from all operating business functions within logical and manageable formats that are aligned to the overall metrics and assures more open and collaborative intelligence. If done properly, this process achieves the objective of covering the full range of data use case measurement with the end goal of ensuring rapid adaptation to future changing consumer and market conditions, with an infrastructure of consistency and unification that preserves a cross-organizational measurement of value and ROI.

The Data Value Vector Decision Workshop

Before scheduling the workshops, a full data discovery and audit is required. This not only serves the purpose of identifying all the data, sources, and organizational usage practices, but it gives the workshop facilitation team the opportunity to work within each area and create strong relationships that will be required as the process moves forward. It is also an opportunity to learn of any external or siloed databases and/or analytical practices that are carried out apart from the internal IT-led database management or a key third-party vendor that would need to be included in the discovery.

Once this discovery and assessment is concluded, and there is a basic understanding of the data and use cases, the workshop facilitators can build a strategy and formulate the content and flow of the workshops. As the data and use cases are compiled, the facilitators will need to pay close attention to the cross-organizational usage of similar data, as it would be wise to include organizations that use the same data in one of the first level workshops—especially where the company is smaller, and personnel are more familiar with each other.

Throughout the discovery process, there is a mandate for openness and transparency between the workshop facilitators, data consultants and the operating functional business teams. The most important theme throughout is to ensure that the Consumer Chain is the primary focus—even for activities that are not directly impacting retail consumer and shopper engagement. If the eventual value proposition is to serve the consumer better, each data use case should support in some way the eventual capabilities necessary to be the first choice of shoppers through whatever channel they use.

As the workshops are held, data from each workshop is compiled and used as the topic content for the next level workshops with higher ranking participants, including overlapping business leaders and key executives from earlier workshop groups, to ensure consistency and continuity. These workshops should be a duration of at least one day each to minimize the disruption of time and focus but will thoroughly cover the end-to-end data catalog to ensure all criteria for data and use case coverage situation is met and accounted for.

Once the entire database has been reviewed, use cases identified, and metrics established through the workshop process, testing can begin to evaluate and model data measurement values. As this is done and validated, there will emerge a more unified and accurate model around data that will be a consistent metric, and account for new data and changes in existing data.

Controlling the Data Value

There are two primary objectives for understanding the true value of the data a company acquires and manages. The first objective is to know the cost to acquire and maintain the data. The second is to know the end performance variable produced by the data usage impact.

The cost to acquire and maintain is far easier to get to, and a figure most companies can come within a high percentage of accuracy to measure—even for data acquired separately by the operating business units. Maintenance of the data typically involves the level of work required to update the data on an appropriately frequent basis. For example, for many of the large mass merchandisers and national chain stores, the cost of point-of-sale data is a known factor as is the cost of ongoing maintenance of software and hardware required to ingest, clean, harmonize, and store the data.

That data could be, at an absolute minimum, weekly or, preferably, *daily* as an overnight upload via automatic maintenance. Otherwise, as in many IT shops, it will be a manually exhausting exercise for internal resources. The cost of internal data, primarily transferred to a central data lake or database, is becoming easier to access, and includes the human resource costs as well as storage, ETL (Extract, Transform and Load) and API (Application Program Interface) data maintenance, or development. It will also include any customization of the data when called for or required. Internal data from ERP systems, supply chain, manufacturing, procurement, shipping, and other sources must be included in the assessment.

Where there are customizations and other changes that impact data quality, those will be considered as well. The end performance variable costs are a primary factor in being able to determine true ROI value for data. This set of calculations will be plugged into the formulae that are going to derive the final figures of value, and can be highly controversial, political, and outright challenged. Many executives feel that any such calculation is, at best, subjectively arrived at.

The most important work of the Data Decision Vector Workshops is to eliminate uncertainty, doubt, and disagreement in both HOW the numbers are calculated and WHAT the end results are. Not only is it critical to understand the end performance costs, but it is also important to understand the impact of any change that is made and/or external factors which might disrupt the normal achievement of results. For instance, the fluidity of the ebb and flow of consumer response to the various stimuli created by promotions, environmental conditions, weather, competitive actions, economic or seasonal events, and most certainly major disruptions like the recent global Covid-19 pandemic, can easily render any feeling of consistency totally unreliable.

Each variable will need to be measured and compared to begin to build a firewall of intelligence that enables at least a better-than-nothing impact factor that can be applied quantitatively to the end performance variable calculations. The point is to ensure that there is a path to generating a quantifiable and increasingly trustworthy ROI figure. It really can't be a hard and fast number that is used in all cases, but more of an intelligent variable that can be automatically or manually "plugged in" to the ROI formulae when necessary.

Even if the standard measurements are used to produce a data ROI figure, certainly adding the right "asterisk" to the result to indicate where abnormalities exist (like the virus quarantine) is a more effective way to view the end result.

Even a consumer products company with a rapid growth rate in a growing category will find that even in a relatively small company environment, the problem of data quality costs millions annually.

The past practices of creating "entrepreneurial" environments, pushed by upper management on to the business leaders across the corporate organizational infrastructure, have resulted in independent decisions that created numerous siloes of analytical tools which often generated individual databases that were not part of the corporate data management infrastructure. From a sales and marketing standpoint, business teams were operating with data that was often unaligned, and even in direct conflict, with, data used by other siloed operating units.

The resulting impact on the company's costs and bottom line were unknown because they were never measured. There were no metrics because there was limited awareness among the teams from sales and marketing due to lack of communication and the virtual nonexistence of collaboration.

In a recent case study of data quality with a global household cleaning and laundry products company, this workshop and data consolidation process was done with two of the many product categories the company had in their portfolio. The results after a full year of operation reflected a much smarter operational environment with sales, marketing, supply chain, and finance organizations all working from the same data lake, using the same metrics, and having maximum visibility to consumer engagement across all sales channels. In addition, the near real-time view of promotional results enabled the company to be more proactive with the retail channel and virtually eliminate out-of-stock problems that were primary causal factors for their promotions to fail.

The Cost of Data (COD)

In Figure 8.3 we show the high level view of the flow of cost calculation for data. While this may appear simple, it is far from it. As the operating business units execute their respective tasks and functions, their use of data varies with the nature of their day-to-day business plans and operations, even when they use the same data.

Demand planners will use much of the same data to create the baseline forecasts the sales account planners use to configure trade promotions; but the end state of their work will generate unique and different objectives with different definitions of contribution to the corporate success. Demand planners will want their baselines to depict the accurate picture of demand across all 52 weeks in the year and relate to the sales and operations plans that determine how much product to build and move through the supply chain.

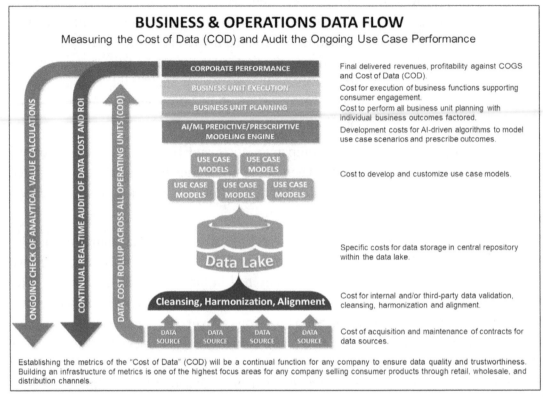

Figure 8.3 The Business & Operations Data Flow Measuring the Cost of Data (COD)

The end state of a promotion will generate specific levels of volume of product sales, revenues, and profitability. Yet both metrics combine to contribute their share of the quantifiable level of success. This is the essence of determining the true value of the data.

Experience tells us, through millions of hours of trial and error, case studies of corporate success and failure, and a demanding class of consumer that there must be an *accountability* for the cost of acquiring, employing, and measuring data to achieve performance objectives. Further, through multiple analysts' reports and papers on the effects of bad data, no data, or the wrong data, we know that this is a huge cost to the corporation and a definite risk to corporate success and survival.

Leading companies are finding that they must take the steps and execute the initiatives to know the cost of data at every juncture of business operations, and to develop the infrastructure to support an end-to-end metrics and measurement system to not only continually monitor data use and calculate the contribution each data element delivers, but also to build in the internal visibility to the functional delivery of each piece of data used across every business organization. Getting to a well-organized project that can uncover data use and determine the costs and subsequent measurable value must be the highest priority of every company's strategic mission.

Considering the current visibility of the tremendous costs associated with bad data, incomplete data, and the inability to measure performance across operating business units, it is no surprise that the quest for ROI on data is now a high priority among the global consumer goods industry. But with a concerted effort within each company to build an infrastructure and business ecosystem to support a culture of measurement and collaboration, finding and managing the ROI on data has become more of a mandate for future success with consumer engagement and corporate operational efficiency than it has ever been.

CHAPTER 9

ATTAINING THE DIMENSIONS OF KNOWLEDGE

Crossing the Rubicon

O ld Julius Caesar decided to cross the Rubicon River in 49 B.C. which started the Roman Civil War, created the Imperial Roman Dictatorship, and ultimately led to one of Shakespeare's greatest works. It committed Rome to a new way of life, to be sure.

Most consumer products companies are already ankle-deep in the Rubicon of changing the telemetry and entering a new generation of analytics. It's about time to cross that river and make the necessary and mission-critical moves to advance knowledge, insights, and intelligence.

The progression of capability along the lines of measurement and analysis of more than one trillion dollars of trade spending globally is always represented in a sort of "wish list" set of steps that define the level of insights and intelligence desired by not only the manufacturers/suppliers, but also the retailers, wholesalers, distributors, and value-added resellers that make up the consumer goods distribution channels.

These "steps" are defined in different ways by different people. But they are levels of measurement capability from the simple collection of basic data to advanced insights and knowledge generated by artificial intelligence and machine learning, internet-of-things sensors, and virtual and augmented reality. Analysts and consultants may argue the various levels and steps required to get there, but most of them say the same thing.

143

Let's call these *Dimensions of Knowledge*.

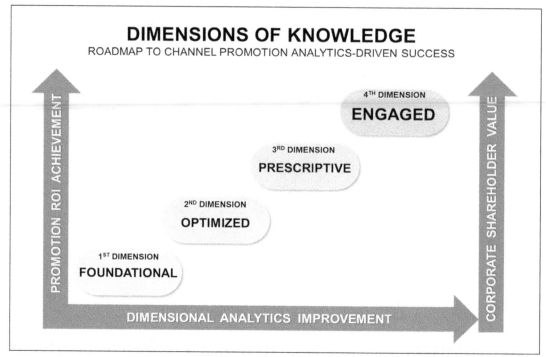

Figure 9.1 Four Dimensions of Promotion Analytics

THE 1ST DIMENSION: FOUNDATIONAL

The 1st Dimension is where most TPM systems are today, or at least aspiring to be. This is considered the minimum capability required for basic analysis of promotional performance and financial return (ROI).

Stair-step, waterfall and ascending ladder graphics are plentiful showing the individual levels of competency of promotion analytics among the top consulting firms, systems integrators, TPx vendors and third party co-op and MDF service firms. Each of them is, on their own merit, logical and intelligent. Most of these charts depict stages of development of the manufacturer's/supplier's roadmaps to more precise and trustworthy analytical tool sets; but they are far more complex than they should be.

Figure 9.1 represents what I have observed after years of being involved with and/ or driving analytics development initiatives across almost all consumer industry sectors and lines of business within the corporate landscape. It not only simplifies the visual but is a more realistic view of what is going on right now.

Because of the variations in the definitions of these "levels," we have seen little or no real research data on the current progress being made up these levels in any usable scale. However, with this distinctive and simplified definition of achievement in analytical prowess for trade channel promotion, most consumer products companies are likely to be on the first level – the 1st Dimension.

144

The 1st Dimension is what I call "Foundational," which essentially covers the basics of promotion measurement. Virtually all consumer goods companies provide all or most of these basic pieces of intelligence in their existing reporting tools.

The 2nd Dimension is where advanced technologies like artificial intelligence and machine learning begin to deliver true "what-if" scenario predictability that the TPx industry today likes to refer to as "Trade Promotion Optimization," or TPO. Although growing in numbers, very few companies, including major global brands, can deliver precise and trusted predictive or optimized promotional plans.

The 3rd Dimension moves beyond promotion optimization into *prescriptive* promotional planning, where the higher, advanced technology combines to leverage more accurate and plentiful historical performance data to create a prescribed promotion for targeted individual and specific objectives.

The 4th Dimension is where the Consumer Chain begins to drive promotion planning and execution. It is where manufacturers and channels are so close to the consumer that sensing demand drives near and real-time autonomous promotional activity, events, and offerings.

The 5th Dimension is a great rock group from the late 1960s who sang the Broadway remake of "Age of Aquarius/Let the Sunshine In" to the top of the charts.

OK, I digress.

But seriously, each of these dimensions signal a complete evolution in the way trade channel promotion is measured and analyzed. The combination of advancements in process, technology, and data will drive how well and how fast a consumer products company can move into each dimension. So far, there is a lot of talk, but little in the way of action. Old habits die hard, and changing major technology, data, and process paradigms has been slow, to say the least.

Today, there is an increased development of more sophisticated analytics platforms by systems integrators, consultants and TPx vendors. Especially around revenue growth management, these are examples of analytics solutions that begin to approach the 2nd Dimension of promotion analytics and appear to be moving upward along the dimensional improvement curve.

In addition to longtime consumer products research companies like Nielsen, Information Resources and NPD, POS data providers like Retail Velocity and Retail Solutions, Inc., have continued innovative data cleansing, harmonization, and alignment development. These efforts are already showing signs of breakout advancements in AI- and ML-driven success stories in CPG and FMCG that clearly embrace the move to the 2nd Dimension of promotion analytics.

BASIC CURRENT STAGE PROMOTION ANALYTICS

1ST DIMENSION

FOUNDATIONAL

- Forecast, Demand Plan, Shipments, Baselines
- Promotion plan timing, tactics, products and costs
- Post-promotion volume, revenue and profitability
- Simple calculation of promotion ROI
- Syndicated consumption intelligence

Figure 9.2 The 1st Dimension of Promotion Analytics

Because promotion spending has begun to capture the attention of the top corporate executives, there are already existing and planned efforts to increase analytical capability, if, for no other reason than to have visibility to spending. You might think this a bit shocking in today's Invisible Economy, but outside of the financial organization, few of those top corporate executives can tell you what the spending IS, much less what comprises it. And they are, themselves, often unable to respond when you ask them what the ROI is on that spending.

"What do you mean," asked the executive vice president of sales for a leading global sporting goods company. When I showed him a simple equation from the research we did on his company's trade channel and co-op advertising expenditures showing a negative 3% return, his eyes widened. "That can't be right," he said, flipping through the pages. "OK, so what happened to generate this loss, and what are you using to calculate that, anyway?"

I showed him that the figures from his syndicated data provider showed a negative promotion sales figure for seven of the last nine promotions against the volume sold at the sell-in. The simple calculation showed a net 3% fewer products sold to the consumer than they sold in. "So where is the extra product, then?" he asked. Looking at the pipeline forecast of his key account manager, it showed a definite reduction, even lower than the baseline adjustments made in the previous quarter. "My KAM shows a 19% incremental volume and revenue gain," he added. "But I see the lowered forecast." At this point, he promptly picked up his phone and called the KAM to find out what was happening.

I did not want to ask the KAM about THAT call.

Remember our discussion about the "Shell Game" in Chapter 5? Not to belittle the sales executive here, but that is what they are paid for. Pushing the volume for the best price possible, including trade promotion spending commitments, and achieving a marginal profit has been the primary measurement of compensation for a consumer products sales executive.

146

He had what he thought was the answer right in front of him, but his data was not deep enough to dissect the *reason* for the net loss. His opinion that the sell-in value was driving the ROI is unfortunately a popular assessment among corporate sales executives. We will examine some case studies that show how these numbers can be deceiving later in the chapter, but the key take-away here is that most trade promotion and co-op advertising management and execution systems, whether a series of spreadsheets, home-grown applications, or a vendor TPM solution, have largely been very light on the volume and quality of post-promotion performance data.

Achieving the 1st Dimension of promotion analytics means having the necessary data elements to establish the full and complete understanding and assessment of *what happened* in the promotion execution. It is literally the initial stage of a "crawl-walk-run" strategy to achieve exceptional analysis of promotional performance and create the primary data infrastructure that eventually powers all the advanced planning and execution of promotions in the higher dimensions.

Forecast, Demand Plan, Shipments, and Baselines

Promotion planning begins with a solid sales forecast—not just the numbers, but a figure that everyone across the company's organizational landscapes accept as the *single version of the truth*. Have you heard that phrase before? I am sure you have, because it is a major step forward from the historical problems in corporate forecasting where sales, supply chain, production, and even finance has multiple versions of the forecast depending upon the point of view. This problem has been addressed so much in the past few decades that, thankfully, most consumer products companies have created processes and technology that enables full visibility, collaboration, and agreement on the corporate forecast across all organizations.

That is a good start.

Likewise, the Demand Plan (the output of a process to predict the volume of product expected to be purchased by the consumer) has improved as well, or at least as much as it can be with what data is generally fed into the systems. This process is highly technical (and it should be) because it involves so many pieces of data, external causal factors, and inherent variability that severely pressurizes the entire organization to make critical decisions that impact the procurement of raw materials, factory production schedules, research and development of new products, management of product lifecycles, and of course, the need to effectively plan, execute and measure trade channel promotion effectiveness.

There are so many books, white papers, articles, blogs, and opinions about demand planning that it would be wasteful of good print for me to spend an inordinate amount of time breaking down the process and function of demand planning. However, for our purposes, establishing the foundational requirements for the 1st Dimension of promotional analytics, let's just say it is a clear mandate to set the right direction and tone for the forecasting of any product.

Demand planning, if done right, is essentially tracking and predicting the entire Consumer Chain. Knowing the demand and the timing and extent of impact thereof on the business is the first major step in the eventual achievement of promotion objectives.

Measuring the shipment of products has become a huge industry all on its own. Warehousing and logistics, especially in the digital world, has taken on a critically high priority for consumer products companies, especially FMCG companies where the products are moving at lightning speed across global supply chains to the demanding channel customers and their consumers. Shipping logistics quality is one of those areas where, in the past, problems in the order management, invoicing and promotion payment and settlement processes have been directly attributed to a late, lost, incomplete, or inaccurate shipment of products.

The shipping process is critical to the promotion cycle because virtually every promotion begins with the purchase and subsequent agreement for shipping of product to one or more distribution centers and/or retailer locations. If the product is not on the shelf when the promotion begins, the promotion fails. Unfortunately, out-of-stock conditions are too frequent, and many of those are caused by failures in the shipping and receiving processes.

Today, systems are in place to monitor and track shipping, including RFID (barcode) and IoT sensor technology to provide near real-time information about the status of the shipment, what products are being shipped, and advance notifications of issues, errors, or problems. That data must be part of the 1st Dimension complement of information.

The forecast and demand plans are used to establish the baseline. For too many companies, the baseline is a "set and forget" type of measurement because there is a lack of near real-time POS or consumption data to drive more frequent updates. A 2017 survey of more than 300 consumer goods companies showed that 61% update baselines only once annually, and another 22% update quarterly.[65] This means that only 17% update baselines more than once per quarter, which also means that static baselines could be the source of inaccurate measurement of incremental volume and revenue performance.

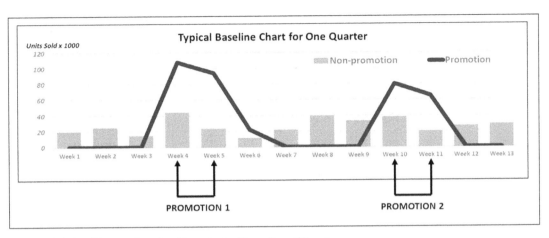

Figure 9.3 An Example of a Quarterly Baseline Chart

The baseline is a very important indicator of sales volume that measures two key performance indicators (KPIs)—product sales on promotion and off promotion. Figure 9.3 is a simple example of a typical baseline chart that shows the anticipated forecast volume without the stimulus of a promotion, represented by the bars, and the volume of product projected to be sold during promotions, represented by the solid line. Most actual baseline charts can show additional data, but for our use, this example works.

Note that there are two distinct promotions taking place. The first happens during a two week period covering weeks 4 and 5, and the second during weeks 10 and 11. Most promotions typically run between 5 and 14 days, usually beginning on Wednesdays. In fact, the most shopping visits occur from Wednesday morning when promotions begin through Sunday, with the highest average spending by shoppers for the week.[66]

Newspapers began noticing this trend in the 1930s, eventually configuring their advertising rates based on what the industry began calling the "Best Food Day" editions because that is when most of the grocery store advertising was placed. Sunday newspapers had the most preprinted inserts with coupons and discounts from the national brand manufacturers. So, you had the beginning and end of the promotions bracketed by the local and national promotions. Consumers had no chance to avoid this promotional "kill zone."

Baselines are the source of a great deal of angst and frustration among promotion planners. On one hand, the baseline is the culminating intersection of consumer demand research, product lifecycle management, shopper purchasing statistics, and historical promotional trends. Syndicated data providers like Nielsen, Information Resources Incorporated and NPD Group all provide both POS and consumption data to the consumer products companies. This data is also used to analyze and configure the baseline to support the forecast of product sold on promotions, helping to validate or confirm the projected incremental values depicted on the chart.

149

On the other hand, the collective doubt of baseline accuracy seen in the halls of marketing and sales planners, as well as demand planning and supply chain executives, often instills fear and uncertainty that the promotion plans will not produce the desired and expected outcomes. More often than not, as you have seen in past data presented here, they do not.

"Throw a dart against the wall and hope it sticks," says a consumer products key account manager for a national grocery chain in North America. "I have to go with it because we have nothing else to go on. I know my account contacts distrust it, and for good reason. We rarely hit the mark, and sometimes by a lot."

Overall, the majority of promotion planning executives think that the baselines are satisfactory tools to help configure the right forecast and promotion calendar. However, almost 40% of those surveyed by Consumer Goods Technology in 2018 were not satisfied with the accuracy of the baselines, and only 17% thought they were very accurate.[67] This shows a clear lack of faith in the current baseline development system, but much of the data used to create it—syndicated POS and consumption data—is based on sampling of markets and locations, averages of POS data, as well as limited detailed historical trade promotion performance records.

This is another example of how and why trade promotion outcomes are extremely difficult to predict, and overall promotion return on investment is so poor. But today, there are few alternatives in place to change that paradigm.

Good times are coming, but they are not here today.

The other practices that make up the Foundational element of the 1st Dimension of promotion analytics have been adopted and maintained by most consumer goods companies for years, but in marginal capacity and capability. That is important to mention here.

Promotion Plan Timing, Tactics, Products and Costs

Trade promotion management software is achieving breakthrough success with new, powerful, and innovative solutions popping up all over the world boasting of advanced AI- and ML-driven analytics, beautiful screen layouts and easy navigation, big data capability, cloud and mobile interconnectivity, and expanded functionality.

The problem, however, is history. There is too little of it, and what there is of it is generally not good.

Most modern trade and channel promotion management solutions today have expanded their functionality considerably, especially around workflow and navigation. However, because the core infrastructure of their technology is often anchored in earlier versions with improvements in the UI and user analytical dashboards, there are still some issues with the breadth and depth of the data the systems capture. In many of these solutions, changing the data models is tantamount to a full system rewrite, which very few of them can afford to do at this point in time.

Even amidst the more elegant UI and array of reports and dashboard views available, the base promotional data captured is often insufficient to accommodate the algorithms of advanced AI and ML scenario modeling. This data is required to handle the multiple variations of promotional tactics, timing, and product grouping needed to generate a precise and trusted prediction of ROI.

The logic of promotion planning so many key account managers and sales reps have is that if a promotion achieved a high ROI before, repeat the same promotion again and expect a result that is at least close to what was achieved previously. This is flawed for so many reasons, but one of the major ones is that the historical data is not detailed enough.

Here is an example of what I am talking about. This is another case example similar to what I presented in Chapter 7 (See Figures 7.7 and 7.8).

A consumer goods company with a strong portfolio of products that are sold in grocery, mass merchandising, drug, and even home center chains, has a very strong track record of success with their trade promotions. Their brand is well-recognized and respected, and they are often high on the category listing for most retailers if not the category "captain" in many of them. Their key account managers are well-seasoned and successful at creating strong promotions, even though many do not achieve the level of ROI they set as goals. One KAM was very frustrated and told me that he could not understand how his promotions were so different in goal achievement while basically being identical from one period to the next. "How can I get some assurance that repeating a successful promotion will do as well, or at least will not fail," he said.

He told me that he was adept at using the new trade promotion optimization tool the company implemented the year before, and overall, it seemed to be very effective. "About one in every four promotions I configure on the TPO will go off the rails. My buyer is beginning to distrust the output from the optimization tool, and I am at a loss as to how to solve this problem," he continued. We worked with the IT team and the data scientists and found the problem.

In two previous promotions, the tactics included a temporary price reduction (TPR), and a display and a demonstration day (where samples of the product were given to shoppers in a small booth next to the display). The two previous promotions last year, run Wednesday through Sunday, were repeated in the exact same grouping of stores featuring the same product grouping and at roughly the same cost. Both promotions scored high ROI and there were very few issues of out-of-stock shelf conditions.

A third promotion that was repeated the same way last month was found to be a complete failure. Less than one-third of the inventory sold-in to the retailer was purchased by shoppers and the ROI was a negative 42%.

Further research showed that there were three factors that were different:

The two previous promotions featured a center aisle display that was positioned immediately beside the demonstrator booth in all but a few of the store locations.

The two previous promotions occurred within one week of a corporate national TV promotion for the same product group, with the most recent promotion many weeks outside any national or regional product promotion or advertisement.

Both previous promotions were weeks away from any competitive product promotions, and the most recent promotion overlapped a "Buy One, Get One Free" promotion from the competitive category leader.

None of these data items were present in the TPM system, therefore the optimization engine and algorithms supporting the scenario model had no visibility to these critical causal factors.

Most TPM systems today have little if no data infrastructure to capture enough of the causal factors that are required to execute an effective prediction for success; yet the assumptions and sales pitches elevate the power of the TPO to a far greater level of capability than they really can provide.

The problem is one of practical software development and domain knowledge. Many of the people directly responsible for the design and development of trade promotion optimization solutions have little or no understanding of this problem. It is not to say they are not domain experts in consumer goods, but that they are not experiencing this on a daily basis and may not put the puzzle pieces together to get to the right combination of breadth and depth of the data models themselves.

So, today, based on my own experience with virtually every TPM and TPO solution on the planet, I have to say that most of them do capture the basic data well, covering at least the fundamentals of promotion data like start and end dates, product groupings, and even a fair array of tactical activity types, but the relationships and hierarchical structures are not often there. Taking tactical activities alone, the TPM solution data models often have them set up on a *horizontal* basis, with individual field types and nomenclature. Instead, we need to see TPM data models for tactics that are *vertical* with hierarchical parent-child relationships that can be interconnected for more granular, hence effective, scenario modeling algorithms that would produce more accurate predictive outcomes.

TRADE PROMOTION TACTICS DATA MODELS

Vertically Hierarchical Structured Promotional Tactics and Mechanics Add Granularity to Analytics

HORIZONAL DATA MODEL

TACTIC/ACTIVITY
Price Discount
BOGO
Percentage Discount
BOG2
B2G5
Instant Rebate
Mail-In Rebate
End Cap Display
Front-End Merchandiser
Checkout Display
Cold Gondola
Shelf Talker
Kiosk
Printed Coupon
Floor Display
Instant Coupon
Online Coupon

VERTICAL DATA MODEL

TACTIC/ACTIVITY		
TPR	Display	Coupon
TYPE		
Price Discount	End Cap Display	Printed Coupon
BOGO	Front-End Merchandiser	FSI Coupon
Percentage Discount	Checkout Display	Instant Coupon
BOG2	Cold Gondola	Online Coupon
B2G5	Shelf Talker	
Instant Rebate	Interactive Kiosk	
Mail-In Rebate	Shipper Display	

Figure 9.4 Two Data Models for Trade Promotion Tactics

Figure 9.4 illustrates differences between the two types of data models. Don't be confused by the two definitions—vertical and horizontal. Both seem to be vertically stacked, but what I mean by "horizontal" is that there are no relationships between one tactic type and another—each tactic is a unique attribute in a flat or horizontal array.

With a vertical model, there are specific hierarchical relationships between the standard tactical identifiers, such as "TPR" for a temporary price reduction, that can further identify *what KIND* of price reduction is being promoted. In fact, using a cross-blend of tactical types, we could now establish a promotion tactical activity as a *coupon* with a flat price discount supported by an end cap display, versus the current typical limitation of simply showing a promotion that consists of a "TPR" with a "Display" and a "Coupon."

Granularity is the key to successful promotion optimization, because the AI/ML engines learn from the variations in the promotional make-up, and the more detail, the more learning, and the more accurate the prediction becomes. The relationships between the tactics, in this case, is critical because it adds a dimension of knowledge that enables more exact and trusted output from the algorithms run.

Individually, with the above "horizontal" data model, the promotion optimization engine cannot break down the definition of the promotional outcome in any more granular way, leaving a great deal of intelligence behind that could more effectively determine why a particular ROI outcome happened. Going into legacy systems and TPM solutions that already have an established data model and making this kind of change is often an impossible task, leaving the consumer products company's sales, marketing, and finance executives without the ability to get to a precise causal factor.

Without this intelligence, we can never get to the higher dimensions of analytics we show in Figure 9.4.

Let's take the issue of products.

Virtually all promotions are built around specific groupings of products, typically known as "Promoted Product Groups" or PPGs. Because category marketing is the general base level of marketing development across major branded consumer products companies, it is critical to understand not only how the whole category performs, but for certain individual products as well, especially if one or two are extremely popular products such as Frito-Lay™ Doritos® Brand Nacho Cheese Tortilla Chips.

PPGs are lumped together in most TPM systems as a single "product" entity, and usually with special designations to identify the grouping to include specific sets of individual SKUs. For the most part, reporting is limited to the PPG level, and not to a specific individual SKU or even a similar grouping of SKUs comprising flavors, textures, and so on. But as with tactical activities, these are horizontally classified, which means that, as a source data item, they can show performance at the group level only, with definitions as to what specific SKUs are part of that group.

However, as with the current typical horizontal structure of tactics, all the analysts can do is run reporting on that specific PPG. Since only one PPG is typically promoted, this does not seem to be a major issue, and it may not meet with a common consensus among the marketing and sales organizations that it makes sense to do it any other way. But if you want to measure certain products within those groups (Doritos® Brand Nacho Cheese Tortilla Chips, for example), there is no way to extract that data. Other flavors of the product may outsell the leading SKU but getting to that data may be difficult *within the current TPM system*. The syndicated data providers can and will break down these individual SKU sales, because the shopper does not buy the entire category—they drop only one of their favorite flavors into their shopping basket.

Where is THAT data?

It is in the POS data that comes directly from the retailer and is captured by the data providers. To bring that data into the mix of analytics on board the typical TPM application, it would take not only customized reporting, but potentially a rewrite of the entire data model. If you consider that the promotion is based solely on the combined PPG, ROI analysis on the individual SKU is going to be near impossible to report.

While this may not seem to be an issue now, talk to a brand manager who sees their branded products losing shelf space to store branded products in the same SKU make-up. They will not be so forgiving.

The consumer products company with this type of limitation cannot get to the 2nd Dimension of knowledge without having a data model that provides this level of granularity and association.

Post-promotion Volume, Revenue and Profitability

Profitability and Loss are the key measure of success for any company on this planet. CEOs like to continually urge their employees to think of themselves as individually contributing to the company's overall success, and that means revenue and profit generation. This is a critical mission for any chief executive.

But over the years, where has that zeal been when it comes to the massive spending taking place on trade and channel promotions? As we mentioned back in Chapter 2, top financial executives have counted trade promotion spending as one of the most frustrating pain points in their entire careers. Efforts they have tried to put in place to curb the exponential growth of trade funds over the past several decades have certainly put pressure on the sales teams.

But their complaints have fallen on the deaf ears of the CEO because the chief sales officers have been in their ears saying that this is a requirement to get the revenues— and the facts indeed prove that to be true. Never mind that the promotions themselves are failures; we walked away from the retail deal with the volume, revenue and profit we wanted, and we have hit our forecasts consistently.

For any CEO, that is music to their ears.

Trade promotion key performance indicators have focused on revenue and volume as two of the chief metrics, and those numbers usually look good. But crank in how well the promotion does, and how much those failed promotions impact future revenues, and you paint a wholly different picture of profit and loss. Until lately, P&L reporting as a fixture in the array of standard reports on the dashboards have either not existed or, as we just mentioned, used high level revenue and profit figures based on the "Sell-In" and not on the "Sell-Out" or sales generated by the retailer in the stores and online.

Recently, I have been engaged in a massive TPM implementation project for a Latin American CPG company where the influence of the financial and internal controls teams was very high in the ongoing design and development of their new TPM system. To their credit, they focused on the importance of P&L across all the account, product, and territorial measurements to ensure that it not only painted the right picture, but that it was detailed enough to enable granular evaluation of individual causal factors.

The combination of the corporate team and the TPM vendor, as well as the systems integrator assigned to the task of implementation put such a high bar on the accuracy and reliability of the P&L analytics, that there will be no issues or problems knowing what the P&L is on a daily basis across the entire landscape of accounts, products and geographies. The way they did it was to break down the data models to ensure that sufficient integration of key performance indicators was accounted for, and that individual financial components of pricing, spending, fund accruals, and costs were all able to come together to generate a multilayer view of profitability in as near a real-time environment as they could make it.

P&L is becoming a high priority focus area in the development of TPx analytics, and as we will discuss in the upcoming 2nd Dimension of promotion analytics, the most important focus of promotion planning will be the generation of P&L as the primary metric for promotion success.

Modern TPx systems must be better at measuring financial indicators. Virtually all TPx solutions have analytical tools that measure the volume, revenue, and margin at sell-in; and they can perform these measurements across multiple factors of product, timing and even tactics (e.g., how much is spent on each different type of promotional activity) by account, sales territory, and promotional program—all great indicators of promotional value.

The good news is that, like the project I recently participated in, all the teams of internal executives, TPM vendor and the implementation consultants are paying attention to this, and even though the cost of customization to achieve better visibility to P&L is high, it seems the consumer goods companies are willing to make the investment.

Simple Calculation of Promotion ROI

We have already mentioned the problems in current TPM technology associated with the lack of an effective data model and the granularity that is often missing in the overall analytical capability. ROI measurement is an unfortunate victim in this situation.

Most TPM technology today captures both the "Sell-In" (initial volume, price, and promotion cost of the promotional deal with the retailer) and the "Sell-Out" (e.g., the actual results of the promotion at retail). For Sell-In, the following primary elements are generally captured:

- Total volume by product
- Standard Price per Unit
- Discounted Price per unit
- Total Revenue generated
- Promotion Allowance

The calculation of ROI on the Sell-In, then, is a simple formula:

Sales Volume x (Standard Price-Discount)-Promotion Allowance = Sell-In ROI

Fair enough, right?

Maybe for now, but as the data capture increases and the historical accuracy improves, the challenge will be to ensure enough granularity to feel confident enough to add trade promotion P&L data to the annual financial report.

Syndicated Consumption Intelligence

For the Sell-Out or actual promotion results, the manufacturer/supplier is at a bit of a disadvantage right off the bat. Most consumer products companies track the volume of product sold in a promotion through the receipt of reports from the syndicated data providers such as Nielsen, IRI or NPD, as we have stated previously. All three of those syndicated providers engage in extensive use of sampling methodology, extrapolated averages, and projections to deliver assessments on compliance with pricing, displays, advertising, coupons, and other merchandising assets.

Overall, it is excellent data and well-constructed algorithms that provide solid measurements of promotional activity in the stores. But as with any sampling methodology, there is risk of inaccuracies, missed data and of course, the latency that naturally comes from the hard work of transforming the store data into usable insights and intelligence.

"So, what!" says the head of trade promotion for a global candy manufacturer. "Everybody knows the problems with [syndicated] data, and there's nothing we can do about it. So, everyone plays in the same ballpark, and until something changes, we have no lesser or greater advantage over anyone else."

Well, yes you do if you have a lot of money and can buy more markets, create custom reporting, and pay for the higher frequency of delivery.

It's true, though, in a very practical way. In today's consumer goods marketplace, with everyone buying promotion performance reporting from either Nielsen, IRI or NPD (or a combination of the three), the generally acceptable definitions of promotions, pricing, competitive actions, and consumer shopping data do project a somewhat level playing field.

That said, the sophistication of the analytics performed against these sampled data can deliver a fair estimation of what occurred during a promotion, and key performance indicators like products sold at the discounted price, what displays were in place, advertising and coupon tactics that were driving the volume. But at the end of the day, the *volume* and *price* are what the typical TPM system gets to configure the retailer's P&L.

What I am referring to here is integrating the data into the TPM system itself—not having the data in form of external reports or dashboards.

Some TPM systems capture this information, but regrettably, most don't. But when they do, it is usually the bare minimum intelligence that is committed to historical archives. Remember, this is the database that future optimization engines and advance AI- and ML-driven algorithms are bumping against. Therefore, calculating the total volume of product moved within the promotion and extended against the discounted price is the general extent of the ROI reported.

Another consideration is that, in most companies I have been around, the very people doing the promotion planning don't even have access to the expanded and more potent results delivered by the syndicated data providers. That is another can of worms, and we will get into that later; but right now, the state of intelligence quality that the TPM systems provide to the promotion planners is fair at best—certainly not as good as it could be.

As with the increase in TPM solutions with expanded promotional data granularity, the ability to ingest higher quality and deeper granularity of data to deliver a higher ROI is improving globally. That is good news to everybody.

EARLY-STAGE ADVANCED AI/ML-DRIVEN ANALYTICS
WITH INCREASE IN NEAR REAL-TIME DATA FROM CHANNEL CUSTOMERS

2ND DIMENSION

OPTIMIZED

- AI and ML-driven predictive analytics
- Increased POS data to provide near real-time visibility
- Integrated and aligned consumer marketing planning
- Integrated near real-time retail execution compliance data
- Pricing, assortment and logistics data in promo planning

Figure 9.5 The 2nd Dimension of Promotion Analytics Optimizes All Promotions

THE 2ND DIMENSION: OPTIMIZED

Figure 9.5 shows the key indicators for attaining the 2nd Dimension of promotion analytics capability which would enable AI-driven optimization of promotion plans that delivers realistic predictive outcomes. The prerequisite would typically be to ensure that all the functionality and capabilities of the 1st Dimension foundational elements are in place and operational.

However, in today's TPM technology arena, there are elements of the 2nd Dimension present in the more modern and advanced TPx solutions, although not entirely meeting the data model foundational requirements in the 1st Dimension. The reason for this is that some of the TPM vendors have been able to build or acquire some level of advanced optimization functionality before they can create the data models to support them. This is not such a bad thing, and in some situations, it does help to prepare the consumer goods manufacturers/suppliers for more rigorous optimization that would take advantage of expanded data sets. It also drives the desire to invest in the building of more granular data models.

AI- and ML-Driven Predictive Analytics

As the subtitle implies, the first level of achievement for the 2nd Dimension is to have a fully capable AI and machine learning engine that can effectively take business scenarios and data to model outcomes. This does not mean doing a database pull of all historical promotions that have the same data and projecting those ROI figures to predict similar success for a duplicated set of promotion plan values.

This is more or less what is happening now that many industry analysts unfortunately tag as "TPO" solutions. They are not.

The distinction between real TPOs versus what we see across much of the TPx vendor landscape today is machine learning. Artificial Intelligence is about providing direction based on experiential learnings—the ability of the technology to learn from previous operations and react by using that learning to enhance the outcomes. Considering the huge amount of data we are talking about here, with POS data from hundreds of millions of transactions, for instance, legacy database operations would take days to pull the answer together and even then, provide no guidance on how to effect change that produces better results.

Given that promotion planning is done by the people who are charged with the selling, you cannot expect them to be marketing experts. Neither can you expect them to perform the rigors of plowing through petabytes of data in an attempt to create patterns, trends and scenarios that guide them to the most likely success factors.

That is what AI does. It learns, adjusts, and responds to constantly changing conditions in the marketplace and rapidly provides smart insights and directions based on those causal factors.

In seconds.

However, if AI and ML technology is being used, even to a small degree, then the definition of real trade promotion optimization will eventually fit the solution. But have no misconceptions about how well these AI-driven analytics tools can perform and how real the projected results will be once the post-promotion analyses begin.

The use of true AI-driven predictive analytics for trade promotion is still a very immature science with high dependencies on the quality of the data which, as we have pointed out, is significantly lacking in most companies.

If you oversee your company's quest for a promotion optimization initiative, make sure you have your vendors test with real data and get them to show you what is possible. Do not make your decision on a demonstration. Do not make your decision on a reference. Have your data scientist in the room and give them the task of verifying the technology with their own testing.

Implementing a TPO is a long and arduous journey. Don't be caught down the road with a limited functional capability because once you deploy, the die is cast. Your company will have to begin the even more difficult process of customization and augmentation—or outright expulsion of the solution in search for another vendor.

Increased POS Data to Provide Near Real-time Visibility

The 2nd Dimension is about getting smarter.

The highest level of technology in the world is only as good as the data it uses. Investing in a real AI-driven trade promotion optimization system is smart, so you want to make sure that the data enables the machine learning to work from the most accurate and trustworthy data available. The alternative is that old saying, "Garbage in, garbage out."

As I have said before, the syndicated data providers do excellent work. Their analysis of the market, competitors, consumers, and retailers is highly regarded and should be. However, the question I have asked over the past few years, as TPOs are making strides forward in innovation and creativity, is about POS data and whether a market and location sampling methodology is sufficient. I think, at the very least, efforts should be made to work toward 100% of the POS data capture, whether it means getting it from the syndicated data provider or through direct acquisition from the retailer.

With the volume and breadth of data covered, and the billions of rows of shopper transactions that must be considered, it has made sense on a historical basis to create viable and representative samples to reduce the time and cost of data wrangling. But no longer, I feel.

We live in a digital real-time world. With AI technology and innovative new high speed database systems in place, there is no reason why those petabytes of data would limit our capacity to be thorough and comprehensive in our examination, analysis, and subsequent actions taken to create the highest possible quality of success in predicting promotion performance.

Given the rising tide of e-commerce shopping, where data comes from every single transaction, perhaps we need to rethink the issue of sampling methodology when it comes to the mining of POS data.

Even with the most sophisticated, time-tested, and trusted sampling of markets, retailers, locations, promotions, and products, the insights and intelligence we would miss from those entities that are not included could be costly.

The argument is going to be that science and experience is driving the sampling algorithms used by the syndicated data providers; but again, even with that quality of scientific method, are we not putting ourselves at risk with the practice of "assumption-based analysis" which is happening now? Certainly, the syndicated data providers could and should lead the way to a more accurate and timely ingestion of data and provision of intelligence; but the bottom line is that POS data especially should cover every retailer, every location, and every market.

Remember, the motto of today's revenue growth management function is ensuring the right product, at the right retailer, at the right price, and at the right time. That sounds like a need to be 100% right.

The way we live today is in a real-time environment. Backward-looking analytics are simply no longer the way to go. Receiving post-promotion analysis weeks after the end dates might well tell us what happened and how, but it is simply too late to do anything about it.

Maybe next time, right?

No. That does not work. In the consumer e-commerce environment, online shopping and resulting action is real-time—what the consumer looked at, how long it took them to look at it, questions they asked, what they eventually purchased and even how they felt about it. If a consumer goods company has a promotion going on that is failing on day one, they need to know about it *that* day, or at least within 24 hours.

With POS data, there are so many important bits of knowledge you can know in 24 hours. You can track the trending purchases, even on an hourly basis through yesterday's data. You can compare the purchases to the levels of inventory you have from either shipment history or in-store audits, and you can quickly determine if there is a risk of being out-of-stock in time to do something about it.

I will remind you that out-of-stock conditions are among the leading causes of promotion failure; and many believe them to be the primary cause. One of the best examinations of out-of-stock conditions (OOS) was a 2007 study conducted by Dr. Thomas Gruen and Dr. Daniel Corsten, and funded by the Procter & Gamble Company. In the extensive study, there are several excellent statistics and recommendations for correcting this painful problem; but one particular statement they made makes my point about POS:

> "The use of point of sale (POS) data is a viable measurement method for many store formats. There are a number of companies that have developed algorithms to estimate OOS from POS data, and some retailers have developed their own in-house systems. POS measurement systems can be sustained, scaled and are able to deliver sales

161

loss and duration measures. The accuracy of estimating OOS using POS data is 85 percent or greater, which is equivalent or greater to the accuracy of manual audits (where human error is present)."[68]

Sampling methodologies and their issues aside, trade promotions and all other forms of channel incentives are, by their very nature, intended to support the local promotion of the manufacturers'/suppliers' products everywhere. So, the argument about scale and coverage can be made that, in this social-media-charged environment, we should see the entire picture in near real-time.

There is a trend among the top consumer goods manufacturers to begin requesting and paying for (in some cases) POS data directly from the retailer. This not only ensures 100% coverage of all locations where the consumers shop, but the coveted ability to see what happened *yesterday* instead of in a few weeks from now. This is the difference between agonizing over a failed promotion that costs both the manufacturer/supplier and the retailer/wholesaler and being able to make changes or stop it on day two.

If there are out-of-stock issues visible from the data, replenishment can be immediate, saving the promotion from further failure and ensuring sufficient product on the shelf for the weekend shopping. Considering problems like Phantom Inventory (where in-store system-reported on-hand inventory is higher than the actual physical stock on-hand), direct POS data can also combine with shipment data to help pinpoint these types of nagging problems.

"We have combined our e-commerce and trade channel reporting systems to deliver a single unified and aligned status for promotion performance," explained the vice president of revenue growth management (RGM) for a paper products company. Her company began changing their POS data acquisition from the syndicated data provider to direct store upload two years ago. "I still heavily depend upon a lot of the analytics we get from [the syndicated data provider], but as far as POS data is concerned, we have already seen marked improvement in our ability to understand what is going on across the entire country in each major geography and demographic."

Her company is moving toward the development of an optimization engine that she hopes will combine all the elements of her RGM practice focus into one analytics tool set. It gives her field sales and marketing teams the ability to collaborate across their channels of distribution to drive smart decisions, generating higher revenue and profitability. The technology being used is not one of the major TPx vendors, rather their own internal development. But for her, receiving direct POS data from her top 15 accounts, as well as the combined e-commerce and multitier distribution (indirect buying resellers) data she currently receives, enables integration into the warehousing and shipping logistics data to deliver a solid 360-degree visibility to the Consumer Chain.

Her IT organization and data scientists are also integrating weather data and syndicated data to build a single database of consumer purchasing trends and patterns. This data will also include in-store audit data that will validate promotion compliance, assortment and planogram compliance, and demographic statistics. Leveraging that data to generate ongoing scenario models, her AI technology will begin assessing all the conditions and results, learning from, and adjusting to new trends and patterns, to produce a higher quality prediction of performance across the entire business.

Integrated and Aligned Consumer Marketing Planning

Every now and then, the CEO has to put on his striped shirt and grab his whistle to referee the next bout between his chief marketing and chief sales officers. Perhaps this is a bit more dramatic sounding than it really is, but the rift between corporate sales and marketing, especially in the consumer products companies, has created significant barriers to a unified and aligned corporate strategy of consumer engagement.

As I documented in previous chapters, the slow drain of funds over the years from the corporate marketing budget to the sales budget to support the never-ending appetite of top accounts for trade promotion spending has created a barrier between the two organizations. Sales plans and executes trade promotion, which is often more than double the entire budget of the marketing organization responsible for advertising, PR, consumer research, couponing, and e-commerce.

The argument is that sales executives do not understand the consumer as much as the marketing organization does, and that is probably true. But the sales team responds that trade promotion funding drives the volume, which drives corporate revenue and profitability, so cash your paycheck and don't complain.

That is a bad attitude, and probably an exaggerated reality. In truth, the marketing organization most likely does know more about the consumer. The research, ad responses, coupon redemptions, mobile and e-commerce responses, and even customer service inquiry data provides critical insights into the Consumer Chain and helps to position the company's products and messaging such that it generates the right demand.

Sales leverages this intelligence in the form of demand plan insights that help configure the right promotional tactics, pricing, timing, and product groupings the consumers end up seeing that drives them into the stores to buy the products. That is the way it is *supposed* to work.

Conflicting promotional messaging between corporate consumer direct marketing and trade promotions often counteracts and cannibalizes a good promotion for both the retailer and the manufacturer/supplier.

The good news is that finally both the marketing and sales organizations are beginning to collaborate and align promotions to ensure support and coverage both at the national and local levels.

Many of the current TPM systems can show both the trade and marketing calendars in one screen view. But the visibility to those two calendars, even on the same screen view, is not enough to create realistic alignment—there is much more work to do.

Promotion optimization technology is the big beneficiary of this improved working relationship. Bringing the retailer into the picture also enables a level of collaborative intelligence that goes a long way to generate the best possible outcomes for promotions. The data that can be made available to the promotion planner and the optimization engine is already proving a high value.

Just a few paragraphs ago, I mentioned the RGM executive with the paper products company who is overhauling her entire consumer and promotion analytics capabilities to prepare for the power of AI-driven optimization of price, promotions, product assortment and retail execution. As I pointed out, she has already merged critical marketing data into the mix, including advertising media calendars, coupon drops, and e-commerce promotions, to build a single strategic and tactical force to ensure the highest quality predictive promotional plans.

In the most recent project for TPM implementation I am engaged in now, the working relationship between marketing and sales is phenomenal. It was not created through this TPM initiative but has been in place for years. The results are telling, too. Every year these executives meet to create a unified and integrated business plan that combines both local and national promotional events and tactics, with the combined goals of revenue, profitability, product share expansion and new product introduction.

Nothing is done without coordination from both organizations, and the driving direction comes from the Revenue Growth Management leadership. This team continues to meet in some form on a weekly basis, sharing ongoing management and compliance of the promotions, which, in a perfect world, seems to be the right way of working across the two organizations in every consumer products company.

Integrated Near Real-Time Retail Execution Compliance Data

Over the past few years, this rather old business practice of Retail Execution (REX) has enjoyed a renaissance of sorts. The practice of sending merchandising reps out to stores all over the country, checking on individual local store compliance with pricing, promotions, product planograms, inventory stock levels, competitive activity, and overall store conditions, has been a heavily manual, expensive, and yet required action by consumer products manufacturers in every sector.

We take a close look at Retail Execution in the next chapter, but it is a critical component of this dimension of promotion analytics.

Today, more sophisticated technology is in place to make this process more efficient and effective. But it is often an overlooked source of consumer engagement intelligence that should plug into the data necessary to optimize future promotions. So how does that happen?

The more advanced REX vendors have advanced planning and scheduling software with state-of-the-art tablet and mobile devices that can capture and track everything that is visible inside the retail location. This includes, but is not limited to the following information:

- On-shelf stock

- Backroom stock

- Phantom Inventory (what the retailer shows on hand versus actual counts in the store)

- Display and positioning

- Pricing (on package)

- Competitive products (shelf stock, pricing, location)

- Competitive displays (location and details of promotion)

- Advertising (in-store flyers or window banners, local newspaper, broadcast, and social media)

Currently, field merchandise reps can only visit a select grouping of the stores in their respective territories, and most likely no more than 20 or so daily. However, new digital technology using in-store security camera access (with retailer permissions, of course) and IoT sensors can automatically track some of the above information and deliver it in real-time. As this technology continues to mature, the ability to gain almost immediate compliance intelligence will change the way promotions are measured and most likely settled.

A major tool company has engaged in a proof of concept (POC) project, with two of the largest home center chains across four major markets, to test the use of video to conduct retail compliance audits. The store's internal security cameras were accessed by the vendor to capture and compile the data. The vendor's software set up recognition routines that enables the AI tools to evaluate the product placement (shelving as well as end caps, shippers, and other places where the product is positioned), displays and even shopper activity.

After two months of testing, the company was able to target locations that were not compliant, and even situations where the shopper touched the product or handled it in some other way but did not decide to purchase it. The test also revealed for the retailers that shelf stock was often bare even with plenty of inventory in the rear stockrooms that could have been brought out but wasn't.

The POC was also designed to provide for immediate reimbursement of promotion costs when the compliance levels reached an established threshold. Of the 42 stores that were tested, only two stores were guilty of failing to erect the displays and stock the shipping display (shipper) that was sent. As a result, the promotion was reimbursed at 95% (40 out of 42 stores compliant), but the reimbursement was made the same evening, so settlement was less than 24 hours from the start of the promotion!

So, if the reward for the retailer is rapid payment of trade promotion, the reward for the manufacturer is better and more immediate intelligence into the status of the promotion on a near or real-time basis. Typical REX systems can deliver in-store audit results quickly, most coming from immediate upload from the device of the rep standing inside the store. Likewise, the rep can access real-time views of promotion plans, giving him/her the ability to stay current on what promotions are in place and what is coming. Many of the merchandise reps will inform the store manager to prepare them to be ready when the next promotion hits and the prepackaged display materials and pricing requirements are received.

From a perspective of optimizing future plans, the key account manager and/or sales reps who are conducting the planning process can leverage REX data to provide a heads-up to their buyer as to which locations are common violators of promotion compliance, which is a good way to avoid problems with compliance and also give the retailer a chance to fix problems of their own with their existing store managers who fail on a regular basis to comply.

Most important, however, is the intelligence gathered from the onsite audits and reviews as a validation of the promotion execution. The infusion of this data, especially with critical local intelligence like weather conditions, store traffic, and other causal factors can heavily influence the promotion's results and provide visibility that would be otherwise unknown.

This is how the AI engine *learns*. The individual follow-on compliance issues are the essence of proof of performance, especially in FMCG industry segments where documented proof of performance is a rarity.

Pricing, Assortment and Logistics Data in Promo Planning

The science of price management is a very mature process. The extensive research and historical tracking of price effectiveness and its impact on consumer sales presents a treasure trove of intelligence that can refine and enhance the precision of predictive analytics for promotions. The current environment in most consumer products companies, of building and expanding the RGM organization to incorporate more functions like promotions, assortment, and retail execution, is where AI-driven optimization systems have the most benefit.

Every single promotion that is configured, other than contractual Every Day Low Price (EDLP) agreements, features temporary price actions that pressure the promotion planners to make the right pricing decision. The other factor is that, in most cases, the retailer drives the promotional price, pushing the KAM or sales rep into negotiations that stretch margins to the breaking point and anchor the entire value of the promotion.

In a typical High-Low promotion (periods of time when the price is lowered off the regular or "high" price standard), price sensitivity is the key to attracting the consumer/shopper. But far too many promotions are "giving away money" because the price negotiations are simply that—campaigning back and forth until an agreed-to number is reached. This process can be devoid of real intelligence, because pricing has usually been left in the hands of the KAM and the retail buyer who are both operating from acceptable "ranges" of price. As a result, someone almost always leaves money on the table.

With price as a major factor in the data model being used, there are two very important factors that must be part of the final promotional price.

First, the extensive research and testing of price levels done by most companies can establish more than just a range, but an actual specific recommended price. Second, looking back at pricing history by comparing promotional TPRs, the optimization engine can learn and reapply logic that helps to validate and justify the eventual price.

This type of capability is beyond what most retailers have, and they do have extensive pricing intelligence on their own. But the reason it is so valuable is because the manufacturer has the benefit of price history and promotion performance results across every retailer in every market—not just the data from the retailer currently in negotiations for the promotional event. Retailers recognize this.

One of the world's top consumer over-the-counter drug manufacturers proved this in a series of case studies in 2019, ahead of pandemic-skewed 2020. The company's RGM teams worked their price optimization data into the promotion optimization engine to leverage five years of historical pricing and promotional activity to determine the ideal price during virtually every period of time, season, and geography.

The test was conducted with five of their top ten retail accounts and lasted two quarters. The retailers agreed to use the output from the price/promotion optimization tool and run at least five promotions across the six-month period featuring three different promoted product groups. The buyers were not allowed to deviate from the price level set by the KAM, which was the optimized price point.

The test consisted of two different parallel analyses—one of the six-month promotions and a second of similar promotions and timeframes across the past two years. Both analyses were compared to the existing and ongoing research that the manufacturer's marketing team and agents ran, testing pricing in panels and groups across the same markets for the same products.

The final analysis showed that both the retailer and the manufacturer lost money compared to the historical performance of promotions at the negotiated price. The current six months showed a more than 8% average increase in margin for both the retailer and the manufacturer. The optimized price became the base that both the buyer and the KAM used in configuring future promotions. This case study, appropriately anonymized, is used to demonstrate the power of optimized pricing in promotion planning and is now being rolled out to the rest of the manufacturer's account base.

Assortment planning is the practice of defining exactly what product and how much of it to carry in a retail store, e-commerce warehouse, or wholesale distribution channel. The work required to understand historical buying habits, cost of goods, demographics, and even changes in neighborhoods, for example, is enormously complex and voluminous. If any business function cried out for artificial intelligence, this one does.

As with pricing, the movement of this practice into RGM organizations has begun, and assortment planning becomes a major factor of promotion optimization because it is the very essence of which product is on the shelf and which is not. Aside from the obvious pain points of out-of-stock conditions, assortment planning is the guideline to what *should* be there and in what quantity. This data has to reside in the same mix as inventory control, because it becomes the basis against which the key product performance metrics and measurements are calculated.

What complicates this issue of assortment planning is the increase in adoption of private label brands in the major chain stores, especially grocery. Edgar is the KAM for one of his company's largest mass merchandiser companies. His category management team provided guidance for him to schedule and execute promotions in the timeframe immediately after the Easter seasonal rush was over. He and the buyer worked out the promotion months in advance—a $132,000 promotion that featured a TPR and a front-of-store end cap display with special shelf-talker tags. The promotion was set to begin on a Wednesday and conclude the following Monday, for a six-day run.

As Edgar was packing up to leave his office on Friday during the promotion, he received a call from the head of the field merchandising team for the southwest region. "So, I got a call from Chip, my field rep director over in Dallas. He told me that one of his reps visited one of the stores running the promotion and saw no sign of any such promotion. In fact, he could not even find any product on the shelf, no display and more than two skids of inventory in the stockroom," he said. "Before I could say anything, he also told me that he had two of his other field reps take a run over to stores in their areas, and by this afternoon, it was obvious that none of these four stores were running the promotion."

In Dallas—one of their top five markets.

Worse than that, he said that in all four stores, there were store-branded products in their slots (shelf positions).

At this point, Edgar was puzzled; but as he tried to figure out what he could do, the field manager told him that one of the reps talked with the manager of the store he was in and was told that the assortment plan now changed and that his products were being moved to another location as soon as a new planogram was created. "I was furious," said Edgar. "I called over to our product management team and was told that, yes, we had a change that was temporary, and we were reconfiguring our planogram to accommodate a change in the retailer's home brand assortment plan," he continued. "Did you guys think of telling us? I have a promotion running right now and it's a huge investment."

The moral of this story is that product assortment is a constant process today, far more dynamic than it was in the past where assortment plans were stable for years. But as in this case, the growing percentage of store-branded labels and the increased prominence of placement of those products on the shelf ave become a serious issues which have to be taken into consideration when the optimization engine is using historical data to model new promotional plans. It also means that there is a mandate for integration of the planograms and assortment plans with internal system and human checklists to make sure the promotion calendars are consulted before any change in the assortment plan is made.

Edgar's promotion could have been a financial disaster and was further complicated because the buyer and their own internal planogram team evidently did not coordinate the planning either. If there was a limited or even no shipment of new product sold-in to support the promotion, it would be a total loss by the manufacturer, and the retailer would have to reimburse the $132,000. Moreover, as product assortment plans shift, the reasons should also be imbedded into the logic so that the optimization algorithms can learn from the experience.

There is an old United States Marine Corps saying that applies when these types of obstacles are encountered: *Improvise, Adapt and Overcome*!

Oorah!

Finally, there is another key component of promotion optimization that is just now really coming into vogue among TPx product designers and developers.

Logistics.

As a major component of the supply chain, the processes of production, warehousing and shipping all contribute to the success or failure of a promotion in many ways.

The product is backlogged in factory production

- The product is insufficiently low in the warehouse
- The product is not IN the warehouse
- The product is shipped late
- The wrong product is shipped
- The shipment is delayed en route
- The truck driver delivers to the wrong address

And on and on, as it goes. But the important aspect of logistics here is that promotions depend upon the accuracy and trust in how the products are delivered to the store—or to you, for an e-commerce promotion. Since shipping issues, warehouse problems and factory backups are common enough occurrences, it behooves the promotion optimization developers to have ongoing integration between the TPO and key logistics systems in each of those areas.

Further issues can be created by the distribution centers and logistics systems of the major retailers and wholesalers. This is typically a black hole in the supply chain; but there are more and more channel companies that are providing near real-time data on distribution center warehousing and shipping logistics to their manufacturers/ suppliers to alleviate and light up this black hole.

Each of these issues mentioned above have the capacity to derail a promotion's execution. In some cases, these problems are ongoing, but most are infrequent. Even so, the scenarios that happen should be mapped and cataloged into the optimization models to add even more intelligence to the overall decisioning process of the TPO. Given this, then, leveraging this historical data enables the optimization engine to foresee issues such as weather, breakdowns or, dare we say, *pandemics*, and factor them into the final predictive outcomes generated.

All these components are critical to the optimization of trade promotion, and although very few, if any, TPOs have the existing capabilities described above, this is what the 2nd Dimension, Optimization, is. Achieving anything less is not being in the 2nd Dimension, is it?

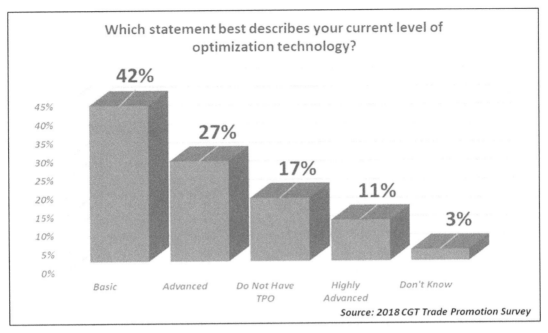

Figure 9.6 2018 CGT/Capgemini Survey on TPO Capability in Trade Promotion

In the aforementioned 2018 CGT Trade Promotion Survey, the question was asked, "Which statement best describes your current level of optimization technology?" The response was somewhat surprising. Of the more than 300 CPG executives surveyed, 38% reported their TPO as "Advanced" or "Highly Advanced." Each of these respondents were left to determine the meaning of "advanced" and "highly advanced" as well as the other measures to their own assumptions of capability.

Forty-two percent said that they had "Basic" TPO capability, however many of them with whom we followed up did not have a specific TPO solution, rather, they had their own internal data scientists perform scenario modeling using some sort of AI. I strongly suspect that this is the same finding from all the other respondents, except of course for the 17% who were extremely honest that reported that they did not have one.

The good news is that everyone recognized what TPO meant, and that in and of itself is a major milestone in the history of trade promotion to date.

THE 3RD DIMENSION: PRESCRIPTIVE

The 3rd Dimension of promotion analytics (Figure 9.7) is all about predictive capabilities around trade channel promotion optimization. Predictive analytics takes historical data and conditions and generates reliable predictions about what is going to happen based on the data at hand. Once you have a prediction for a promotion displayed on your screen, you have to decide if that is what you want to do.

PRECISE AND TRUSTED PRESCRIPTIONS FOR PROMOTION SUCCESS
BEYOND PREDICTIVE AND OPTIMIZED TO TRUE COLLABORATIVE PLANNING PRACTICES

3RD DIMENSION

PRESCRIPTIVE

- Time-tested algorithms shared by channel and marketing
- Increased data capture from all promotions and events
- Daily, near-100% POS data capture and reporting
- Dynamic inventory alerts and threshold monitoring
- Social sentiment and real-time ecommerce integration

Figure 9.7 The 3rd Dimension of Promotion Analytics is Prescriptive Decision Making

That is the job of *prescriptive* analytics.

Prescriptive analytics takes the same data used for predictive analysis and delivers direction with options and potential outcomes. It dives deeper into the data using AI and machine learning capability to not only tell you what is likely to happen but moves beyond that and tells you what you should do now based on that prediction.

Predictive analysis is what you can expect to happen given the existing data.

Prescriptive analytics answers the "So What?" It tells you what you can do now and how to do it in potentially multiple options.

You need both.

Time-Tested Algorithms Shared by Channel and Marketing

We have covered the various pieces of data typically found within the internal operational history of a consumer goods company. However, prescriptive analytics should also include more information from the channel reseller as well—the retailer, wholesaler, distributor, and indirect reseller.

Ideally, this will go beyond POS and include more information about shopper loyalty data, shopper movement data, and to some degree, purchase history. This data is usually not shared; however, as we move further into the capabilities and rewards of prescriptive analytics, we may see retailers loosen the lids of some of this data.

"I have no problem sharing some of our loyalty data providing it is secure and we get to select which data to provide," said the marketing director of one of the northwest US' largest grocery chains. "It's a trade-off, in my opinion," he continued. "If I can see a value that increases revenue and profitability, I'm all ears."

The responsibility does not just lie with the manufacturer/supplier, to be sure. Smart retailers know that they have a lot to gain from the combined intelligence of the manufacturer's entire global value chain, and we are seeing more collaborative initiatives around sharing data and advanced optimization of price, promotion assortment and execution.

172

Marketing data was discussed earlier, but as we defined prescriptive analytics, the historical trends and consumer patterns can be put to great use driving predictive optimization scenarios to more execution options. Marketing does indeed know the consumer very well, and if a consumer products company wants to leverage the Consumer Chain better than they do now, this is the fastest way to get that done.

Prescriptive analytics takes the hard work done by the optimization engine and hits the afterburners of insightful delivery that brings the entire collaborative team to a smarter decision about what to do, where to do it, how to do it and when.

Increased Data Capture from All Promotions and Events

If there ever was a reason to spend the time and money collecting even more data, prescriptive analytics is the overwhelming reason to make that happen.

POS data delivered by most retailers is, for example, almost summary level data. The syndicated data providers may capture more individual pieces of information from their POS feeds, but as we mentioned earlier, the value has to be balanced between having all of the locations and the sampling methodology they use. Still, the value proposition for expanding the information is obvious—the more data we have, the more scenarios we can create, and the higher likelihood we will get a more dependable and trusted direction.

AI is a technology that learns, so the important thing is to begin to build that expanded database, and that will mean increasing the capabilities of the trade and channel incentives management technology to accommodate the broader scope of scenarios required for the machine learning to grow. As I work with the more sophisticated analytics teams and technology, one thing I consistently see is the increased value and benefit of insights that are derived from these expanded scenario models.

That said, a 3rd Dimension database must be large enough to manage all the data mentioned above in the 2nd Dimension stage. Every TPM implementation begins with the development of interfaces between the primary data source systems. Designing, developing, and testing integration is a long and tedious process, but the outcomes more than justify the effort and cost. Most TPM vendor platforms have basic out-of-the-box integration toolsets, and this usually includes prepackaged interfaces for the more well-known data source systems like the enterprise resource planning (ERP) systems from SAP, Oracle, Microsoft, and so on. Those systems will contain foundational data like customers, products, revenues, sales territories, accounts receivable and accounts payable.

Trade promotion history is usually maintained in the TPM vendor's system database or, where internal technology is used, any combination of internally developed or legacy systems of record. But integrating with the broader array of data sources like direct retail POS, syndicated data providers, external marketing agencies, and retail execution systems will require individual design, development, and testing.

Keep your eye on the prize. That prize is the benefits your future analysis of performance, both predictive and prescriptive, will have. The simple formula you want to achieve is to be able to provide specific directions for a promotion that states:

If you create a promotion with this customer, in this timeframe, promoting these products, deploying these specific tactics in these markets at this cost, you will have a 95% chance of attaining a minimum of 250% ROI on incremental revenue and profitability for you, and a 300% ROI for volume and profitability for your customer.

These numbers mentioned are only examples, but this is the objective of prescriptive promotion planning and the fundamental purpose of the 3rd Dimension of promotion analytics.

Daily, Near-100% POS Data Capture and Reporting

Although we made this statement earlier, it bears repeating. POS data is the most accurate and immediate intelligence a consumer products company can have to determine the success of a promotion.

One of the more popular blog posts I have ever written was on the subject of promotion plan timing. In the FMCG industry, the lowest level of timeframe planning is the week. Everyone knows that there are 52 weeks in a year, 13 weeks in a quarter and 7 days in every week. Right?

But in the business of trade promotion planning in the FMCG industry, typically, the most granular data you get from the syndicated data providers is the week. That has been the measure for such a long time that the blowback on my post's statement that we must eventually go to a daily tracking was intense.

Remember writing letters? You write a letter and drop it into the mail. A couple of weeks later you get a reply, and you were fine with that. Imagine a Generation Z kid today texting a friend and not getting a reply within five seconds. Frustration. Within five minutes? Devastating!

The same is true in trade promotion these days. Promotions no longer run for weeks. They run for days, and often less than seven days in duration, crossing weeks (which makes it even harder to determine weekly performance). For all consumer goods analytics, it has always been a practice of managing promotional performance from the rear-view mirror. Receiving reports on what happened during a promotion a few weeks ago is better than not ever knowing, there is truth to that. But we live in an age where virtually every measure of life these days is real-time.

Some activities are yet to be easily managed on a daily basis, but now promotions can be by receiving POS data directly from the retailer overnight. This provides a near real-time look at how the promotion is doing within the week it is running. It is invaluable data and provides insights that drive potential corrective actions NOW, not after the promotion ends in failure. My blog post argued that now is the time to make this happen. There are companies that can and do deliver full coverage POS data daily to the consumer products companies, and here is where the syndicated data providers can change their methodology to a 100% POS coverage, even for the retailers they do collect it from, and report it immediately thereafter.

The blowback I spoke about was primarily technology-based. For the syndicated data providers, their analysis and reporting tools take time, and are no doubt highly valuable insights; but how long can we sustain a trade-off between insightful intelligence and latency?

Not long, I think.

Daily analysis is the very essence of the 3rd Dimension of promotion analytics. While it is not necessary to have yesterday's data to create the annual promotion plan, the AI machine learning technology does need the granularity of this data, and having it is mission-critical.

The same problem exists for multitier distribution, where wholesalers and distributors resell the products to their customer base, except the problem is more difficult to solve. Most distributors highly value their top customers and limit communications (and even knowledge of their existence) between those customers and the manufacturer/supplier. Since there is no direct contractual purchasing relationship between the manufacturer/supplier and the indirect reseller, finding out what is going on at the store level is very difficult, if not impossible.

POS data from those indirect-buying resellers have to come through the wholesaler/distributor. In these cases, there are reporting systems and vendors that provide this data, but again, it can typically be weeks after the promotions. The wholesaler/distributor controls the amount of data and is generally unwilling to provide pricing, promotion payments, and fund availability for those indirect resellers. Typically, volumetric data is provided and of course, if known, the field merchandiser reps can visit those stores and report critical data such as pricing, assortments, promotion compliance and competitive product data.

But times must change for the wholesaler and distributor as well. They perform a needed service and role in consumer goods, and that is to serve and support the smaller retailers who cannot afford a direct contractual relationship with the manufacturer, but still want to provide the products and services to their customers in their markets. Of course, buying from distributors is not limited to small independent retailers. Many large retail chains maintain buying relationships with distributors to purchase inventory they cannot get directly from the manufacturer, such as emergency replenishment or buying excess stock at lower prices than they could from the manufacturer.

In all cases, POS data is becoming the currency of intelligence, and the ability to gain that information on a daily basis across 100% of the retail locations is a consideration every consumer products company must make. The cost may or may not be less, but the value proposition of having immediate knowledge of product sales is worth it.

Dynamic Inventory Alerts and Threshold Monitoring

We discussed out-of-stock conditions and the impact they have on promotion success. One of the most important values that daily POS data will bring is reducing the timeframe of knowledge about the potential of empty shelves during promotions. With the current structure of intelligence, the risk of not having near real-time sales data (POS) is too high to continue.

There are very good technology vendors out there which can provide inventory tracking and reporting solutions; and most consumer products companies have some capabilities in this area. But knowing when and where the inventory is at all times is one of the most important data components required for effective prescriptive analytics.

Through logistics data, manufactures know what is being shipped to the retailer, either at the store directly or to the retailer's distribution centers. Using this data against POS data provides at least a somewhat trustworthy picture of what *should* be on the shelf and in the stockroom for every retail location. The tracking of on-hand stock, versus in-transit stock, versus distribution center warehouse stock can be combined to create that picture, and in many cases, this is how the "shipped" data is generated for forecast planning. Most supply chain systems provide monitoring of inventory with specific threshold levels that trigger alerts when they are reached.

But when POS data is part of the composition of analytics delivered by either the syndicated data providers or internal systems after the promotions are run, how do you compare the knowledge of out-of-stock conditions that occurred during the promotion with the visibility of a potential out-of-stock situation occurring now?

The answer is that there is no comparison. Finding out about an out-of-stock condition after the fact is one thing, but being able to know in the first 24 hours of a promotion if there is a lack of stock that threatens any one day of a promotion is worth the extra cost of the data in near real-time, is it not?

Indeed it is. However, it is not easier said than done. But it IS something we have the technology to do now and should be.

Social Sentiment and Real-Time E-commerce Integration

You've read the numbers in earlier chapters. E-commerce is eating up more of the brick-and-mortar retail share of sales every day. For the consumer products company, it is a growing channel of distribution and has to be aligned to all forms of consumer engagement. For the consumer products companies, the strategic and tactical business plans include selling through an omnichannel environment today, and the sophistication of marketing in the e-commerce channels has exponentially improved over the past two decades alone.

But as I work with manufacturers and suppliers across all sectors of consumer goods, I continually see that dividing wall we talked about between sales and marketing, in place between e-commerce marketing teams and trade promotion planners. Leading consumer products companies have tactical plans in place to leverage the marketing budgets to segregate promotions between trade promotion and e-commerce and given the nature and uniqueness of e-commerce, there is generally a separate organization within marketing that runs the e-commerce channel promotions.

In the meetings and workshops I have attended and given, I always try to bring trade promotion planners and management teams into the workshops with the e-commerce team so that we get a great all-around perspective of the consumer. I must confess that this is very difficult to do. I may end up with one person from e-commerce, and typically not someone who can make decisions or policy. It is very frustrating, and I hope this pattern does not continue. It can't.

Going back to the most recent project I mentioned earlier with one of my Latin American clients, they do have the full team in place, and even have weekly meetings in the form of a joint committee that includes trade marketing, sales, category marketing, direct-to-consumer marketing and e-commerce executives. These are not only decision makers, but key stakeholders and policy influencers who work together better than I have ever seen it done before.

The output is a clear, concise, and workable strategic and tactical plan to promote their products across every channel of distribution they serve. They are a market share leader in most of their product categories, and it is no wonder how they got there with this type of collaboration.

They are the model for how it should work. They look at the entire promotion calendar and balance their promotions to ensure the right mix of tactics and timing, making sure to build cross-channel product and brand support, and avoiding conflicting pricing and promotional offers. This ends up being a very strong annual calendar and their customer base really appreciates being brought into the collaborative planning process.

The final component of ensuring prescriptive analytics quality is dealing with social media. Aside from the usual use cases like advertising in the major social media platforms, social sentiment analysis is now a mission-critical mandate to include promotions planning.

A former colleague of mine at Capgemini always reminded me that you cannot predict social sentiment. His background in the marketing business is deep and I respected what he said. What we focused on then, however, was the current state of social sentiment around a particular brand or product. Overlaying this intelligence with the outcomes of the promotion can add a dimension otherwise unattainable to the analysis of the promotion—either during or after the promotion concludes. Here is an example of what I mean.

A major poultry producer, a leader in packaged chicken, turkey and other poultry products had a promotion beginning in early December 2019. The promotion featured a price reduction on packaged whole turkey with messaging around the idea of eating turkey more than just at Thanksgiving. There was a series of displays and a national television advertising promotion all scheduled during the same two-week period in the heart of the holiday season. During the first two days of the promotion, the POS data showed tremendous sales at all their major grocery and mass merchandiser chains across the USA. The promotion began on a Thursday and continued through the next week, to take advantage of television ads during the college and professional football games. In addition to the TPR and displays in the stores, the company executed a social media campaign complete with recipes, dish photos and stories of turkey dinners.

After a strong weekend of sales, new shipments of products reached the stores to support the second week of the promotion. On Monday, there was a rash of social media posts and comments about the spoilage rates of turkey and the serious medical problems that can result in eating spoiled turkey. These posts, many of them, were made as comments and opinions of the company's own social media stories supporting the promotion. Millions chimed in, and the majority of the posts were negative, with thousands of stories of hospitalizations and even deaths caused by eating leftover turkey.

The POS data showed a huge decline in the purchase rate, and after a strong weekend performance, the promotion died on the heels of the social media explosion. These stories are common now, and in conversations with the company's data scientists, they mentioned this could have been avoided with a simple examination of similar situations across social media. "We could have done a search and run a simple 'what-if' algorithm to apply machine learning to determine extensiveness of the negative posts." He pointed out that this is so common and that most of these posts are always negative. "Seems everyone has a bad story to tell," he said. "We could have predicted this and refrained from running a social media campaign across the major platforms."

Social sentiment analysis vendors do an excellent job providing data about social media trends and patterns. This data can easily be included in the mix for predictive analysis, with the prescriptive output being to avoid the use of the top social media platforms. However, that said, the use of major social media platforms in the company's programmatic advertising strategy has strong positive influential history for effective consumer engagement and should always be considered.

The smart money is going to be on the ability to leverage the prescriptive analytics technology to help with the decision-making on where to put the promotions, what messages to provide and when to run it. Social media is still a very dynamic and unpredictable media in many aspects, and the analytical capabilities we have today are rather immature. But with the growth of technology, and capabilities we have to provide immediate intelligence on social media sentiment and content, it is only natural that it should be a major component of the data feeding the 3rd Dimension of promotion analytics.

CONSUMER CHAIN-DRIVEN PERFORMANCE
AUTONOMOUS CONSUMER-DRIVEN PLANNING AND EXECUTION

4TH DIMENSION

ENGAGED

- Integrated consumer-driven RGM-based promotions
- IoT-based monitoring and consumer demand sensing
- Real-time dynamic baseline adjustment
- Enrichment of causal data driving marketing mix
- Predictive supplier/materials and value chain optimization

Figure 9.8 The 4th Dimension Is Engagement with the Consumer Chain

THE 4TH DIMENSION: ENGAGED

Entering the 4th Dimension of promotional analytics, the consumer goods industry manufacturers and suppliers must focus on the consumer more than they ever have. Up to this point, trade promotion, as with co-op advertising, market development funding, and business rebate programs all deal with the relationship between the manufacturer/supplier and the channel customer. This business-to-business (B2B) relationship has worked for more than a century to provide financial aid and support in the form of subsidized promotional assets designed to attract shoppers.

This B2B relationship has been covered in depth within the pages of this book already; but suffice it to say that the light at the end of this long tunnel is the face of the consumer. So, as we look at all the ways to leverage technology to deliver the right product at the right price, to the right location at the right time and in the right quantity, we also have to consider the end-game—inciting the consumer to buy the product.

As illustrated in Figure 9.8, entering the 4th Dimension of Knowledge means the consumer goods industry players have now crossed the line from making this all about the channel to all about the consumer. And with all the money spent on trade promotion, co-op advertising, and market and business development funding, this is the pinnacle purpose of analytics.

Integrated Consumer-Driven RGM-Based Promotions

This is a mouthful.

Revenue Generation Management (RGM) practices are all about getting the right product into the right channel at the right price and at the right time. As such, trade channel promotions have been used as the incentive for the channel customer to buy enough volume to meet the forecast and agree to promote the product in their stores to meet the sales forecast.

That is the present thinking and the present strategic objective.

All the information I have provided in this chapter is in preparation to conduct the final mission: to create a sustained relationship with the consumer, converting them to become a loyal customer and, therefore, generating a long-term financial success for the company.

What this means is that future promotions will focus on achieving the objective of winning the competitive battle for the hearts and minds of consumers at every link in the Consumer Chain. Going back to Chapter 4, we gave examples of what the consumer thinks, feels, and desires at every one of those levels, and discussed the practical application of domain expertise and knowledge to put your company at the top of the consumer's mind when they reach each stage represented by those links.

The concept of the *Demand-Driven Supply Chain* is not new, but the driving objective is to set the supply chain strategy based on consumer demand. Most definitions call it "customer demand," which makes me wonder if that means *channel* customer versus the consumer. Certainly, that retailer, wholesaler, or distributor is where the money goes, isn't it?

But no, I think it is intended to apply to consumer demand. I always love what the late Roddy Martin says about the demand-driven supply chain. He pushed the change from a traditional, transaction-based, inside-out order-to-cash concept of supply chain management to the more modern outside-in approach, where external inputs drive demand sensing which in turn drives better visibility, analytics, and execution.

Roddy would also always say that the difference in achieving a true demand-driven strategy is more about the company's being leadership-driven than pure IT-driven, where, as we are indeed seeing now, the business leadership in sales, marketing, RGM, finance, and operations are making the key decisions for technology and functional innovation.

For a company to become truly consumer-driven, the adoption of a real demand-driven supply chain is a necessary step; but more importantly, is the adoption of all previously discussed requirements around predictive optimization and prescriptive promotion planning. The place to start is the Consumer Chain (Chapter 4). Translate every link in that chain as a data component required to drive predictive and prescriptive planning.

IoT-Based Monitoring and Consumer Demand Sensing

In the old TV series, *The Twilight Zone*©, host Rod Serling would begin with an introduction:

"You're travelling through another dimension, a dimension not only of sight and sound, but of mind; a journey into a wondrous land whose boundaries are that of imagination. That's the signpost up ahead—your next stop, the Twilight Zone!"

Unless you are a millennial, generation X, Y or Z—or are not an old TV show junkie—you may remember that, and you may even think you can hear the weird music played under old Rod's voiceover as you read through the introduction.

Consider that same introduction as appropriate in this topic, except that the signpost up ahead says *"Internet of Things."*

IoT is already well-implanted in our daily lives, as we pointed out earlier. But in the context of the 4th Dimension, autonomous consumer-driven planning and execution of promotions, it promises an exciting future of opportunity. Today, IoT is in use already in warehouse management, store traffic monitoring, shelf sensors, factory production management, and even in our cars and trucks.

Leveraging the technology of IoT as a viable way to increase the efficiency and effectiveness of consumer engagement would fill a room-sized whiteboard of use cases. Rather than fill the next several pages with IoT use cases, let's take a look at some realistic ways in which IoT can soon begin to drive data from the Consumer Chain into the planning and execution of trade channel promotion and all channel incentive programs globally.

- **Packaging Sensors** – Even though we already have RFID and other barcode-type labeling technology that helps track product, on-package sensors could continue to track the product from the factory to the store. But the exciting thing is being able to track the product after it is sold from the store to the pantry to the trash. How is that for increasing the visibility of the product lifecycle?

- **Digital Video Cameras** – We mentioned this previously but given the coverage of security cameras across the world, imagine being able to digitally monitor product shelving, displays and even price labels using advanced video and digital IoT technology. This would reduce or even eliminate the need for human store visits for promotion compliance.

- **Digital Shopping Carts** – Sensors embedded in the shopping cart can detect packaging sensors to provide real-time shopping content, alert store stocking teams when inventory on the shelf is reaching minimum thresholds, and even provide advance checkout as the product is dropped into the cart.

- **Maintenance Sensors** – For mid-to-high ticket price items like appliances, auto parts, consumer electronics, and lawn equipment, sensors can detect certain product maintenance and replacement needs, alerting the consumer to update, upgrade, repair or replace, stimulating the Consumer Chain's first link, "Identifying a Need."

This list is growing every day, but you can see how IoT technology is creating higher quality intelligence by providing data capable of fueling the critical predictive and prescriptive analytics we are covering here.

Real-Time Dynamic Baseline Adjustment

Baselines are part of the 1st Dimension, Foundational level of promotion analytics. I described some of the problems associated with maintaining the baseline and the concerns over the accuracy of the data portrayed in the baseline. Those issues are well-documented and a part of hundreds of surveys on supply chain and demand planning done globally.

But we know that baseline development is the intersection of demand planning, supply and operations planning, and historical channel sales, and that they are the guidelines for sales forecasting and promotion planning. The incremental volume and revenues shown in these baselines form the foundation of P&L reporting, do they not?

If they are so critical, why is the average update timing for FMCG and large consumer durables companies so long? Sixty-one percent of the respondents in a 2018 survey by Consumer Goods Technology and Capgemini were either dissatisfied or not confident in the baseline accuracy.[67] Why?

Because, as we later learned, the timing for updates was too infrequent to provide confidence in the numbers. "This market changes way too often to set volume and revenue standards one time a year or even quarterly," says the head of sales for a household cleaning products company. This seems to be a popular complaint among key account managers and sales reps charged with the responsibility to plan and execute promotions.

It is not a simple fix, evidently, because the entire set of sales forecasts rides on these figures; and the process of changing the forecast from a fixed target to a dynamically moving target is something most sales executives want to avoid. But it still does not solve the problem of inaccurate reporting based on flawed baselines.

The answer is not just faster turnaround of POS data. The baseline is just that—an estimated base number for projecting forecasted and incremental volume and revenues. Actual volumes and revenues from POS data can then be overlaid to show and compare actuals to forecast estimates. The quality of the data itself is the culprit here.

Receiving sampled, averaged, and extrapolated POS data from a limited set of markets stretches the boundaries of accuracy beyond what they should be. To use this data for the compilation of the baseline is simply basing forecasts on data that could be skewed significantly.

Going forward in the 4th Dimension, the baselines should be given more attention. Annual baselines should be adjusted at least quarterly, and for many companies, that is the operating standard. Who really knows the delta between what is currently used for baseline-setting and what it would be if full, 100% POS coverage was used as the basis for baseline projections? Even at a 1% variance, a spending level of anywhere from 15% to 30% of gross revenue could be multiple millions of dollars for many companies.

Enrichment of Causal Data Driving Marketing Mix

We have already discussed ways to increase the capture and enrichment of causal data from every corner of the consumer goods channel. The problem goes deeper into the corporate infrastructure than adding and/or upgrading technology.

For more years than I care to count, I've heard marketing executives tell me that they know more about the consumer than anyone in their company. They are vehement in their argument and passionate about how frustrated they are to see the money spent on trade promotions they know will eventually fail to engage the consumer.

"Look, I get the need to spend our money with the retail buyer to get a deal," says the CMO of a multibillion dollar lighting products company. "But why is there so little attention paid to the actual promotion? I mean specifically the content, the messaging, the positioning. We work our teams hard to understand what drives the demand and how to position our products to draw the customer in, but what happens? Some price-only deal and a bunch of products stacked at the end of the aisle in a sloppy display that we pay hundreds of dollars for each store to put up?"

Frustration. And absolutely, the marketing team knows more about the consumer than the salespeople do. Yes indeed. No KAM or sales rep would disagree with that.

But my next question to these folks is always asking if they collaborate regularly with the sales teams to help them create smarter, more productive promotions. The answer is always a "waste of their time" theme. And that may well be the case.

183

But now, we are in a time in our industry where the luxury of independent promotional strategy and execution is no longer sensible. In order to maximize the company's assets to engage at every point in the Consumer Chain, the CMO and the CSO have to bring their organizations together, preferably under the RGM team leadership, to build a corporate strategic objective that takes advantage of each channel's individual viability and special competencies.

It is less a factor of technical innovation than it is *leadership* innovation. As we mentioned earlier in this chapter, many consumer goods manufacturers and suppliers are beginning to add metrics for the success of the promotion in the retail stores to the compensation schemes. This may be a trend as more and more companies begin to compel their KAMs and sales reps to work harder and collaborate better to build a truly successful promotion.

We shall see.

The good news is that these conversations are going on at a level I have not seen before. Trade organizational meetings are beginning to feature these alignment issues and we are beginning to see realistic networking begin to solve this problem. The technology is with us now and getting better every day.

Predictive Supplier, Materials and Value Chain Optimization

The modern Value Chain begins with the earliest stage of a raw material and ends with the consumer's purchase of the product. It is everything in between those two points.

There are so many great books on supply chain, manufacturing processes, procurement, distribution, and retailing that we need not repeat any of that information here. That said, the Value Chain must support all the dimensions of promotion analytics we have described herein.

The last major component driving operability in the 4th Dimension is a value chain that is fully linked to the sources of data used to predict, prescribe, and measure trade promotion effectiveness. It means being able to include data on raw materials availability, and the ability to adequately procure those materials.

As we speak, there is a huge shortage of computer chips, so thousands, perhaps millions of laptop and desktop computers sit in warehouses unable to be sold because the brains are not attached. And what good is a computer without its brain, yes?

Being able to provide intelligence on the pre-factory production activities of the value chain will dictate and impact everything that comes next, including the ability to get product on the shelf. This includes the ability to know if the raw materials are bad, or full of bacteria or some other bad thing that will make us sick or kill us.

Imagine how many peanut butter and jelly sandwiches were lost when it was discovered that one of the most popular peanut butter products had ingredients from a field of dangerous substances. One field. One set of raw materials out of the hundreds of millions of peanuts from other fields. It took quick action to remove all the brand's peanut butter products from the shelves, even though only a few contained peanuts from the infected fields.

If you don't think that type of data could have been welcomed in the process of predicting the success of a promotion, you have not been paying attention. And I know you have.

The price of entry into the 4th Dimension is being able to have visibility to every aspect of the value chain, from stem to stern. From seed to shelf. And at every point in between. It is not data we can readily identify in all cases, but it is improving, and I do see how track-and-trace solutions, for example, are helping identify specific SKUs of product rather than wiping the entire shelf clean and gaining horrible social media standing in the process.

The difference in the attainment of the 4th Dimension, and the previous three, is the ability to know the consumer from the point of identifying a need, to the satisfactory consumption of the product. It is a tall order, but one that results in a 100% success rate and positive ROI achievement for every promotion executed.

Contrary to what many pundits say, this is an achievable goal for all sectors of the consumer goods industry.

CHAPTER 10

TAKING IT TO THE STREETS

The genesis of modern trade channel promotion is the concept of a manufacturer subsidizing all or a portion of the retailer's promotion of their products in their local market. Tantamount to the success of such an offering is the ability for the manufacturer to verify and validate that the retailer actually promoted the product—proof of performance.

The operative word is *compliance*.

Historically, the process of proof of performance was simple—submit a series of documents showing the actual advertisement, price and cost of the ad, and verification or certification of publication. In many consumer durables industries, this is essentially how it is still being done today, with a bit more sophistication in the types of documentations and the copy of the actual newspaper page, broadcast script and notarization of performance or online screen prints. This method seems to work for both manufacturer/supplier and channel partner.

In the world of FMCG, not so much.

We covered the significant changes in the way FMCG companies execute trade promotion back in Chapter 3, where we introduced the process of deduction from invoice for trade promotion, and the reduction and virtual end to retailers submitting claims documenting proof of performance.

Most consumer products companies now utilize the services of their field merchandising teams to visit a rotating representative sampling of stores to check physically and visibly to see if product was on the shelf, prices were accurate, displays were in place and inventory was in the backroom.

At some point, the formal definition for this process and practice became known as *Retail Execution* (REX).

Retail Execution is one of the major set of tasks and responsibilities of another area called *Direct Store Delivery* (DSD). DSD is the business model where a consumer-packaged goods company has its own distribution system and fleet of vehicles that takes product directly to the individual retail stores. You see them everywhere—the trucks driving up offloading soft drinks, salty snacks, cookies and cakes, ice cream, and beer, for example.

A major component of the process and functionality they provide is to do _exactly_ what the REX process is, but of course the DSD drivers also have the task of stocking, taking re-orders, and managing the cash. In today's digital world, everything is rather automatic; but still, it is a big job.

Another Fine Mess You Got Me Into

It is bad enough knowing that more than 70% of trade promotions fail. We have discussed several reasons for that, none the least of which includes the poor compliance manufacturers/suppliers deal with every day. The statistical numbers in REX are, frankly, equally sad and much more to blame for the overall promotion failure than retailers would like to admit. With all of the pressure brick-and-mortar retailers already feel from e-commerce, contending with the ordeal of making their individual location store managers support every promotion at 100% is like herding cats.

The truth hurts, though. It's not working.

According to a recent survey from Quri, approximately 25% of retail sales are lost due to poor execution on the store floor.[69] This equates to an average, across all retailers, of $3.7 *million per store* per year in lost revenues. We already know the damage to revenues and profitability caused by Out-of-Stock conditions, so mathematically speaking, this is not a minor problem. According to a 2019 survey from Trax Retail, 65% of the consumer-packaged goods manufacturers say that poor retail execution costs them between 1% and 5% of their sales revenues each year.[70]

Retail Execution is a mission-critical mandate, but the way it is handled today makes one think that it is not. Poor execution hurts everyone in the mercantile orbit.

So, how does it affect YOU?

If you are a retailer, you already see the financial damage, don't you? You miss the opportunity to sell more products, make more money, generate higher profits and make your customers happy.

If you are a manufacturer/supplier sales executive supporting the retailer, failed compliance costs *you* future sales volume and, quite often, makes you pay for the excess inventory your retail account did not sell due to poor compliance.

If you are a corporate financial executive, you've just spent valuable trade promotion funds on yet another failed promotion, wasting millions (check the individual average retailer losses in the previous paragraphs) and most likely will have to ask for more money to make up for it.

If you are the field merchandising rep whose job it is to check the compliance of individual retail locations, you may be up long after quitting time, running to more stores to ensure future promotion compliance.

And, most important of all, if you are a consumer, and the store you shop at fails to execute the promotion, you will lose the chance to buy at a discounted price or worse, not be able to buy the product at all because of the empty shelf.

It is a solid lose/lose/lose/lose/lose proposition.

Begging for Attention

For too long, this practice has been relegated to low level priority in the overall scheme of promotion management. The longtime term, "TPM" has always meant *Trade Promotion Management*, accent on the "management." In that acronym alone, we fail to recognize *execution*, although too many will argue that the word "management" applies to managing the execution.

OK, nice try.

But in the modern context of trade promotion, we now call it "Trade Promotion Management and Execution," (TPx) which at least brings the word "execution" into the definition. That is a good start.

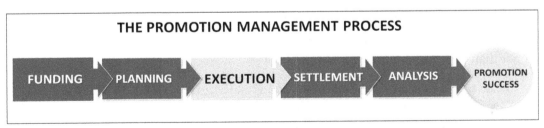

Figure 10.1 Retail Execution Is the Mission-Critical Center of the Promotion Management Process

In Figure 10.1, Retail Execution is literally at the center of the end-to-end trade promotion management process. No positive outcome for any promotion is possible without strong validation of performance and compliance with all promotional tactics and requirements. The leading consumer products companies have already embraced the need to elevate their attention to REX.

It is about time.

There has been a clear resurgence within the corporate operational priorities for Retail Execution in the past five or so years. My colleagues at the Retail Execution vendors may challenge the time-frame for this growth; however, they know better than anyone this is true because the RFPs for REX solutions are on a hockey-stick-like rise in that timeframe. As with trade promotion spending in general, attention on how to maximize the value and return on that investment has a clear focus on the issues around compliance.

The increased elevation and reengineering of RGM organizations have contributed to this increased priority. Because the RGM teams are ultimately responsible for creating and delivering the actions and policies required to increase revenues and profitability, they are beginning to own those REX process and technology assets.

It makes sense. Just as RGM is becoming the leading organizational placement for trade promotion management, product assortment planning, and price optimization, managing the REX function eliminates bureaucratic levels and solidifies the communication lines between each of these disciplines, and the teams with boots on the ground and eyes on the shelves.

While moving REX to RGM is certainly a trend, the number of companies actually putting this practice into place is still very low. Most companies struggle with this problem, and it is not limited to FMCG brand organizations. One of the world's largest tool manufacturers fights these retail execution issues every single day.

"It's not fair to me or my sales managers to have to deal with our top accounts' failure to comply with our promotions," says the executive vice president of a top power tools company. "Even the top DIY accounts have their issues controlling individual store managers who continually ignore the mandates for promotions. I heard the numbers—something like twenty or thirty percent failure rates, but I think it is even higher than that," he continued.

In fact, he's right. In the aforementioned Trax Retail study of 2019 of more than 300 CPG executives, the prevailing intelligence is that instead of the 40% noncompliance often seen in past research, nearly 70% noncompliance is more likely the case.[71] Given the historical lack of solid measurements we have had as an industry over the past 40 years, I would say that we may now have finally found a willing environment for not only measuring compliance accuracy, but giving it the credence it so deserves in the overall quest for high ROI within the Invisible Economy.

What's the Big Deal?

The *deal*.

That is, the trade promotion deal, and specifically, the value thereof.

All of the rich, advanced analytics and technology we now have to assess the historical performance, model scenarios, and predict outcomes is fantastic, to be sure. But at the end of the day, that is to say the end of the *promotion day*, if the shopper can't see the display, the lower price, or worse, the *product,* then it is all for naught. Retail execution is the practice of making sure the shopper experiences the benefits of the promotional offer, isn't it?

IMPACT OF RETAIL EXECUTION ON CONSUMER GOODS COMPANIES

RETAIL EXECUTION ACTIVITY	INEFFECTIVE	EFFECTIVE
• Stock availability checks and audits – On-Shelf, Storeroom • Promotional display checks and validation • Price accuracy audit • Planogram and product positioning checks • Competitive product information capture • Store condition observations and evaluation • Store manager meeting and update on future product/promos • Product re-orders, where necessary • Shopper activity observations and notation	1. Lost sales 2. Inaccurate pricing 3. Poor product placement and planogram compliance 4. Consumer frustration 5. Wasted promotion spend 6. Missed competitive intelligence 7. Lack of communication	1. Increased sales 2. Price effectiveness 3. Strong promotional messaging and positioning 4. Category competitive intelligence 5. Near Real-time intelligence 6. Better customer relationships 7. High ROI on promotion spend

Figure 10.2 Impact on a Typical Consumer Goods Company of Inefficient Retail Execution Compliance

It is easy to get deep in the weeds analyzing each of the detailed problems associated with REX; but at a high level, Figure 10.2 gives a summarization of the negative and positive impact to the consumer goods company for failed promotion compliance. Being somewhat kind to the terms used to depict frustration, anger, confusion and outright rage with retail failures to adhere to promotion compliance, consider the term, "ineffective" to describe the lack of adequate capability the manufacturer/supplier has to measure and check for compliance. Aside from obvious results such as lost sales, missing stock, and frustrated consumers/shoppers, there are other important factors to consider.

191

Pricing, for instance, is one of the top problems found with instore audits of promotion compliance. If the promotional price negotiated at the sell-in process is not shown on the shelf tag, product packaging, or worse, in the POS system, there is a string of dangerous follow-on problems too numerous to mention here. But the bottom line is that price discounting is by far the number one promotional tactic used today. Even with the sophisticated POS systems where price is automated and controlled across the entire store network, without a display or ad or any other form of communication to the shopper, there is a high likelihood the incentive to buy is lost and the deal goes south.

Failure to check for compliance will also result in the lack of intelligence about how the product is positioned in the store. Is the planogram[7] accurately in place or properly represented? All too often, retailers lack control over store managers and unfortunately, ultimately what the interior of the store looks like, and especially where the product is placed on the shelf.

The intensive work done by corporate category marketing and merchandising teams, in collaboration with the retailer's own marketing, merchandising and category staff, is one of the most important aspects of the relationship between the manufacturer/ supplier and the retailer, wholesaler or distributor.

This has to be done right.

"My rep called and said that the display is missing and our products are in boxes stacked next to the ice machine," said the key account manager for one of the company's top convenience store chain accounts. "She told me that the boxes were not even opened and that they were exactly as shipped," he continued. "I'm on deal with that product now!" What he means is that the product has a promotion going on right now, which also means he is about to lose the benefit of the money spent to promote the product. If this is a trend, his promotion dies an ugly death.

This may be an extreme situation; however, product positioning failures are common. In reality, they are just as frustrating to the store headquarters executives as they are for the KAMs.

The other major areas of impact from a lack of effective compliance verification are the obvious lack of competitive intelligence lost and the missed communications with corporate trade marketing, finance, and sales executives jointly responsible for the success of the promotion. This is why great care goes into the scheduling field reps, and the ability to be agile and flexible enough to quickly go to the store location to fix a problem.

Of course, the virtual opposite is true when and where the manufacturer implements a strong REX solution and provides sufficient field coverage to ensure a satisfactory percentage of retail locations covered in any given week. Naturally, the ability to validate and audit compliance helps to ensure the promotion is effective, but it also enables the capturing of intelligence about the retail locations that consistently fail to comply.

Most companies maintain some sort of record of noncompliance, and the more sophisticated the solution or tool used, the more effective and accurate the list of noncompliant "culprits" is. The retail HQ executives want to know that as well, although their own list is most likely more extensive and more highly communicated internally.

The bottom line is that the more accurate the compliance audits, the more intelligence is useful, and consistent problems can be corrected and solved. This elevates the promotional ROI and makes the category marketing, sales, and finance executives more comfortable and confident in their promotion planning and execution.

And it makes the CEO happy.

The Extent of the REX Problem

In Figure 10.2, there is a summary of the usual activities and operations that are conducted by the consumer products company's field merchandising reps and associates. These may vary in priority and complexity across the different consumer products industry sectors, but generally they represent at least a variation of the agenda for a rep's visit to a store location.

- **Stock availability checks and audits—On-Shelf, Storeroom:** Checking and counting inventory both on the shelf and in the back of the store to provide eyes-on assessment of real-time inventory positions.

- **Promotional display checks and validation:** Verify that the displays are in place, the content is accurate or has not been changed from the promotion message and, if necessary, erect the display from extras typically in the rep's car or truck if possible. Photos of the display are automatically acceptable for proof of performance requirements.

- **Price accuracy audit:** Verify the promotional pricing (or even the regular pricing) is accurate and visible to the shopper. In some cases, this may mean visiting the store manager and checking the POS system to ensure the right price will be scanned.

- **Planogram and product positioning checks:** Check the product locations around the store, making sure the planogram is being adhered to, and the product is not in a damaged or misplaced state on the shelf. Also check for permanent display case damage or abuse and order replacements if necessary.

- **Competitive product information capture:** During the walk-around in the store, capture competitive product information, photographing products, checking pricing, inventory (on shelf and in the stockroom if possible) as well as any promotional displays, demonstrations or other visual assets.

- **Store condition observations and evaluation:** Take note of and photograph the store conditions like cleanliness, clutter, difficult shopper traffic routing, security, personnel activities, and external parking and/or other areas (such as fueling pumps, car washing bays, and so on).

- **Store manager meeting and update on future products/promos:** Visit with the store manager to provide updates on future promotions, new products, and company news, as well as get their feelings and opinions about promotional shopping activities, weather related issues, or other factors that could impact the store's performance.

- **Product re-orders, where necessary:** In some cases, but very few, the merchandise rep may be able to take or make re-orders of product from the store manager. In these situations, it is usually to avoid potential imminent out-of-stock issues prior to or during a promotion. Most of the financial, order management or cash management would be done in the form of a DSD business model, not REX. There would be no cash or payments handled by the REX merchandising rep.

- **Shopper activity observations and notation:** While the rep is at the store, they will observe shoppers, especially if they are hunting for one of their company's products. This is not generally intended to create direct one-on-one communications with the shopper, but sometimes it happens. Typically, this activity is observe-only—from a distance.

For any FMCG or other consumer products manufacturer, there is a weighted evaluation of the criticality of each of the issues, concerns and problems associated with Retail Execution compliance. In Figure 10.3, the Trax Retail survey measured the relative values in both criticality (highest importance and/or priority) and frequency of occurrence of these problems.

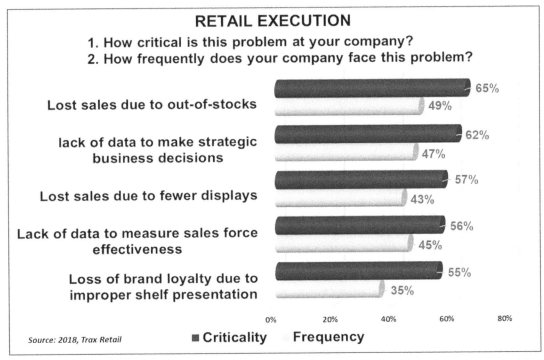

RETAIL EXECUTION
1. How critical is this problem at your company?
2. How frequently does your company face this problem?

Source: 2018, Trax Retail

■ **Criticality** **Frequency**

Figure 10.3 TRAX Retail Survey on REX: Problems, Criticality, and Frequency Faced by Consumer Products Companies

The out-of-stock issue mentioned as the highest criticality in the list of issues has not changed in rank for decades.[72] What is very interesting in this survey is that the second highest issue in terms of criticality and frequency is "the lack of data to make strategic decisions." Sixty-two percent of the survey's respondents say it is a top concern, and just less than 50% say it is a frequent occurrence.

Do you see that?

Nearly 20 years ago, in 2002, Hand Promotion Management conducted one of the most extensive surveys done on trade promotion management and execution, with over 1,000 consumer products executives responding. A similar question was asked about retail execution issues. Out-of-Stock issues were clearly the top vote-getter, but the second, third and fourth were "Loss of sales due to missing displays," "Product positioning and Planogram errors," and "Pricing Errors," respectively. There were no mentions of lack of data or failure to collect data on any strategic planning issue.[73]

But now, with the emphasis I have been telling you about on analytics and advanced AI- and ML-based predictive and prescriptive analysis, you can see how critically important data has become for consumer products company executives now. In fact, in the Trax Retail survey response, *data*, or the lack of it, for measuring salesforce performance is now a top five issue.

What this shows is that REX today is a far higher priority because executives need to *know* what is going on in a more controlled manner and with more frequency. This is precisely why there is an explosion of new REX vendors in the global marketplace today—all touting advanced analytics and real-time mobile field systems to capture and deliver information to all of the key stakeholders responsible for promotion success. And this is a good thing, indeed. The stiff competition between the long-time REX solution vendor leaders and the emerging technology-driven vendors will make REX more efficient and effective, driving innovation across all sectors of the consumer goods industry.

Now, about the retailer.

I told you that these retail and channel resellers are very concerned with compliance themselves. The problems they face are like walking on razor blades because their entire profitability is at risk when the promotion fails.

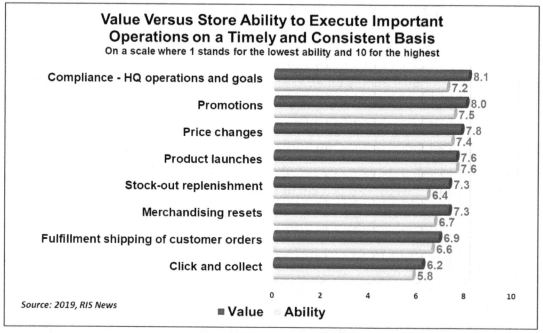

Figure 10.4 RIS News Survey: Operational Compliance Issues Faced by Retailers

In June 2018, retail industry guru Joe Skorupa authored a piece on a survey done by RIS News magazine on retail execution (Figure 10.4).[74] This is an extremely important work because it covers several key performance indicators the retailers use for retail execution. To believe that the retailers are somehow less concerned with execution as the manufacturer/supplier is downright lunacy. Skorupa makes a great case for how retailers gauge the monumental efforts they must go through to support the promotion and to ensure 100% compliance across their entire network of retail locations.

This survey is significantly broader in its definition of store operations that constitute *execution* for the retailer. As you can see, adherence to the corporate HQ goals for operating execution is the top action, and rightly so. This activity covers all of the standard operating procedures, policies, personnel, community, and financial requirements for each location.

In Figure 10.4, the value and ability to execute for promotions and pricing are the second and third highest priorities respectively. Promotions have a perceived value of 8.0 out of 10, with a confidence in ability at 7.5 out of 10—interestingly lower than the retail executives' beliefs in the ability to execute HQ policies and procedures (7.2 out of 10). But that is not surprising. Promotional payments are the lifeblood of retailers' profitability, so you can bet most retailers are good at that job.

Pricing is next, just behind Promotions at 7.8 and 7.4 out of 10 respectively. Price changes, specifically, are always an issue that has to be a priority. As mentioned in the consumer products RIS News REX survey we just covered, getting the price right across 100% of the stores in the network is not an option—it is financial life and death to the promotion, hence the profitability of the store.

Surprisingly lower on the chart is Stock-out replenishment. So right here we have a bit of an issue between manufacturer/supplier and retailer, do we not?

All retailers struggle with out-of-stock conditions (OOS). This is fact.

OOS problems often come from logistics failures like shipping problems, back-orders, and factory production problems. But they are also problems caused by the retailers as well. Failure to frequently check shelf stock, especially during a promotion, or the inability to quickly move product from the storeroom out to the shelf are ways the store contributes to out-of-stock conditions.

Phantom Inventory was discussed previously, but here is where it heavily impacts the shelf status and whether or not the product is actually there or not. Phantom inventory, in layman's terms, is when the internal inventory systems of the retailer report higher stock levels of products than are physically there. Inventory controls systems, especially those with heavily manual controls by the store managers, can often be off the mark by a lot.

One of the top mass merchandisers in North America had a legacy inventory system that always seemed to work well and was overlooked for replacement many times by IT in favor of more advanced analytics, enterprise resource planning, factory, or warehouse systems. The system enabled individual store managers to make changes in the store's stated inventory based on formal and informal checks throughout the year.

These informal checks were verified during key store inventory audits and reconciled against records that were available in the systems. However, there were

197

problems associated with shipping, logistics, distribution center outages, and other factors that often misreported corporate inventory in total. Store managers also had the power to make emergency replenishment orders and often those orders were never fulfilled in total, resulting in differences between manual replenishment orders that went through different order management systems than the corporate procurement systems managing the order and shipping of goods directly from the manufacturer.

The results were that actual store inventories were 12% off, and that meant when a shopper noticed an empty shelf and asked the associate if there were any products in the store, the answer was, "Sure, there's one in the back, I'll go look."

After waiting a long time, the associate emerged with an apology that they did not have one, but their store over on Main Street had one. The shopper leaves and will most likely order online.

Lost sale.

Who Executes the Execution?

The statistics on retail execution are growing in complexity and coverage. However, one particular statistic is evidently disagreed with often in the consumer goods manufacturing industry—responsibility for actual instore execution of compliance audit and verification. The top two groups that are shown as having the primary responsibility to walk into the store and conduct the activities of retail execution are (1) the sales organization, and (2) independent merchandising organizations who deploy thousands of people to visit the stores.

The problem with the statistics that show the responsibility assigned to the field sales organization is that there simply aren't enough of them to make even a small dent in the huge volume of retail locations all over the continent. Unless the company is a multibillion dollar global conglomerate with thousands of salespeople all over the world, the total makeup of the sales organization is small—less than 100 people including KAMs and sales management executives.

And who, among them can afford the time to drive all over creation and spend 10- to 12-hours daily visiting between 10 and 20 locations?

None of them.

Unfortunately, there are thousands of consumer products companies that *do* charge the field sales organization with that responsibility, including the collection of proof-of-performance documentation, arguing deduction and settlement issues, and running down missing shipments and orders. On a recent project where I was mapping the current state processes, it was learned that the sales reps spent one-half of their time on these activities. Fifty percent of their time was taken from them when they could have spent it analyzing performance and figuring out how to sell more.

198

The other group typically shown to have the responsibility is the merchandising and execution vendors who *do* have thousands of people at their disposal across the continent to make those visits and conduct that compliance validation. There are enough of them to ensure that they see a suitable sampling of retail outlets to make it a viable scope of execution compliance in the marketplace. This is one of the major reasons why both small and behemoth consumer packaged goods companies hire brokerage service firms.

These organizations can be costly, but when compared to the time lost by sales reps doing less compliance validation and losing valuable time analyzing performance and increasing sales, what is the trade-off?

Brokerage firms, especially those in North America, often handle the chores of retail execution for both small and large consumer products companies. These companies are essentially sales organizations which do not take title to goods, but handle many of the trade promotion, retail interactions and analytics required by their principal client firms. They engage with large field organizations which are the "ground troops" for retail execution.

The brokers typically have their own legacy retail execution management platforms, but often use REX vendors to provide the technology that goes into the hands of these field merchandising representatives. Armed with tablets, mobile phones, and rugged hand-held devices, they are the ones who perform all the REX activities. The brokers will act as the eyes, ears and hands of the consumer products manufacturers and take a percentage of the revenues as their fees.

For each manufacturer, a broker will have a group of representatives assigned to work directly with the national and regional account managers to provide the heavy services related to sales and marketing of all, or a major portion, of the manufacturer's product portfolio. In addition, the brokerage firm will have a large staff set up on a regional basis who will engage with the field merchandising reps to schedule their calls, follow up on the output from each visit, communicate the manufacturer's/supplier's strategic, tactical and execution plans, and assess individual performance.

The large amount of intelligence generated from each of these visits is typically coming from either manual or automated systems that connect to the mobile devices carried by the field reps.

Manufacturers/suppliers leverage these reports and intelligence to generate insights into future promotion planning, as well as work with their retail customers to improve on retail execution compliance performance.

The retailers are very careful to make sure that there are strong and secure communications to and from either the brokerage firms or the manufacturers/

suppliers. The sensitivity of compliance data makes it very important to ensure that it is communicated up and down through the proper channels and managed by the right people. For the retailer, for instance, retail execution is a mission-critical role with a focus on three important people in the mix.

In the 2019 RIS News Study (Figure 10.4), the question was asked about the perceived value of the three people most involved in store operations, including retail execution.

On a scale of 1 being unimportant and 10 being extremely important, each of the three people were evaluated:

Store Manager:	***9.0***
Store Associate:	***8.7***
Region/Field Manager:	***7.7***

The store manager is generally responsible for everything that happens and everything that fails to happen at his/her store. So naturally, the retail perspective gives them the highest responsibility for execution.

Likewise, the store associates are in the store and responsible for carrying out the physical demands of the promotion execution including ensuring the stock is constantly on the shelf, displays are erected and in the right place, the price is accurately displayed on shelf tags, display verbiage and signage is accurate, and that the area is clean and neat. But the region/field manager is lower on the scale, even though he/she is on the "firing line," "in the trenches," or any other cliché that denotes they are working hand-in-hand with the manufacturer/supplier.

The answer to "who" is responsible for retail execution is a coordinated team that works together to make sure everything is done right, on time, and ready for the consumer/shopper.

Tools of the Trade

In today's modern trade promotion, co-op advertising, and channel marketing fund incentive programs globally, the technology has advanced considerably. Even so, most companies still employ the use of heavily manual processes, including the use of spreadsheets and internally-developed simple data capture tools that easily run on mobile phones and tablets. These are highly inefficient considering the demands and requirements of compliance for the dynamic Brick-and-Mortar retail promotion environment.

To think that more than $1 trillion is spent globally in the Invisible Economy, and such an inefficient set of tools and processes are used to verify compliance, when more than 70% of the promotions fail is what many would call ridiculous—ludicrous and irresponsible really. Yet it is what it is, as so many want to say today.

But like the cavalry to the rescue, the past decade has seen a resurgence of interest in REX and a growth spurt of highly sophisticated technology driving new and aggressive vendor solutions all over the world.

I won't put rankings or names of those emerging vendors here; because, not only would it be unfair to leave one of them out, but there are so many coming on the scene that, by the time this book goes to press, the vendor universe may well double!

The technology has certainly impacted the quality of performance for retail promotion compliance. Old legacy ruggedized hardware devices that were designed to read bar codes have merged into more functionally robust devices like tablet computers that have real-time interfaces with corporate systems and, in some cases retail systems, to provide up-to-the-minute views of inventory, promotion scheduling, POS data, and even coupon redemption data.

The new technology aligns retail trade promotions with consumer marketing events, direct-to-consumer promotions, and national advertising calendars to provide real-time updates of instore audits for compliance. These updates are transmitted directly to the trade marketing and settlement teams to help with validating promotional deductions, payments, and other settlement transactions.

Onboard cameras, interfaces with store security cameras, and digital kiosk feeds all combine to provide even higher resolution and real-time visibility of shopper traffic, purchases, display compliance and even on-package price verifications.

Retail execution vendors are now enjoying a very busy season responding to RFPs for REX management. "I've never seen it like this," says the head of sales for one of the largest REX vendors in America. "Most years we will get between 5 and 10 RFPs to bid on each year; but in the past three years, we have averaged more than 20 RFPs per year." He also noted that his company won nearly 50% of those RFPs as well.

Another vice president of sales of a major REX/DSD vendor solution confirmed it saying that their company has received more than 40 RFPs so far in 2021, and they are implementing more than 15 REX solutions in six countries at the present time. "I can tell you that we have engaged with two major systems integrators to help with these implementations, and they have received several more RFPs themselves than they have in a single year," he said. "The Covid-19 pandemic may have had something to do with the increase based on the need to ensure compliance in the supply chain, but the overall importance of trade promotion is what I think really drives this."

Going back to the RIS News Retail Execution Study (Figure 10.4), the responses revealed that most companies used mobile devices to manage execution but did not specifically call out a particular type or brand.

The question asked was about the extent of mobile device equipping within the stores:

Store Managers:	*57%*
Store Associates:	*33%*
Region/Field Managers:	*77%*

When asked about how the level of device distribution will be done over the next 18 months, 20% said that they would increase the equipping of store managers, with 23% saying they would not increase the mobile device equipping of store managers. Store associates were the lowest level equipped with mobile devices, but the response was that 30% would increase that level and 37% said they would not. Finally, regional/field managers had the highest level of mobile technology, with 13% increasing it over the next 18 months and 10% holding steady at the current rate.[75]

One interesting caveat of the RIS News Retail Execution Study is that of the importance retailers give to store managers in the execution operations. The survey figures show that the store managers were 9 on a scale of 10 for importance as the key resource for execution. The regional/field manager was rated the lowest at 7.7 out of a scale of 10. I am in agreement with Joe Skorupa, the author of the article on the RIS News Targeted Research Report that the store managers should have the highest level technology, including a dashboard and "console" he/she can check at any given time to see the status of the promotions.

The future is bright for compliance, in my opinion. Even with the horrible numbers we see in both compliance and overall promotion failure, I can see where technology and expertise will save the day. I am a big fan of Retail Execution solution providers and I am betting they will begin the process of merging their technology with trade promotion, analytics, and financial management systems vendors to provide full and consistent execution support that will eventually deliver 100% compliance.

This is another major step to make the Invisible Economy more visible.

And we all need this to happen.

CHAPTER 11

A NEW CHIP OFF THE OLD BLOCKCHAIN

When you talk about the Invisible Economy of consumer goods, you are talking about big numbers. I am not referring to just the near $1 Trillion payout from manufacturers/suppliers to retailers, distributors, wholesalers, and resellers, but the volume of transactions as well. Think about it. How many individual different products are carried in a Walmart store? Target? Best Buy? Tesco? Carrefour? Kroger?

Hundreds of thousands is the answer. Each of those products has identification tags, prices, shipping history, manufacturing lot numbers, and of course purchase transactions. Every day a gazillion transactions are generated and processed by computer systems all over the world, some linked, some not, and most highly sophisticated in functionality and capability.

Big numbers.

In Chapter 8, I covered analytics—the telemetry of consumer products. Amidst all of those insights generated from all of that intelligence, the world's mercantile systems crank away every millisecond and in every language, telling us what has happened, what is happening, and what will happen. Managing all these transactions and all of this data requires tremendous technology and cost, people power and intelligence, and careful planning and execution.

We have come a long way since the first generation databases and mainframe computer systems, and we are about to move into the next generation of technology—blockchain.

If you have heard the word, but have no idea what it is, join a very large club. Most people in the developed world probably have; but it will soon be as common in tech vernacular as mobile phones are today. Blockchain technology is real. Since its creation by Satoshi Nakamoto in 2008, blockchain has primarily been associated with the cryptocurrency, Bitcoin, and has served as the platform for managing Bitcoin transactions.

One of the best descriptions I have heard of blockchain comes from Max Thake, who has written some excellent papers on how blockchain works and where it is destined to be in the global business environment:

> "Blockchain is a distributed ledger or database,
> replicated over all the nodes in the network. This distributed
> ledger forms a linear chain of blocks of transactions in an
> unalterable, chronological order. Transactions are bundled
> into blocks of transactions to be validated. Validated blocks
> are added to a chain of previously validated blocks."[76]

In a bit less technical language, blockchain is a new way to record transactions that are immutable, public, and supposedly difficult to hack or steal because everyone has access, and the transaction is more streamlined and highly accountable. Transaction fraud is almost impossible, especially changing the transactions after the fact. It can consist of any type of digital asset, so the future application of the technology is wide open.

In this chapter, we will look at the realistic potential for this technology in the application of trade channel promotion management and execution. This is not going to be a deep technical treatise on blockchain; rather, more of a straightforward, simplified, and practical discussion on how, where, and why this technology could, should or would be applicable to trade channel promotion, cooperative advertising, and channel marketing incentive fund programs.

Is This for Real?

OK, let's begin by saying that blockchain, as with any emerging technology, is touted to apply to virtually any aspect of human life. It is hailed as a miracle cure, of sorts, for all types of transactional activities including industries like financial, healthcare, retail, high-technology, and consumer goods.

Speculation about adaptability across all phases of consumer goods is rampant, and in some cases, a bit bizarre. I will spare you from the danger of getting too carried away with such dreamy ideas, but for trade promotion, there are some very realistic and game-changing use cases we will discuss.

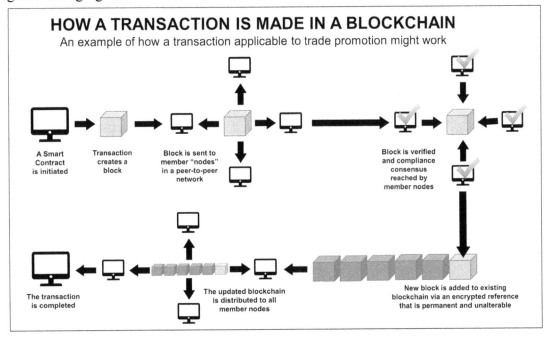

Figure 11.1 How a Blockchain Works

Blockchain pundits contend that the technology is a more secure, faster, and highly flexible network over which data can be transmitted. For trade promotion, throughout its recent history, transaction speed and security have not been much of an issue. However, cloud-based technology has made it possible for several major TPx vendors to move to a cloud platform. Even with the advantages in cost and performance in the cloud, consumer products companies still restrict the sensitive information which consists of trade funds, expenditures, and performance to on-premises databases and processing technology.

"No way am I going to expose my co-op and trade promotion data to a blockchain platform," says the CIO of one of the world's largest soft drink manufacturers. "Heck, I don't even have it out on the cloud, and frankly, I'm scared to death that our multiple firewall technology and security can't protect it 100%," he said.

He has a point.

With recent nightmarish breaches in data at major corporations, even the most secure, firewall-protected data seems vulnerable. Manufacturers seek to protect their sensitive trade promotion funding, spending, and plans as a priority, and are often leery of new technologies that offer multiple access points.

There have been several developments in blockchain technology that have focused on security and reduced vulnerability to hacking, and many companies are beginning to initiate blockchain projects across the entire business landscape.

It is real.

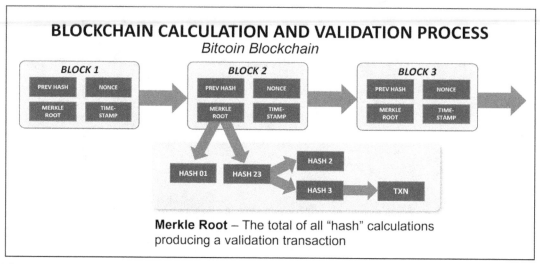

Figure 11.2 Blockchain Calculation and Validation Process Example

The original blockchain concept is based on transactional calculation formats that were discovered in 1993 called "Proof of Work," where the consensus is achieved through a series of complex mathematical calculations called "hashes" or simply a "hash." I said I would not get technical, but to point out one issue that many IT executives have with blockchain is that the process shown in Figure 11.2 illustrates the deep complexity of validating and, therefore, reaching the consensus that blockchain has as an advantage.

You can see that the process illustrated in Figure 11.2 takes time, and with every single transaction on the blockchain going through this consensus process, it simply takes a lot of power—real, expensive, and sometimes unavailable electrical power. That, of course, translates to cost; so, this technological disadvantage would need to be evolved into a more efficient, faster, and less expensive technology. We have had blockchain now for several years, and in a very short time, it is reaching a level of maturity.

In fact, one of the ways you know any technology is maturing is the appearance of a second, third, or fourth iteration, or variation of the product, in the market. As use cases begin to pile up, weaknesses in the original blockchain technology begin to show up because the applications are new and were most likely not included within the original functional scope. One of the most important developments is the creation of the Directed Acyclic Graph or DAG.

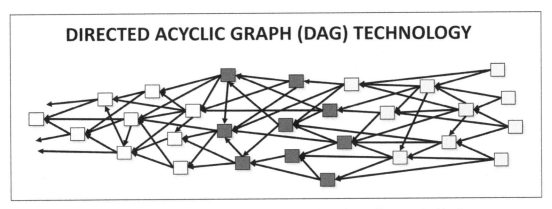

Figure 11.3 How Directed Acyclic Graph (DAG) Technology Connects Nodes

DAG is a type of blockchain, but instead of a singular linkage between nodes or "blocks," the DAG connects to multiple other nodes, giving it more of an appearance of a tree than a single, in-line horizontal chain of blocks. This enables a higher level of flexibility and, with the DAG design, is also much faster. Both attributes are critical to trade promotion management and execution use cases. We will discuss DAG in a bit more detail later, but let's break down the main value proposition of blockchain.

Because the blockchain was first created for Bitcoin, the transactional components had to be forged in speed and security. There are five attributes of a blockchain. These are:

1. **Distributed Ledger:** Every member of the blockchain can access and view the data, giving higher visibility to every transaction and protecting, to a degree against hacking.

2. **Immutable Records:** Once the blockchain has verified and logged the transactions, they cannot be changed. If an error exists, a new transaction will correct the error and the entire share group has visibility to both records.

3. **Consensus Algorithms:** The data must be run through a series of algorithms that produce a consensus agreement by all who share the network before it can be added to the blockchain. Once it reaches consensus, it can never be changed or deleted, giving the blockchain a high level of security against fraud and embezzlement—everyone sees it!

4. **Security Permissions:** Having the functionality of consensus and shared ledger, the addition of permissions enables a more secured series of validations and authentications; but, at the same time, enables broader variability and flexibility in the data itself.

207

5. **Smart Contracts:** The "Smart Contract" is a built-in mechanism that provides a richer set of terms and conditions, enabling higher security, but also connects and synchronizes the transactional relationships and validates compliance more efficiently and effectively than most other automated business rule-based transactional systems.

A third technology that is likely to become relevant to trade promotion is IOTA.

IOTA is a distributed ledger technology created for Internet of Things transactions that is designed to accommodate extremely high volumes of transactions and inputs.

The Internet of Things has significant trade promotion application especially around inventory management, manufacturing, product tracking and even to the Consumer Chain, where at-home connections with pantry, refrigerator, and freezer product-use tracking will eventually be part of everyday life.

However, in this case, IOTA becomes super relevant as new innovations such as the development of the *Tangle*[77] enter the marketplace. It can handle the much higher scale and speeds required to pass real-time signals across a network from device to device. The Tangle was developed to take advantage of the open-source IOTA to aggregate millions of devices into a single distributed, but accountable network. It uses DAG technology as a platform and enables billions of transactions across millions of devices to recognize and identify each other, pass information to and from multiple devices, and do it all with a greater level of accuracy and trust.

To turn this vision into reality, the Eclipse Foundation and IOTA Foundation created the Tangle EE Working Group. This consortium includes some of the top computer hardware, networking, software, energy and academic companies and institutions in the world. The mission is to focus on future use case development for IoT.

Most Likely Use Cases

Conceptionally, blockchain has significant merits for trade promotion. Using the idea of smart contracts for trade promotion plans could be an effective answer to the problems created by terms-rich promotion agreements, tactical promotional activities, corporate governance, and business rules. Agreements for specific performance requirements expected for each promotion committed by the manufacturer/supplier and the retailer, wholesaler, distributor, or value-added reseller are difficult to execute today. Smart contracts ensure more consistency, improved compliance verification, and a more detailed data set.

One of the more appropriate use cases is settlement and deduction management. Deduction managers, who spend so much time chasing down unidentified deductions, cost companies millions each year with a continuing poor record of reconciliation.

But with smart contracts, where the full scope of terms, business rules, performance conditions and requirements are digitally imprinted on the system, deductions can be transacted immediately, even without moving away from the A/R process, thus eliminating time and cost of deduction management.

In consumer goods industry sectors like consumer durables, fashion, high technology, software, consumer telecom, consumer electronics, automotive aftermarket, and household products, there is another potential use case for blockchain. In these industries, the settlement consists of a process where physical (or digital) claims are made that are fully documented with proof of performance and cost.

The time and effort required to audit documentation and validate compliance is long and tedious. With smart contracts, the terms and conditions can be automatically validated without human involvement, including the decrementing of funding and final settlement accounting. Month-end closing, which is always made more difficult where cooperative advertising and market development funds are transacted, would result in a more efficient and certainly faster process.

Of course, the original purpose of blockchain was to manage a cryptocurrency—Bitcoin. You now know that trade promotion is the second largest line item, after cost of goods, in a consumer goods company's financials; so, one of the most obvious use cases would be transacting promotion spending itself.

But this is where we have to draw a line.

By its very nature, trade promotion spending is one of the most highly protected business processes in any company selling products through the channels of distribution. The idea of a distributed ledger, open to public viewing with "consensus" protocol is, on its own, a non-starter for trade promotion management.

In 2018, I interviewed the executive vice president of finance of one of the largest canned goods manufacturers in the world about the idea of using blockchain for trade promotion. "The idea of blockchain is interesting, and although I'm not a tech guy, I can say that my IT organization is rapidly building use cases for this technology," he said. "But I've told them they need not knock on my door just yet. The one thing that keeps me awake at night is that someone would gain access to our trade funds promotion plans, and quickly extrapolate our entire revenue strategy with our account base. I can't have that."

That is beginning to change with the people I talk to today. They are more informed about the technology, especially the newer forms of blockchain like the DAG format. As we stated above, DAG technology is structurally a better fit with the idea of trade promotion management and execution than blockchain, and seems to be more functionally aligned with the typical infrastructure of several trade promotion processes.

Remember, the end function of trade promotion is a financial transaction. The phrase "trade spend" is what we are all about here. So why wouldn't blockchain be a perfect platform to convert modern currency-based trade spending to cryptocurrency?

Some executives are going so far as to admit that cryptocurrency could become at least a type of exchange for trade promotion spending. Others remain more skeptical. "Don't hold your breath," says the CFO of a major meat products company. "There are so many variables that come into play here—like how would we be able to control the blockchain nodes to achieve the level of consensus required, how would we stop the multitiered slowdowns and how could we manage the credentials that allow the blockchain to create the security?"

The problem to which he refers is that public view and consensus we talked about. Trade promotion compliance, in his world, is full of overrides, changes, reversals and an extraordinary turnover of retailer and/or reseller personnel at the channel points.

He fears even a blockchain has a limited capability and, at worse, could cause dangerous overpayments, higher deductions due to dropouts, loss of credentials causing failure to comply, and undermine the confidence that is so important for the blockchain to work.

The idea of some other "actor" coming into the transaction from the outside scares the bejeebers out of most CFOs.

He also points out, wisely so, that any attempt to jump into blockchain operational use today would be a continual battle with updates and changes, even more than with the early TCP/IP infrastructure of the internet in the 80s and 90s. One example of that is the case of the June 2016 hack of DAO (Decentralized Autonomous Organization) resulting in a loss of $60M in the ether market. DAO was running on the Ethereum blockchain platform, where security vulnerabilities led to several changes and updates in the platform. As a result of those changes, Ethereum is one of the most secure blockchain platforms in a maturing cryptocurrency technology marketplace.

As we discussed at length in Chapter 8, for trade promotion, the emphasis right now is on the advancement of artificial-intelligence-driven cognitive and machine-learning predictive analytics in planning promotions. Still, blockchain is gaining momentum among both IT and upper C-level executives who are continually looking for ways to reduce costs and improve stock value.

In the trade promotion vendor space, most of the focus is on improving customer business planning and analytics capabilities, but there are some of the larger vendors who are looking very closely at the potential of blockchain as a platform for trade promotion management and execution. Says one CEO of a trade promotion management solution vendor, "Our priority is to drive the percentage of high ROI trade promotions to the near 100% level." He states that they have exhausted their future technology budget in shoring up their promotion planning and optimization technology, and blockchain is only a lunch discussion they are having.

On the channel side, blockchain does generate interest among the more progressive wholesalers and distributors, who struggle with their own reseller customer base in providing the support of suppliers' trade promotion, co-op advertising and market development fund programs. This is one of the most difficult situations for both the wholesaler/distributor and the manufacturer/supplier and has been for 100 years.

In a recent call to the CTO for a consumer goods distribution company, he said that he has a team considering blockchain as a network to manage promotion activity by their own retail and reseller customers for trade promotion performance compliance. "Our research on the blockchain indicates that we may be able to create documents that identify specific tactics, costs, time, media and other details as smart contracts to prove performance and get paid trade funds directly without all of the work we have to do internally."

He goes on to say that this could drastically cut the time and expense they incur from their suppliers who do not pay them until they can prove compliance at the indirect level. "Blockchain has some attractiveness as a closed network of our own, using the power and capability of that technology to do the work we hate to do manually now. It just makes sense to us, and we're investing in the research to make that happen."

POS, POP, and POW!

In April 2018, I was asked by the Promotion Optimization Institute to give a presentation on the application of blockchain to trade channel promotion. Just as I have done in this chapter, I began with a high level layperson's overview of Blockchain technology. I showed the differences between the blockchain and DAG processes for the purpose of preparing the audience to understand how each could be applied to TPx use cases.

When I began talking about one of the most viable use cases, Point-of-Sale (POS) data, I think the crowd began to see some real potential. I caught their eyes widening and felt the afterburners firing in their brain synapses, so obviously I struck a nerve.

All downstream data plays a huge role, if not one of the most important, in trade promotion today. Point-of-Sale (POS) data has become the primary pool of data and intelligence for both retailer and supplier companies to understand immediate impact of trade promotion execution. Some providers are looking at the blockchain in the context of transacting POS data in near or real-time with significantly higher capabilities to analyze promotion, sales, inventory and consumer marketing data. The idea of a consensus-based distributed ledger network to deliver real-time insights into consumer shopping activity, promotion response, and supply chain optimization has gained momentum among revenue growth management, trade marketing, and demand planning executives and stakeholders.

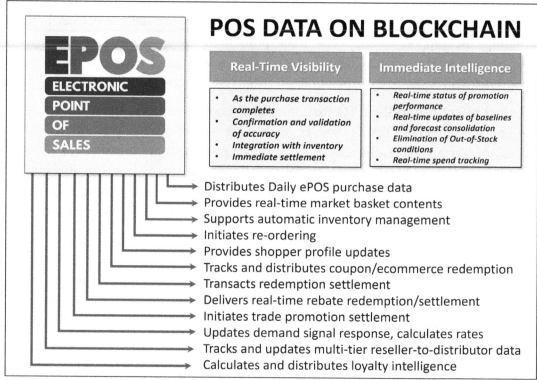

Figure 11.4 POS Data on Blockchain Can Remedy Many of the Biggest Problems Facing TPM

Given the volume of POS data, combined with shopper marketing, in-store traffic, category life cycle, and online purchases, blockchain may be an appropriate medium to transmit all this data. This may end up being the first major use case for blockchain in consumer goods.

I agree that this should be explored as a priority before any real design thinking happens around funding and trade spending. This aligns with the emphasis on analytics and should gain support across the entire enterprise.

As we described in Chapter 8, the POS data most manufacturer/supplier companies receive today is at a bare minimum: product; selling price; promotion status; time of day; etc. But what if ALL the data that a retailer captures as the product slides over the scanner could be immediately transferred to a DAG blockchain, available for all of the subscribers to view, in real-time and without question of accuracy, sampling methodology, extrapolation calculus, or missing locations?

While the idea of automatically sharing ALL of the POS data may not sit well with the brick-and-mortar retailer community, efforts are already underway to improve collaborative planning with their manufacturer/supplier counterparts. This could, or at least *should*, be a viable step to take. As long as some of the more sensitive data on shoppers (such as credit card information) can be culled, it seems a wise way to use blockchain technology, does it not?

Leveraging the power of the consensus and smart contracts elements of blockchain, the retailer could make far more information available to virtually every supplier which sells to the retailer, wholesaler, or distributor. We are talking here about including loyalty data, payment information, demographics, and perhaps even some unstructured data such as weather conditions, social sentiment, and localized events—all potentially impacting the success or failure of a promotion.

Let me repeat: In. Real. Time.

Now, think about having that level of intelligence to not only drive insights that generate smarter, more effective promotions, but also to immediately validate compliance. The huge problems of Proof of Performance (POP) have driven more people mad than road rage. Leveraging the retail stores' security cameras and digital shopper tracking systems, data captured could be used in an AI-driven analysis of display positioning, pricing, and on-shelf inventory levels.

Again, not to be too technical, the process of adding cryptocurrency coins to the blockchain is called "mining." A "miner" is someone who adds transactions to the blockchain. "Proof of Work" (PoW) is the process the system undergoes to confirm the transaction and create the consensus validation.

The embedded PoW calculation functions in both DAG and blockchain that perform verification and consensus are important to consider here, because the downstream data we are discussing, including POS and consumption data delivered by the syndicated data providers, can all benefit the industry on both sides of the channel. This does not exist outside of heavily manual, and incredibly time-consuming, transactional systems we have today in ERP, TPx and supply chain planning. Being able to validate the data, ensuring its accuracy, is a key cornerstone to data integrity; and it is an important factor in being able to confidently prescribe high ROI-achieving promotions.

Cryptopromotion

During my talk at the POI conference in 2018, a member of the audience asked, "Do you see a situation where trade promotion and co-op advertising will be paid using cryptocurrency?"

My answer was "Yes, maybe, but certainly not now." That was over two years ago as I write today; but realistically, the answer to that question depends upon so many variables, economic conditions, and frankly, the ability to do so, that it remains largely speculative.

IBM is one of the early promoters of blockchain as a technology that can be applied to the retail and consumer goods industries. They have an entire platform built on the open-source Hyperledger Fabric from The Linux Foundation.[78] There are already several industrial applications, and IBM has also targeted trade promotion as one of its focus initiatives for its blockchain strategy.

At Capgemini, I worked with the IBM Blockchain Team. Their August 2017 white paper, "Using blockchain to disrupt trade promotions"[79] is still a very appropriate first pass on the idea of blockchain technology use case development. The document lays out several strong use cases for trade promotion. They, like so many of the world's largest consulting firms, have a strong case plan for how blockchain can work in trade promotion; but the actual real applications that have gone live are limited and scarce, to say the least.

Using cryptocurrency in place of regular currency to fund $1 Trillion of global trade spend is beyond ambitious in thinking and most likely a generation away. There are significant problems with the technology now, such as the impact of errors in the block transactions and of course, the major knotty problem of eliminating the current "everybody can see everything" aspect of blockchain itself. These issues must be overcome, before either the manufacturers or the channels will trust blockchain, or any derivation of it, to manage trade payments. Most likely, applications of store purchases by shoppers using cryptocurrency will be the starting place for dealing with the promotion money element of consumer goods industries.

Speaking with a blockchain and cryptocurrency domain expert recently, I gave him the "clinic" on trade promotion, explaining how it works and its role in consumer marketing. After a few days of research on his own, he now believes that the scope of trade channel promotion presents one of the best opportunities he has seen in this emerging field.

For consumer goods trade promotion funding to be a cryptocurrency source, where manufacturers offering trade promotion incentives could benefit significantly through the creation of a new cryptocurrency specific to promotion spending, there would have to be several deep structural changes in blockchain infrastructure and money-handling operational functionality. He believes the eventuality of a cryptocurrency trade promotion settlement methodology is real. From what the industry is saying and projecting about trade payments on blockchain, this may soon be more of a reality than it seems now.

Pros and Cons for Blockchain Applications in Trade Channel Promotion

Blockchain, as I have said many times before, is a *foundational* technology. Like the internet back in the late 1980s and early 1990s, the dreams are alive and well, and the application pundits alive with speculation about virtually every aspect of life itself, but no doubt for consumer goods and trade promotion. Where does it lead, and how should we realistically consider what makes sense in the near future?

BLOCKCHAIN TECHNOLOGY USE CASES	
Trade Promotion Planning and Instore Retail Execution	
Use Case "PROs"	**Use Case "CONs"**
• **Smart Contracts for promotion plans**	• **Unproven technology and applications**
• **Shared data for instore Retail Execution activities**	• **Requires external "Oracle" for decision and approval**
• **Rapid tracking and compliance**	• **"Timestamp" issues and potential for malicious nodes**
• **Immediate settlement**	• **Smart Contracts are not yet stable on DAG/Tangle**
• **Real-time intelligence**	

Figure 11.5 Blockchain Technology Use Cases for Trade Promotion and Co-op Advertising Management and Execution

Right up front, it appears that three very important "hot spots" in promotion management are:

1. **Funding and Budget Management**

2. **Promotion Planning**

3. **Retail Execution and In-store Compliance**

In Figure 11.5, the value proposition, or "PROs," for these use cases are:

> **Smart Contracts for promotion plans** – As mentioned earlier, this is a great use case because there are so many problems arising from the inability to align, link, synchronize and honor the terms, conditions, and business rules of contractual agreements. These include specifically problematic areas such as price discounts and product assortments. A smart contract would digitally track and automate compliance in a way that KAMs and sales reps responsible

for planning would not carry the burden of having to check the contract language every time they want to create a promotion plan.

Shared data for in-store Retail Execution activities – The merchandising reps in the field cannot visit every store, every day. They can't do it every week; but the roll-up of data after each visit often takes some time to get into a form or report, dashboard, or communication that is usable. DAG technology can clearly advance the capture, storage, and access of this critical data for use by AI-driven algorithms that can convert the intelligence into insights and alerts, such as in a case of impending out-of-stock conditions that would need to be immediately corrected.

Rapid tracking and compliance – To reiterate, promotion performance data, in the form of POS, or even syndicated data provider consumption analyses, can not only immediately update everyone on the status of the promotion, but can also prevent promotions that are failing, or change tactics to turn a promotion into a success.

Immediate settlement - Leveraging in-store camera and shopper tracking data, near real-time validation of display, pricing, and other tactical compliance can verify performance and enable immediate settlement without the need for claims, deductions taken, or payment requests.

Real-time intelligence – This is a priceless commodity. Today, the entire industry is set up to receive information about promotions weeks after the performance. Everyone agrees this is not conducive to effective and efficient management, but ongoing status quo perpetuates the practice. With blockchain or DAG technology, the availability of data on a near or real-time basis speeds the potential for reaction by both the retailer and the manufacturer/supplier responding to the most damaging scenarios that impact the failure rates we see across the entire promotional landscape today. The promise of real-time intelligence is not a panacea, but instead is already in practice and producing results today. Applying blockchain and/or DAG, Tangle and IOTA technology eliminates the problem of "rear-view mirror" reaction and looks to bring us into an entirely new paradigm of intelligence and insights. In a word, it *fuels* the advanced analytics we are building today.

The value propositions for these applications would be reduced costs, higher security, and the ability to manage much higher volumes of data—required in the coming change to more direct POS acquisition from retailers and more rows of data in each POS upload. As with all of the other pundits' claims of a better tomorrow with blockchain, these are clearly speculative. However, the speculation comes from a great deal of study that has been done for the past five years.

On the downside, there are clearly negative aspects of moving to a blockchain. The "CONs" may not be as well-accepted as the "PROs" above, but still command intense scrutiny as the industry moves forward in the development of new blockchain applications. These include:

Unproven technology and applications – Not much, if any of these trade promotion applications, has been done in case studies we have today that stimulate confidence and assuredness of functional improvement. While there are several cases involving financial transactions on blockchain, committing the investment of dollars in trade funds and spending to a blockchain, a DAG or Tangle network has yet proven to be wildly successful, at least from what I have been able to uncover in my research. Nothing would make me happier than to hear of a highly successful, practical, and working application of blockchain in trade promotion.

Requires external "Oracle" for decision and approval – In order for the smart contracts to work with outside data, there is a need for a third-party element, called the "Oracle." The downside here is this is a third-party *outside* source used to validate or verify the data. Most people do not know this because across the wordscape of many deep explanations of blockchain, especially smart contracts, this does not often come up. Still, it makes sense; but again, it is a requirement that, like so many of the processes within a blockchain, requires processing time, cost, and power. It can slow down the function, yet it is a requirement for third-party processing. In our case with trade promotion and consumer goods, it applies to POS data, syndicated consumption data and of course, any other supply chain, marketing, or product data that enters the blockchain. To think that there is a requirement for an outside "coordinator" to intervene in a settlement transaction will make most CFOs shiver.

"Timestamp" issues and potential for malicious nodes – This is a big negative for traditional blockchains, where an outside source can hack in and create a "node" that can alter delivery of the data packets, create wrong data, and prevent new legitimate entries. Blockchain trust is a major factor, and there are several excellent products that help to prevent these malicious nodes and keep the blockchain running smoothly. Timestamping is the validation and authentication factor used to identify a blockchain transaction. Although no guarantees, the timestamp is a very good deterrent and usually holds up in a court of law.

Smart Contracts are not stable on DAG/Tangle – The prevailing wisdom seems to say that since DAGs are lacking in total order, smart contracts are problematic, if not downright impossible to work. That is, so far, with what is termed "Blockchain 3.0," or the version of blockchain attributed to DAG type technology, no smart contract operation seems to be viable.[80]

The overriding "CONs" here are a combination of process "potholes" that can create problems and errors, the need for a third-party outside "Oracle" to validate data entering the blockchain, and the high risk associated with the inability to manage a key component of trade promotion operation—the contract. All these combine to give IT and C-level executives a bit of a pause before rushing into this technology.

While blockchain provides some wonderful promises and, to be fair, some already proven results in being able to manage huge piles of data, and provide secure, actionable intelligence, the mandates of modern trade channel promotion telemetry and measurement analytics are stringent and weigh heavily upon executives that want to maximize consumer engagement.

BLOCKCHAIN TECHNOLOGY USE CASES
Consumer Shopping Engagement/Experience and Performance Analytics

Use Case "PROs"	Use Case "CONs"
• Data could be shared (requires segmentation) • Consumer profile data on Blockchain works to align all • Validation for projections and predictions benefit all • Speed of insights and accessibility lifts "all boats" in the market	• Sensitive nature of some data will be a risk • Retail collaboration may be limited or unachievable • "Oracle" or "Coordinator" could be a difficult issue • Some countries have extreme regulatory environments

Figure 11.6 Blockchain Technology Use Cases for Consumer Engagement/Experience and Performance Analytics

Let's look at two critical areas of intelligence and analytics:

1. *Consumer Shopping Engagement/Experience*

2. *Business Analytics*

Processing large arrays of data is one of the top functional reasons to deploy blockchain. The potential upsides in consumer products can change the course of operations taking place today, especially around managing the influence and response to the Consumer Chain and the associated analytics that provide intelligence and drive insights to action.

The "PROs" for blockchain include:

> **Data could be shared (requires segmentation)** – Important capabilities like having visibility to near real-time promotion performance, POS, advertising responses, social sentiment, compliance data and consumption analyses—all in one place, and all accurately represented—is the key to achieving a unified and aligned consumer engagement ROI.

> **Consumer profile data on blockchain works to align all** – As we discussed in Chapter 4, the future success of promotions and ROI goal achievement will be to have a direct pipeline to consumer demand. Knowing buying patterns, product and brand preferences, shopping locations, spending levels, and overall consumption statistics is vital for precise and trustworthy prediction and prescription of promotions across all channels.

> **Validation for projections and predictions benefit all** – At the end of the day, being able to rapidly visualize the response, whether it is POS, social sentiment, competitive reaction or call center content, for all channel promotion activities drives improved intelligence within the AI algorithms and logic used to form the predictive and prescriptive planning. Each channel plan, no matter what the tactical activities and media are, will benefit by the cross-channel intelligence and insights into how to effectively engage the consumer.

> **Speed of insights and accessibility lifts "all boats" in the market** – An important derivation of value from the blockchain, DAG and Tangle technologies provide the ability to improve the overall quality of data in every market. The value of this data goes beyond the competitive boundaries when you consider that, even today, consumer products companies seek immediate

and high-quality intelligence about the overall market and how the consumer reacts—not just to their own strategic and tactical promotional efforts.

Together, these "PROs" like real-time insights, higher quality data, and lower costs. "My sales and marketing people have to trust the data, first, before they can be satisfied with any set of results we give them," said the CIO for a multinational CPG conglomerate. "It goes beyond the word integrity, to a level of trust that I have not seen yet." She was desperate to improve not only the database and analytical technology she had, but to go above and beyond that to achieve a vital consensus from her peers that they can have confidence in the outcomes of the actions they take from the insights and intelligence they receive.

On the "CONs" side of Figure 11.6, similar issues exist for the use case of trade promotion management across the consumer engagement, experience, and promotional performance analytics applications.

Sensitive nature of some data will be a risk – One of Blockchain technology's value propositions is the shared nature of the data and the visibility everyone has of it. But on the other hand, that can also present some challenges as well. DAG technology helps that somewhat, but every consumer goods industry player treats their promotion funding and spending with the highest level of security and propriety. Private blockchain networks may seem to solve some of this; but again, the nature of the "beast," as it were, is that, even with the so-called "consensus" functionality helping to ensure accurate and trusted data, the risk of being hacked is a constant threat.

Retail collaboration may be limited or unachievable – At this point, it seems that blockchain networks that are private in nature, operated as an intercompany ledger, would not permit the channel customer to participate. This would mean that effective collaboration on promotion planning with access to real-time data would be restricted or, in some cases, impossible to permit. This is a very "sticky wicket" that must be worked out before any blockchain technology can be viable for an omnichannel collaborative planning effort between the manufacturer/supplier and the retailer, wholesaler, or distributor.

"Oracle" or "Coordinator" could be a difficult issue – The simple question is WHO or WHAT is the "Oracle" or so-called coordinator whose role it is to provide third party validation of the data before it becomes the consensus. The conceptual view of an external point of validation is not, in and of itself bad. But the *application* of this concept is another barrier that has to be dropped before blockchain can be a viable technology for effective trade promotion data management.

Some countries have extreme regulatory environments – Like any new technology, blockchain conceptual operations may run afoul of certain regulatory statutes across the different countries. The regulatory focus now seems to be on cryptocurrency and the financial side of things; but clearly, with the emphasis these days on privacy, data regulations will not be far behind.

The risks may not be fully understood at this point, but clearly there are always going to be issues that will have to be addressed, and most likely this is the reason why there is so much talk, and very little action. All the major systems integration consulting firms are lining up blockchain initiatives and, in some cases such as the IBM Blockchain Platform, already have active engagements and live operations in place.

The TPM vendors and co-op advertising outsourcing service firms all have identified potential areas where they will consider building blockchain applications. But until the technology and the issues around data are more clearly addressed, what you will see is a continuation of projections of what blockchain technology can and should be for trade promotion and channel incentives management.

My two cents is this: Blockchain technology, in some form, is going to be the next wave of technology evolution for trade channel promotion. The major areas where I see this occurring include:

- **Promotion Settlement** – Potential for cryptocurrency tokens to be used for promotion settlement and fund management.

- **Promotion Planning and Execution through Smart Contracts** – This is where I believe the most immediate opportunities lie. Almost every TPx implementation struggles with integrating complex contract terms into strategic and tactical promotion planning and execution. It speaks heavily to the calculation and management of P&L.

- **Data management and Intelligence** – Solving the data security issues will open the flood gates to faster, more accurate and trusted intelligence.

- **Consumer Shopping Experience and Engagement Management** – We are already seeing the benefits of blockchain technology with shopper experience. Translating this into in-store and online shopping to achieve alignment with the Consumer Chain will increase and enhance the quality of prescriptive promotion planning.

- **IoT** – This almost ties the bow, so to speak. Leveraging blockchain technology to track, reconcile, share, and expand on the operational data coming in and out of every device is already something that is beginning to reap benefits now. For trade promotion, there are clear use cases around transportation and logistics, out-of-stock resolution, and compliance that I predict will be a huge business in the coming years.

So what?

What you do is take action. If your company has a blockchain team or initiative, join it. Be part of the planning for this new technology application, and more importantly, be part of the *design* of the next generation of blockchain technology coming down the road—like a 40-ton tractor-trailer rig at 100 mph!

Specifically, I would suggest the four following actions:

1. Consider blockchain and cryptocurrency in your future roadmaps.
2. Structure your programs to accommodate the smart contract.
3. Make sure you have an IT organization that is planning for blockchain and cryptocurrency.
4. Consider blockchain and cryptocurrency technology when planning new or upgrading trade promotion management functionality.

While you may believe this to be a purely IT initiative, it isn't. In fact, the more realistic process-oriented thinking that goes into blockchain technology readiness projects, the more successful they will be. Learn all you can about it and be the resident expert on blockchain in your specific group or organization.

Right now, there are so may barriers and doubts about the potential of blockchain technology, that there is always a chance the next innovation you need is going to come along too late. That is why this chapter deals with this issue, and why it is so important for the future of trade channel promotion.

If it sounds like I'm "beating the drum" for the adoption of this technology, join the percussion section with me.

CHAPTER 12

How Do We Get to the Endgame?

The "*Invisible Economy*" is too large to ignore.

A recent study showed more than 83% of consumer goods companies believe that trade promotion spending will remain the same or increase in the next five years.[94] The increase in technology, especially advanced data science, increased data quality, and the continual flood of digital transformations in the consumer goods industry promises to push both suppliers and channels to increase smart collaboration toward improving the ROI on this second largest line item in a consumer goods company's financial statements.

What is the "Endgame" and how do we get there?

Think about what we have covered in this book so far. We have picked apart virtually every function, process, issue, and problem around the management, execution, and analysis of trade channel promotions. I showed you how we arrived where we are now, and how a consumer products manufacturer/supplier can identify, attain, and sustain success with every promotion, and achieve the perfect combination of high ROI and successful consumer engagement.

The "Endgame" is being able to plan and execute a consumer promotion that will dependably achieve near-100% of whatever specific single or group of objectives and goals are set.

It is a confidence level that assures everybody in the loop, between manufacturer/ supplier and channel partner, that the data, processes, policies, procedures, practices, and key performance indicators are precise and trustworthy—consistently hitting the target and doing it efficiently and effectively. It is full collaboration between every single group within the manufacturer/supplier organization, the channel partner and external support vendors.

Are We There Yet?

How many times did you ask your parents this question? Or, if you are a parent, how many times have *you* heard this from your kids?

The answer is a lot.

Reaching the endgame is a definite point in time that will be easily measured. So, what *is* that measurement?

The answer is a lot of different ones.

Before we even define the "Endgame," we must agree on the key measurements that will mark its achievement.

Throughout my entire career, I have seen hundreds of presentations on "ROI" and the definitions thereof. All of them are good, I will have to say. But invariably, while I see someone presenting their view of ROI achievement, I see others in the crowd shaking their heads negatively. I can't say that they disbelieve the presenter's definition of ROI; but you and I both know that they will have their opinions of it, just as they are apt to have their opinions differ on the way to achieve it.

Testing this issue, I thought it wise to track and measure where we are in terms of the definition of, perhaps the most critical of measures, ROI—specifically, ROI for trade channel promotions. I received over 300 responses to my little survey question: "What is the single most important metric in determining trade channel promotion ROI?" I was happy to see that the spread between sales, marketing, and finance executives and stakeholders responding was almost one-third each, with sales slightly higher at 32% of the people responding. Marketing represented 29% and finance at 22%.

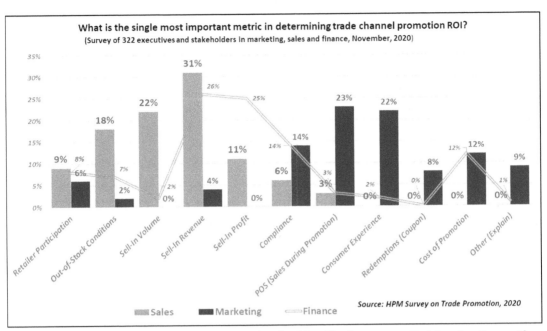

Figure 12.1 November 2020 Survey Results for Key Performance Metrics for Promotion ROI

I was hoping to see something closer between sales and marketing than what I received. Looking at Figure 12.1, you can see there is a clear preference for the metrics around the sell-in process for sales executives, with 64% of the total responses pinning ROI on volume, revenue, and profitability achievement on the initial deal with the channel partner.

This illustrates the point I have made all along about how the sales organization, especially key account managers and sales reps view trade promotion altogether.

Only 4% of the marketing respondents, on the other hand, saw the sell-in as having any real value in determining ROI. For them, the definition of trade promotion ROI was more aligned with the consumer response—to the actual product sales in-store during the promotion (23%), coupon redemption (8%), and of course, consumer experience (22%). As shown,12% of marketers saw cost of the promotion as a higher measure of TPx ROI than sales, who never mentioned the cost of the promotion as a key ROI metric.

That one made me scratch my head.

If you look at the Finance line on Figure 12.1, notice that their concerns are revenue (26%), profit (25%), compliance (14%) and cost of promotion (12%). That makes sense.

It is also notable that, aside from the marketing team, neither sales nor finance executives and stakeholders included the *consumer* in their priority metrics. There are several trade organizations which are addressing this infusion of consumer engagement into analytics. They now have more sessions in their conference agendas which are focused on the consumer engagement aspect, including loyalty management and social media applications. Many of the breakouts and panel discussions include both sales and marketing executives talking about how they collaborate to build more effective promotions for the trade channels and in direct-to-consumer media activities.

Still, we are all far apart in our definitions of what constitutes the key metric of ROI for trade channel promotions. And that is not only sad, but indicates we have a very difficult hurdle to overcome before true overall success is achieved. We have to be aligned across these three key lines of business so that we work together to appropriately prioritize and enhance the analytics for everyone across the business landscape.

Are we "there" yet? The trouble with settling on "there" is knowing the destination.

Throughout the course of this book, we have broken down virtually all the major areas of focus and concentration applicable to the development, funding, planning, execution, and measurement of channel promotion success. Almost any treatment of a targeted key performance indicator (KPI) is going to draw some disagreement, and that's fine—as long as we are at least considering what the KPIs should be.

ACHIEVING CONSUMER ENGAGEMENT EXCELLENCE
Building the Most Successful Omnichannel Promotion ROI

CONSUMER EXCELLENCE	Accurate Monitoring, Analysis and Responsiveness to the Consumer Chain
EXECUTION EXCELLENCE	Integrated, Near/Real-Time Compliance Verification and Communication
COLLABORATION EXCELLENCE	Secure, Accessible, Comprehensive, and Efficient Communication Platform
OPTIMIZATION EXCELLENCE	Trusted, Accurate Prediction and Prescription of Promotion Outcomes
TPx EXCELLENCE	Comprehensive, Effective Management of Funds, Planning, Settlement
ANALYTICS EXCELLENCE	Cross-Organizational Tools Delivering Real-Time, Actionable Insights
BASELINE EXCELLENCE	Accurate, Timely, and Trusted Demand Plan and Baselines
DATA EXCELLENCE	Clean, Harmonized, Aligned and Omnichannel Coverage of Data

Figure 12.2 Achieving Consumer Engagement Excellence Through Omnichannel Promotion Success

Working with hundreds of companies across multiple consumer products industry sectors, I have created what I think is a solid summary of what "there" is. "There," in real terms, is an environment in a consumer products company where all four dimensions of knowledge exists, and where, on a daily basis, the practice of deep analytics takes place among all of the organizations that comprise the corporate value chain.

Figure 12.2 is an overview of what it looks like for a company to achieve the 4th Dimension of Knowledge, beginning with precise and trusted data and culminating in the ability to predict, prescribe, and respond to every single link in the Consumer Chain. Let's not call it "Promotion ROI," let's call it *Consumer Engagement Excellence*.

ROI is, of course, one of the most important metrics in the achievement of Consumer Engagement Excellence. As a corporate executive, you want to be able to stand before the CEO and board of directors and say that, not only are we generating high ROI on promotion spending, but our entire organization is in lockstep in every single promotion, event or program offered, and now we are able to effectively predict and respond to demand, and our market share has grown better than forecast. Inherent in each of these levels is the ability to measure and report the KPIs that drive the company's achievement of those objectives.

Data Excellence

Chapters 8 and 9 are all about achieving data excellence for channel promotions across any consumer products sector. Achieving data excellence means being able to source, ingest, clean, harmonize, align, and be granular enough to drive the artificial intelligence engines to create and sustain effective machine learning.

It means being able to handle both expected and predicted market forces and environments, but also the unexpected as well—a Covid-19 pandemic being an ugly and painful example we are all dealing with now as I write this book. In the broadest sense, the KPIs define the data requirements, but smart companies must think ahead and factor in potential scenarios that, frankly, do not exist yet.

In today's Omnichannel marketing and selling environment, it is unacceptable to keep data in siloed environments. Every database must be carefully vetted for application and relevance, and access available to every executive and stakeholder responsible for any aspect of consumer engagement. No longer can we tolerate individuality in database management or analytics.

IT has borne the brunt of this frustrating problem, doing their best to consolidate databases and come to some sort of structure for universal accessibility, but most often, to no avail.

There must be a central authority for data, period. Any deviation or attempt to create a separate database and analytical tool set is going to effectively torpedo the end goal of data excellence.

Don't do it.

Baseline Excellence

I showed you the results from the 2018 CGT/Capgemini Trade Promotion Survey about baseline accuracy and trust. They were not great. Only 17% of the respondents believe that baseline accuracy is a reliable metric for postpromotion measurement. With a figure like 37% of the responding executives thinking that baselines are not accurately portraying even the nonpromoted volumes of product sold, how can anyone trust the incremental volumes and revenues?

Baseline excellence is simply defined as accurate volumes of product sold based on the expected demand—every day of the week. If those numbers are off, then say goodbye to accurate forecasts and trustworthy postpromotion performance analyses. In this day and age, if we cannot overlay the projected baseline to actuals at the end of every year and see only a single-digit variance, then there is no way to get to the 4th Dimension of Knowledge, much less accurate promotion spending ROI at any point on the journey toward Consumer Engagement Excellence.

The frequency of baseline updating is critical because the modern consumers' responses to promotions are changing constantly, forcing both manufacturers/suppliers and their channel partners to continually review and respond to changing market conditions and shopper dynamics. Many, even those in supply chain demand planning, will argue that you cannot have a "moving target" by updating baselines more than quarterly, as some suggest.

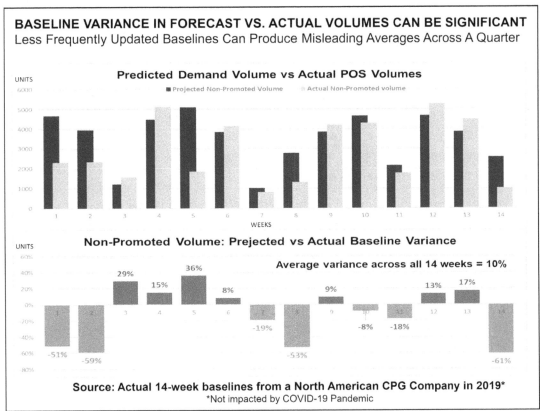

Figure 12.3 Baseline Variance Between Forecast and Actual Non-promoted Volumes

The baseline chart in Figure 12.3 is a real example of the problems faced by promotion planners. You can clearly see how much variance exists between estimated or forecasted and actual nonpromoted product volumes across a period of 14 weeks—one week beyond a typical quarter. Overall, when you measure the quarter, the variance is just about 10%. But as you can see, there are wild swings in weeks 1, 2, 5, 8, and 14, with exactly half of the 14 weeks

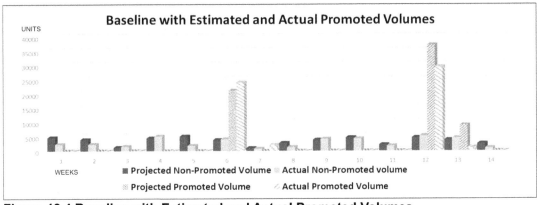

Figure 12.4 Baseline with Estimated and Actual Promoted Volumes

Now look at the same 14-week period with the estimated and actual promoted volumes overlaid. Notice that there is a significant variance in the promoted volumes in week 6, to the good by 13%. In fact, in week 7, the promotion was evidently carried over with 2,100 units sold against zero estimated. What happened there?

In a two-week promotion during weeks 12 and 13, the wheels came off. The actual promoted volume was 21% less than predicted in the first week, and totally off the second week by a negative delta of 87%. In week 6, the promotion simply created higher interest among shoppers, and that is a rather normal situation—one that most promotion planners and retailers hope for.

However, in weeks 12 and 13, what you don't see here is that there was a serious out-of-stock issue caused by the retailer's own distribution center shipping blunder, so for almost the full second week of the promotion, there were no products on the shelves throughout the store locations in four major markets. This information was known during the first two days of the first week, but unfortunately, no action could be taken, and the baselines were not updated to show the impact. As a result, weeks and months later when the baselines and demand plans were evaluated, this data was not available, and the baseline updates were adjusted to an assumption that this was not a strong week for future promotions.

But what these two charts show are the problems often faced by demand planners and promotion planners alike. The timelier and more accurate the information, the more effective the planning will be. In a quest for 100% predictable ROI, this is a critical piece of the puzzle.

In Chapter 8, Figures 8.2 and 8.3, I discussed the issues around effective data and the impact on baselines as a key factor in the attainment of the foundational 1st Dimension of Knowledge. We have also covered the lack of focus many sales executives have on the actual results from the promotion they plan—the in-store success and failure. In 2020, Hand Promotion Management measured the responses of more than 300 consumer products executives across sales, marketing, IT, and finance. Figure 12.5 represents the responses to the question of how frequently do you achieve your objectives for (a) volume, (b) revenue and (3) profitability. Three of those survey questions involved the knowledge these executives had of the rate of success (or failure) of the actual store promotions.

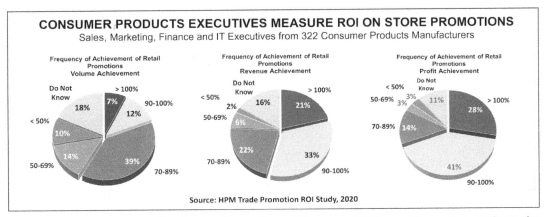

Figure 12.5 Consumer Products Executives Measure ROI on Store Promotions by Volume, Revenue and Profit 2020

Figure 12.5 shows the responses to all three questions. Here are the key takeaways from the responses:

- 39% believed the retailers accomplished <u>volume</u> objectives 70-89% of the time.

- 18% did not know if the <u>volume</u> metric was achieved.

- 54% believed the retailers achieved at least 90% of their <u>revenue</u> goals in every promotion, with 21% believing they averaged higher than 100% return in <u>revenue</u>.

- 16% did not know if the <u>revenue</u> metric was achieved.

- 69% believed that the retailer achieved at least 90% of their <u>profit</u> goal, with 28% thinking that they averaged higher than 100% achievement of <u>profitability</u>.

- 11% had no idea of the retailers' <u>profitability</u> achievement.

Remember that brick-and-mortar retailers depend upon trade promotion funds for the bulk of their profitability, so don't you think consumer products executives—especially the *sales* executives—should know this?

In that same survey, we asked the executives to tell us whether or not they had visibility to cannibalization (where the promoted product negatively impacts sales of another product) and Halo (where the promoted product drives sales of other products not on promotion). About one-fourth of the executives said their companies measured cannibalization with only 13% measuring Halo. 36% did not measure for this metric and 27% did not know.

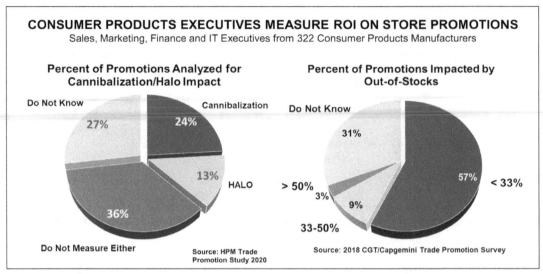

Figure 12.6 Consumer Products Executives Measure Cannibalization and HALO Effect on Store Promotions 2020

All these measurements impact the development of an accurate baseline and demand plan. In all fairness to these companies, we also found that some of the measurements that the respondents indicated were not measured, actually *were.* That is not unusual, however it does show that more attention must be paid to the baseline and demand planning process.

The way to achieve Baseline Excellence will be argued for years to come, but here is my two cents on how to move the needle forward:

- Have near real-time POS data from every retail location.

- Automate the baseline updates daily (or at least weekly as a first objective).

- Enable direct, real-time communications with merchandiser reps in the field to gain intelligence that will impact promotional performance.

- Increase forecast accuracy through multiple model validation.

- Deploy good baseline modeling software with AI- and ML-driven capability to model multiple scenarios and historic performance.

Analytics Excellence

We discussed the route to achieve analytics excellence back in Chapters 8 and 9; however, the most important point to resurrect is to create one single database and eliminate all siloed and independent analytics functions that do not access and use this single database. It sounds daunting because it is.

Every business leader across the organization will find 100 reasons for why they need their own data, and each one will be legitimate. However, the paradigm has to change, and the single data lake or database of intelligence will be the way of the future.

Why else did we spend two decades building "big data" systems?

Because even then, we knew that siloed databases and rogue analytics tools across the enterprise will, at the end of the day, contribute to an unaligned strategic and tactical plan across trade promotion, marketing, sales, supply chain, logistics and finance. This is not to say that all data should come from a single source—that is, of course, ridiculous. But it should all come through the same funnel and be available in one place.

Jeff Beckett is the founder of Retail Velocity in Ann Arbor, Michigan. For more than 26 years, his company has excelled in the collection and provision of quality data from POS feeds directly from the top retailers on the planet.

"The quality of the data is much more than a raw point-of-sale data feed," said Beckett. "The data must be collected, cleansed, resolved, harmonized, integrated, possibly enriched, THEN made available for export to either Machine Learning or Artificial Intelligence engines OR client applications (ERP, DP, TPx)." His company created a powerful tool that accelerates the intelligence and drives insights into action for his CPG customers.

"The only useful demand data is the pure point-of-sale data (in-store or online), he explained. "Almost all other data is modeled and should not be used for key decision making."

Beckett continues, "Trying to use modeled data for optimizing Trade Promotions is similar to playing horseshoes or cornhole (you get a point for being close, but that's not the best solution). I've already discussed the importance of using the cleansed/harmonized POS data, and that will be the ONLY reliable method for outcomes let alone business decisions."

I know this seems impractical in so many ways, but there is no route to achieving 100% accuracy in prescriptive promotional ROI without having all the intelligence coming together in a unified set of tactics and strategy. This is also a very difficult business decision because it invariably means moving away from vendors who may have had long tenures in supporting the enterprise. That is the sad part, but unless you can integrate these vendor tools into one single, accessible, and monitored system, it will simply have to be done. Business leaders will need to recognize, embrace, and accept this reality.

My two cents on an analytics strategy:

- Consolidate ALL databases into a single data lake, accessible and available to all business leads and stakeholders as appropriate.

- Ensure that data from all sources is funneled into a single cleansing, harmonizing, and aligned system.

- Leverage AI and ML technology to create and model all business scenarios across the entire corporate landscape.

- Create a collaboration platform and require total cooperation among all groups within the enterprise.

- Build a data and analytics consensus group, mandating representation and support from the heads of each group (e.g., marketing, sales, finance, supply chain, etc.), that provides oversight and control of not only data but analytics output.

No rogue analytics.

I can't stress the data issue enough. It is the difference between success and failure in not only trade promotion, but marketing, supply chain management, demand planning and tracking financial P&L.

My parents would have been able to validate my lack of mathematical skills, and that has not changed much over the years. But I have had the benefit of sitting across the conference room table with some of the brightest minds in the world, and I have seen the way they approach promotion optimization as a true data science.

In one of those meetings, I walked up to the whiteboard and asked, "Can you guys give me a very simple formula that anyone can use to get to an overall ROI figure for promotions?" I acknowledged all the variables (we had a full whiteboard on all three walls at this point—the bank of windows was the fourth) and asked if they could help me write this formula.

	KPI	WEIGHTED FACTOR	MEASUREMENT/METRIC
OVERALL BASE PROMOTION ROI	• Sell-In Revenue	20%	Percent achievement of forecast (A)
	• Sell-In Volume	20%	Percent achievement of forecast (B)
	• Sell-In Margin (Profit)	30%	Percent achievement of forecast (C)
	• Retailer POS Volume	30%	Percent achievement of promotion plan (D)

(E) Cannibalization Effect: (D) − (E) = Impact (G)
(F) Halo Effect: (D) + (F) = Impact (H)

$$(.2A) + (.2B) + (.3C) + .3(D-G+F) = Base\ ROI$$

Figure 12.7 Calculating Overall Base Promotion ROI

I wanted a weighting factor so that there would be a true sense of realism to the measurement and wanted them also to factor in cannibalization and the Halo effect. Walking to the whiteboard, one of my data scientists took the blue marker and wrote what you see in Figure 12.7. Stepping back, I looked around the room and saw a lot of heads nodding. "This is about as close as you can come to a basic formula," said the data scientist. He was a former Procter & Gamble and Coca-Cola analytics guy for several years. After a lot of discussion, and some examples plugged into the formula, everyone agreed on two things:

As a top-line example, this is really a suitable way to approach it.

None of them would commit to designing it into the client's measurements.

The refusal to commit to designing this logic for their respective companies came from their distrust of the data they worked with, so naturally, they were reluctant to say outright that they would make this the law. To them, having a simple formulaic expression on a whiteboard was yet a far cry from writing the algorithm. But at least everyone agreed that this is the basic idea.

Emphasis on the POS data is a key factor here, which is why it has been given a higher weighted factor. The folks in this room saw the data from the survey represented in Figures 12.5 and 12.6, and all agreed that profit is a key end value that held more weight as well. You may find a far different set of weighted factors, but you have to admit that this is a strong statement, and one that helps to center the eventual success of the promotion as a major piece of the puzzle for determining overall ROI that everyone can understand and agree upon.

So, I offer this suggestion and recommend that you take this simple formula to your own data scientists and work from there. If you have not already begun a serious initiative to design and develop a promotion optimization algorithm, it's not a bad place to start.

Trade Promotion Management & Execution (TPx) Excellence

There is no excuse to run a trade promotion program on spreadsheets.

None.

Don't do it.

I could stop here, and this would be enough said—but let's look at the present environment. There are several very strong TPx vendors in the world today. Many of these companies have invested millions of dollars in new technology, higher quality user interfaces and navigation, and of course, more powerful AI-driven functionality and analytics.

This book is not going to provide you either the names or recommendations for any of these vendors, because some vendors are more applicable to your industry, channels, customer base, and strategy than others. But you must move through the process of finding the best trade promotion, co-op advertising, market development fund, or rebate partner you can in the most immediate timeframe your company will allow.

Remember the old phrase, "Don't try this at home, I am a professional" that so many now make fun of?

For trade promotion and co-op advertising program management, it is highly accurate and applicable. Your IT organization may be comprised of the most talented and bright developers in the universe, but please, do not allow them to build a trade promotion management system. It will be a legacy decision you will regret for years, and at the end of those years, you will end up going with a TPx vendor anyway. So, save yourself and your IT team from making this fundamental mistake.

There are two ways to accomplish partnering with a TPx vendor—outsourcing to a service firm or licensing/purchasing software.

Trade Promotion, Co-op Advertising, and other fund-based promotional programs can be managed by a third party administrator in the form of a subscribed service. Many of these companies have been engaged in third-party administration of trade channel and co-op advertising promotions for many decades and are a highly cost-effective way to manage TPx.

These companies have an internal technology that performs all the functions of an end-to-end channel incentive promotion program, including strong analytics capability. They include services to assist in promotion program creation, advice and counsel for future channel promotions, and maintain well-trained domain experts who can handle all aspects of the TPx function.

Typical administrative services include:

- Strategic and tactical promotion program development (terms, conditions, guidelines, governance, and operational requirements)
- Integration and management of master data
- Claim and deduction settlement processing
- Customer service communications with channel customers and agents
- Allowance fund accrual, management, and accounting
- Promotion performance monitoring and analysis

These companies provide all of these mission critical services and enable your internal teams to remain lean and efficient while they handle the day-to-day issues, concerns and problems of a typical TPx/Co-op/MDF program. Many of these companies also handle other aspects of the business including warranty processing, literature production and fulfillment, marketing development, media buying, and rebate processing.

"I'll tell you this," says the CMO of a top paint manufacturer. "I've used these people [co-op service firm] for more than 20 years, and they have saved us millions of dollars in costs, just from the fact that they know what the media costs are locally and make sure we don't pay more than what it's worth." He also pointed out that the company intervenes in difficult situations around their co-op advertising programs. "What I like is that these guys handle all the communications with our customers, because they actually receive and audit the claims. They can act on our behalf and engage with the customer in sensitive situations that I would not want my salespeople to have to deal with."

He also pointed out that they provide daily reporting of activities and create a very strong bond with the company's customers such that their own customers see the administrator as a competitive advantage. "I've checked the cost of licensing software to manage this and, for us, going the outsource route has a much lower cost per transaction and total cost of ownership."

The industry sectors where you will likely see these companies excelling include consumer durables, fashion, hardware/DIY, home fashions, sporting goods, high tech and consumer electronics, automotive and auto aftermarket, and even commercial products like HVAC, farming implements, and tractor-trailer trucks, to name a few. More and more consumer packaged goods companies are opting for these service firms rather than software licensing or purchase, so keep this option open when you are considering making a change in your channel promotions.

For the FMCG and CPG industry sectors, the prevalent method of managing trade promotion is through internal or vendor TPx software. Most companies continue to manage their trade promotions through either spreadsheets or internally-developed legacy software applications. However, the intensity of competitive trade promotion practices and consumer engagement has relegated most of that type of technology to the category of obsolescence.

For that reason, the market for trade promotion management software has heated up considerably. Twenty years ago, there were only four or five major TPx vendors capable of full end-to-end promotion management. The increase in number of TPx vendors looks like a hockey stick since 2005.

When Hand Promotion Management conducted an in-depth evaluation of TPM software vendors in 2017, I covered the companies that had at least 10 major clients. I may have overlooked some companies that did very little to promote their solution and/or to ever attend any of the industry trade group meetings and conferences. In my study, I had 26 companies. However, I know that number has increased considerably. I am in conversations with at least four other software companies who want to enter the TPx marketplace in 2022, so there is evidently a global demand that is increasing as more companies recognize the futility of managing trade promotions on spreadsheets or old legacy systems.

Mark Osborn, Global Vice President, Business Development & Strategy at SAP, has been involved in trade promotion management for more than 20 years, beginning with his work at 3M in their trade promotion organization. He has seen the growth in trade promotion management first-hand from the perspective of an outsource firm (Gelco) and through his current work at SAP.

"Trade management is evolving into a larger Revenue Growth Management process that considers promoted activity and incremental volume from promotions along with baseline and non-promoted volume across all channels, physical and virtual. Further, significant advances in direct-to-consumer engagement offer Consumer Goods companies significantly more opportunities to interact with and promote to consumers in ways that are shifting the balance of power in the industry away from retailers and directly to consumers themselves. My sense is that corresponding advances in technology for reaching, engaging, and learning from consumer interactions will result in far more targeted and far more effecti ve spend, but in areas that are not or may not be considered what we would traditionally call trade promotion."

He's not alone in those assessments. Trade promotion software has now advanced to a highly sophisticated level, with AI-driven machine learning planning functionality and advanced analytics that leverage POS and other consumption data to help executives achieve higher levels of ROI on trade spending. And, as I said many times in this book, the expansion of revenue growth management with the inclusion of trade promotion is also driving the pace of TPx implementations throughout the world.

These companies also run the gamut of size, from smaller TPx vendors which concentrate on the small- and mid-market CPG companies, to large functionality footprints that are designed to manage trade promotion for multibillion dollar global conglomerates.

Most TPx software includes the ability to manage the primary functions of trade promotion:

- Integration with primary enterprise systems such as ERP, retailer-supplied POS, supply chain management, and syndicated data providers

- Accrual, budgeting, allocation, and accounting management of trade funds.

- Contracts and business rules governance

- Promotion planning

- Claim audit and compliance processing

- Deduction management

- Promotion settlement

- Analysis of promotion performance

Many TPx vendors are beginning to build and implement at least some form of scenario modeling using advanced AI and machine learning technology, but as I wrote in Chapter 9, we are still on the very early edge of true promotion optimization. Clearly, we will get there, and given the significant amount of attention and development from the largest global consulting firms today, that objective will be reached soon enough. I will have a bit more to say about this in the next section.

There continues to be a growing list of TPM/TPO solution vendors operating in the world today, and many of Hand Promotion Management's clients engage us to help them determine the best fit for their trade promotion, retail execution and revenue growth management initiatives.

The largest TPx vendors are working to expand their offerings to cover more of the functionality we have covered in this book. More venture capital is coming into this industry supporting new vendors and expanding advanced analytics and promotion management functionality. According to Pam Brown, Promotion Optimization Institute's Chief Commercial Officer, "There has been a shift in the last three years to move from siloed sales planning to holistic enterprise planning, and Revenue Growth Management sits at the heart of this change."

One of the more common projects I take on these days is to work with consumer products companies to help them evaluate their internal processes and business requirements around trade channel promotion management and execution to determine what the best fit will be for a future TPx implementation. Globally, so many good TPx vendors are filling key operational and functional niches, and it demands a very detailed evaluation of need and requirements before taking on what is now a very difficult corporate initiative.

But the question continues to be asked, "when and how do I need to look outside for a TPx solution vendor?"

So, you need to seek out a TPx vendor solution WHEN:

- You use spreadsheets or internally-developed legacy trade promotion management applications.

- You cannot control your fund management without significant human labor, or your present system is not 100% accurate in fund accounting. *100% Accurate.*

- Your business grows to at least $1 billion USD in revenues.

- Formal promotion planning has to be done in different applications.

- You cannot confidently answer the following questions:

  - What is your total overall ROI on trade spending?

  - Which tactics produce the highest rate of return in promotion sales (POS)?

  - What is the average and total cost of each promotional tactic you run?

  - What is the turnaround for claims, deduction, and total settlement transactions?

  - What is your average write-off amount for unauthorized or unverified deductions?

  - What is the number, total and average amounts of chargeback transactions per month? Quarter? Annually?

  - What percent of promotion plans are claimed or deducted for the exact amounts planned?

  - How many man-hours does it take to manage trade promotion per day, week, month, quarter, and year?

  - What is the average profit & loss by individual promotion, account, sales territory/KAM, brand, category, promoted product group and channel, by month, quarter, and year?

  - What percentage of the total budget is expended for trade promotion by account, sales territory/KAM, brand and category by month, quarter, and year?

  - How long does it take to complete the planning cycle?

- You have difficulty with visibility to and management of the customer account or product hierarchies—especially when they are complex and voluminous.

- You cannot quickly and efficiently reorganize the sales geography or account assignments.

- You cannot effectively access and analyze historical promotion activities and details.

- You do not have any access within the current TPx management infrastructure to include compliance audit results and proof of performance documentation.

- You cannot quickly calculate the cost to manage trade promotion overall, by brand and category, by sales area, by function (e.g., fund management, planning, and settlement)?

These are the top-10 basic questions I begin any trade promotion vendor search advisory, plus potentially many more depending upon the special circumstances that may exist. So far, in my more than 40 years of doing this, nobody has been able to answer all these questions, and, for the largest percentage of my clients, most of the questions.

This is not intended to portray any company in a bad light, but quite the contrary. Once a company engages me to help them determine what their options are for a vendor search, it is not unusual to have so many of these key questions go unanswered when asked. But the fact that they recognize the need is a tribute to solid logic and a desire to drive better promotion ROI, and more effectively and efficiently manage the promotional functions.

Now, let's take the second half of the question—WHAT to do when considering a vendor selection initiative for TPx. Assuming that the "When" questions are answered, at least to a satisfactory degree that management buys off on a vendor selection, here is what I typically advise as the right process for an effective TPx vendor selection project.

Select a specialized team of business leaders and key stakeholders to populate both a steering committee and a working business team that will remain with the project throughout selection, design, implementation, testing, and launch.

Select a representative group up and down the chain of command to ensure not only strategic, but tactical and day-to-day operation.

Have representation for all levels in the Steering Committee (not all top executives, please).

Clear the decks—your team will need to be committed to the project with priority given to the TPx initiative, and appropriate backups in position to ensure smooth ongoing operations.

Hold workshops and build a value stream process map of all current "As Is" business processes and functions that are involved in trade promotion management and execution. These will include, at a minimum:

- Contract terms, business rules, governance, and internal controls.
- Fund budgeting, allocation, accrual, maintenance, and accounting.

- Customer account and business planning.

- Promotion planning for all funded channel incentives offers.

- Claiming and payment settlement, accounting, and communications.

- Deduction research, settlement, accounting, and communications.

- Master data and integration management.

- Analytical tools, metrics, and measurements including corporate P&L.

- Include key metrics of time, personnel resource requirements, and materials costs.

Hold a series of future state "To-Be" process value stream mapping workshops for all the above functions

Formulate current and future business requirements around trade promotion management and execution, leveraging the values created in both the "As-Is" and "To-Be" value stream process maps.

Create a detailed request for proposal (RFP) based on the requirements, processes, and business controls. Include the metrics for measurement of responses from the TPx vendors.

Research and determine the top 5 TPx vendors to which the RFPs will be sent—no more. Have a reserve group of at least 3 additional vendors in case one of the top 5 decides not to participate.

The RFP will request responses from the selected vendors in two formats:

1. Written response, within 30 days, to each point in the RFP along with a preliminary estimate of cost (ballpark) based on the requirements and process.

2. Preliminary presentation and demonstration of the TPx solution functionality.

Steering Committee and Business Team will analyze and measure the results, then will select two vendors as "finalists" to provide detailed demonstrations with dummy master data. Timing should be 30-45 days. This will include a full and comprehensive estimate of costs for full implementation and standard "hypercare" or post "Go Live" checks and corrections to operational "bugs" and other issues that develop for a minimum period of 3 months.

The top two vendors will demonstrate the system functionality and present the cost proposal to the full team. This can take up to two full days and should enable a full and complete evaluation of capabilities and cost.

The final selection of the TPx vendor is made and the work begins on design blueprinting and implementation.

There are several considerations and questions that revolve around implementation, and although we need not delve into that level of detail, one of the top items will be the need to identify an implementation partner. Most TPx solution vendors have relationships with major systems integrators that could be made part of the RFP cycle. Alternatively, the implementation may be carried out by the company's existing consulting and integration partner. That decision needs to be made as early as possible. I typically lean toward a joint presentation of both the TPx solution vendor and their chosen systems integration partner. That way, the company has visibility to functionality and cost of the TPx system as well as the cost of implementation.

If at all possible and depending upon the scope of the trade promotion business operations, it would make sense to include at least one outsource option in the initial bid cycle. Otherwise, there may be an efficient and effective solution that is overlooked for more expensive and time-consuming implementation.

Two years ago, I had dinner with the CIO of one of the world's largest pharmaceutical and personal care companies. We had just wrapped up the first day of workshops preparing her team for a TPM system implementation. "I've had four TPM installs in my past," she said. "I've had three large ERP projects too, but I have to tell you, the TPM installs were harder." She pointed to the complexity and the broad coverage of functions that trade promotion spans, and how tough it was to coordinate and synchronize all of the integrations, financial issues, control issue, supply chain, and demand planning and analytics.

She is absolutely right. Being involved in many ERP projects myself, I can not only sympathize, but empathize with the entire team involved in TPM implementations. The moral of this story is that this is a super critical function, and the teams that are selected to work on a TPM implementation project have to be committed and dedicated. This is a full-time job, and don't think otherwise.

There needs to be a business executive who takes the lead on these projects. It must be their full-time job because it will require it. Strength in management, patience and above all, encouragement are mission critical skills and character needed to lead the TPx implementation effort. It must be someone everyone knows and respects, and it has to be someone who can communicate openly and positively throughout, because there are going to be many bumpy roads and more potholes than the Long Island Expressway.

That said, the leadership throughout the project has to be a full-time job. Do not try to "work this into the daily routine" because it is not routine. It demands attention and focus. You are dealing with the second largest line item in your company's entire financials, so treat it with the level of respect and importance it deserves. When the leadership is full-time, the project typically ends on time. When it isn't, it doesn't.

Whether or not an outsource service firm is selected or a TPx vendor solution is implemented, there is too much at stake to attempt to take on a major development of TPx functionality internally—seek external domain expertise and technology. It's like the old motor oil commercial where the mechanic warns that if you don't use quality oil, the option is "pay me now, or pay me later." Make the effort and commit the time and talent. It is worth it.

Optimization Excellence

While we are on the subject of trade promotion management and execution, we have to take the next step in the journey to consumer engagement excellence by optimizing the Invisible Economy. This is the "Trade Promotion Optimization" or "TPO" you have heard now for several years. As we related back in Chapter 9, there are, unfortunately, many vendors which tout their "TPO" when it is really not an advanced AI-driven machine learning engine.

Going back to a point Retail Velocity's founder, Jeff Beckett, made earlier, the value of the data is key, and with so much riding on it, the effort has to be made to get it in the most accurate and trustworthy state it can be in. "Raw, or rarely cleansed, and never harmonized, is widely available in the top 600 retailers around the world. Not all retailers can provide the data in a file, but for a few years software companies have been able to use various techniques to "read" the information and make it immediately usable," he points out. "Daily data is required when attempting any accurate trade promotion efficiencies, let alone optimization."

The difference between real optimization and what often passes for it in the TPx world today is not just technology, but a combination of domain expertise and advanced predictive data science that delivers a prescriptive plan with a high degree of potential in delivering a trusted outcome.

Hans Van Delden, Senior Vice President at Strategy&, part of the PwC network, has a great response to the question of what constitutes key learnings a consumer products company must have before trade promotion optimization can be mainstreamed.

"First, leadership needs to believe that trade promotions investments can be optimized. If leadership views it as a sunk cost or an immovable object, then it's unlikely the sales teams will invest the effort to optimize their trade spend. Optimizing takes work and if the work is not valued, then there is not much incentive to do it, especially when your discretionary time is already scarce.

Second, it takes a highly skilled analyst to optimize trade investments well. He/she needs to be proficient across several domains:

- Use of modern computers and applications
- Trade promotion mechanics: merchandising vehicles, payment terms, etc.

- Planning with consumption and shipment volumes

- Planning base & incremental volume

- Basic economics metrics such as contribution, ROI, and retailer margin

- Basic optimization concepts: objectives, constraints, scenarios

- Ideally, the ability to use a predictive model effectively

- Tools can do the complicated calculations and streamline the optimization process, but the analyst needs to be able to understand these domains so they can use the tools effectively.

Third, TPM/O tools are data-hungry, calculation intensive simulation systems. They don't just work 'out-of-the-box.' Someone must 'feed the beast.' Sales Operations (or a similar function) usually fulfills this role. These people are critical to the TPO process."

Amen.

Reviewing Figure 9.5 in Chapter 9, you can see the attributes of an effective trade promotion optimization functionality. These embody all the essential requirements in the development and implementation of advanced TPO systems

After all is said and done, the validation of promotion optimization excellence is the production of a prescribed promotion with an outcome that can be trusted to be accurate.

Collaboration Excellence

Collaboration comes in two forms—real and imagined.

There are three primary groups in any consumer goods company that must work together every day if consumer engagement excellence is to be delivered. These are trade promotion, corporate marketing, and the channel customer (retailer, wholesaler, distributor, value-added reseller, etc.). We also discussed this issue in detail back in Chapter 9 as one of the centerpieces of optimized promotions.

Just as with the dangers facing multi-siloed databases and analytics tool sets, planning promotions apart from interaction with the corporate marketing and direct-to-consumer event planning is begging for conflict and misaligned strategic messaging. Another client of mine has what I think is one of the most effective collaboration efforts I have ever seen, and one that should be a model for what we are talking about here.

The company is a $14 billion (USD) maker of toiletry items with highly recognized brands across 12 different categories. They were the category captains for their top 10 accounts in 9 of those 12 categories.

Ten years before, they ran into problems running trade promotions featuring price reductions that conflicted with coupons and rebates offered directly to customers through corporate marketing promotions. Unfortunately, this ran unchecked for years and created some nasty ill-will with their leading accounts, so much so that these conflicts led to their being dropped as category captains by 7 of their top 10 customers.

The CEO invited the CMO, CSO and chief revenue officer (CRO) to a fishing trip in the mountains of Colorado for a week of relaxation, fun and excitement.

Sometimes there's fun and excitement, sometimes there's just *excitement*.

That is what happened up in the mountain cabin. The CEO worked the plan to have these three key leaders build a strategic and tactical plan of action that would forever prevent conflict but would unify these three important organizations into one smooth working cohort whose mission it was to engage the consumer at every level of the Consumer Chain. The outcome of that week was a very strong unification and process that has no doubt contributed to the success this company enjoys today.

They also caught a lot of fish!

This is how the company collaborates today:

- There is one promotion calendar for the entire company.

- Cross-organizational teams of executives and key stakeholders are created and maintained for the full year. These include:

  - Data Compliance – Compiling and selecting relevant historical, projection and performance data for preparation of future planning meetings.

  - Trade Marketing – Manage day-to-day activities between trade promotion and corporate marketing.

  - Financial Management – Manages the funding and financial accounting for all promotion, marketing and event activities and plans.

  - Consumer Engagement – Plans, executes, and analyzes cross-channel promotion, media advertising, coupon and rebate programs. Includes retail execution and customer experience monitoring within the retail channels.

  - Category and Brands – Working directly with corporate category and brand marketing, trade promotion and the ad agencies to ensure alignment with messaging, category, account, brand and product positioning, and product assortment.

- Steering Committee – Responsible for oversight and operational management. C-level executives, line management and selected experienced stakeholders.

- "Data Compliance" teams from RGM, marketing, sales, finance, and trade promotion create and prepare the data analyses for the annual Integrated Business Planning meetings.

- The Integrated Business Planning is a week-long offsite meeting where the entire year is planned, including forecast finalization and demand plan finalization.

- Trade promotion and marketing plans are shared with each account on a secure collaboration portal in preparation for planning and commitment meetings.

- Promotion Planning is a joint team exercise on the collaboration portal with the account's team members (buyer, merchandising, marketing, and product assortment) where the final trade promotion plans are committed and agreed to.

- Weekly meetings are held by the Trade Marketing teams to monitor detailed progress of all promotions across all channels and tactical activities.

- Compliance is monitored and reported weekly.

- POS data is received directly from the top 10 accounts for all locations and all markets.

- Monthly meetings on the collaboration portal with the key account management teams and the account's management teams.

- Problems with settlements, deduction issues and other compliance issues are treated with 100% high-priority and communicated immediately and continually until resolved.

- Analyses and dashboards are shared on the secure collaboration site, including information that helps the account understand how the individual products and promoted product groups perform across the region and globally.

- C-level executives from the customer account and the Steering Committee meet two times each year to elevate key issues and maintain excellent working relationships.

This is a recipe for success. There are issues and problems that arise, of course. But the way this company works with the customer accounts is amazing to see. In all but one of their top 15 accounts, they are back in the category captain's seat. ROI is high, and new promotion optimization tools are being shared and tested in a collaborative manner I have not seen anywhere else.

This is the way it should work. This is Collaboration Excellence.

Execution Excellence

In today's modern consumer products omnichannel environment, there is no reason why proof of performance, verification of price and display compliance and field-level in-store auditing communications cannot be real-time, or at least near real-time. The technology exists and the process is well-accepted. In e-commerce, for instance, compliance is immediate and accurate, driven off the actual promotion online and corresponding consumer purchase.

But as pointed out in Chapter 10, there has been slow progress over the years with automating and improving these vital business processes in the brick-and-mortar channels. We also mentioned that a resurgence, of sorts, has taken place and the number of opportunities for retail execution improvement has grown to become one of the most highly-prioritized focus areas in the consumer products industries.

The definition of execution excellence is being able to integrate key component systems and databases to provide instant visibility to promotion plans, marketing events and schedules, pricing data, competitive analyses, and inventory shipping and logistics into the hand-held systems used today. This should enable on-the-spot decision making, driving the field reps and merchandisers toward the most appropriate actions to take during their visits.

Manual verification of performance and compliance is where we are today across the brick-and-mortar channel landscape; but, leveraging new technologies, IoT and in-store camera and sensors, we have to get to a point of automatic validation at a level of 100% coverage—not some smaller percentage of store locations. The results of this technological capability will be more accurate, immediate, and comprehensive verification of compliance, at far less cost to both the retailer and the manufacturer/supplier. It impacts financial compliance by driving faster deduction and claim processing and may even eliminate the need for claiming or deducting in favor of off-invoice transactions generated immediately.

We have a long way to go to be at that point, but the good news is that you can see it progressing to that point. We have the technology, the understanding, and the ingenuity to solve this long-standing problem in consumer industries.

Consumer Excellence

The culmination of all that we have discussed in this book is the ability to predict and prescribe the right response to every link in the consumer chain (Remember Figure

4.1 in Chapter 4?). This is a realistic expectation every consumer products company should have, and a goal for every aspect of consumer engagement we have covered in this book.

Data accuracy is required for precise and trustworthy monitoring of the consumer's journey toward purchase and loyalty. Near and real-time analysis of the Consumer Chain is mission-critical, and every operation and function of the trade promotion management and execution process must adhere to and comply with the strategic and tactical plans put in place to produce the outcomes we have detailed.

A devotion to the consumer is paramount in the achievement of this level of excellence. It means thinking about the end results of a promotion before you plan the event. It means being able to predict with near 100% confidence in what the consumer will do before committing to the demand plan. It means increasing the focus on what and how the shopper feels when they are in the store by the field merchandising reps carrying out their daily store visits. It applies to the collaborative planning between sales and marketing to ensure that the customer does not see or experience a conflict. It means thinking more about the consumer's lack of ability to buy the product than worrying about the logistical issues with out-of-stocks.

All those actions must take place, and clearly, each one of them has its own relevance; but true consumer excellence comes from putting it all together and making the consumer part of the thought process for every single project, function, operation and analysis performed by the sales, marketing, finance, IT and RGM executives and stakeholders.

It must be the one thing you ask of any function and process, analysis and communication made—is this going to improve our consumer engagement and drive loyalty?

If the answer is yes, then you are on your way to achieving consumer excellence.

Managing the Change

You've heard the term, "Change Management" often, I am sure. If you have followed these guidelines and recommendations toward achievement of Consumer Excellence, then you already know that the impact of making those changes to the workforce, processes and technology are significant.

If you have not yet begun the journey, then you must know that the amount of change that takes place because you have now completely reengineered the mission, purpose, and intent of your trade channel promotions is going to bring hundreds, perhaps thousands of people into a much different and more challenging way of life in the workplace.

Managing those changes requires everyone to understand the mission and accept their individual roles and responsibilities that will flow from these changes. It is going to be a top-down, bottom-up effort that depends upon three critical things:

1. Leadership

2. Planning

3. Communication

Leadership is a key component of that change. We already discussed the leadership role in the transition from one form of trade promotion management and execution to a new, more automated and advanced level of technology, process and functionality. But while the leadership of that transition is critical, there is a step-up in intensity required to manage the organization, technical and measurement changes across the entire company landscape. The leader has to be someone trusted and highly visible in the organization, but able to dedicate and commit their full measure of time to the employees' adjustment, acceptance and execution of their new ways of working.

Individual "change managers," or whatever functional title these key people have, will need to be in place to drive change throughout their individual organizations. While this means setting up a vertically hierarchical structure, leaders will need to be cognizant of the horizontal leadership—where the entire company sees managers from each organization embrace and work their teams through the changes. This also means being able to personalize the change—work individually with key stakeholders, new employees and those who may openly resist the change to bring everyone into understanding and acceptance of each new area of responsibility and functional execution.

Many change management consultants will tell you that the plan for managing change is as important, perhaps even more so, than the plan of change itself. That, I agree with. Unfortunately, I've seen where change management is relegated to a few memos from the top management about new responsibilities and how great the change will be for the company, but that really does not cut it. It will have to be detailed and thorough, making sure that there is a solid plan for action for each and every change. Think about the detailed milestone chart you have for the TPx implementation. That is precisely what is required for the change management.

Plan for what you know, and plan for what you don't know. In other words, use your implementation teams to project what they believe will happen that impacts their employees, the customers and, of course, the consumer. You may not know everything in advance, but you will be ready with an action plan and a proper measurement system for every single change—both planned and unplanned.

You have to communicate everything. The communication has to be timely, thoroughly covering every element and facet of change, and completely transparent. Transparency is a key, because one of the most feared things about change is about how that change will affect the employees personally. Regular meetings need to be held with not only those for whom the change impacts the most, but even those who work in the periphery, so that they understand what will happen and how that will affect the organization as a whole.

Change management is about setting and sustaining an atmosphere of understanding, acceptance and eager execution of the new technology, processes, roles, and responsibilities. It is most important that everyone knows that each contributes to the overall success of the company and the engagement of the consumer through their respective roles and responsibilities. Make it fun. Make it exciting and make it a positive experience.

In his great new book, "The Power of Goal Zero," Sam Smolik provides some of the most important and best lessons on leadership and management to achieve true operational excellence I have ever read. In his book, he makes a profound statement that I will always remember and hope you will as well. He tells about working as a team in the achievement of the improvement of the quality of his company's Enterprise, Health and Safety (EH&S) programs and how important each individual was to accomplishing the company mission.

He tells his team:

"None of us was as good as all of us."[81]

This is a great theme for accomplishing excellence in consumer engagement, because as I have stated throughout this book, it takes a team of committed, dedicated and hard-working people to make any project successful—especially something as complex as trade channel promotion management, execution and analysis.

Have We Arrived?

"Consumer Excellence" is our destination.

The answer to "Are we there yet?" is, "Not yet."

But it's just around the bend.

There, is the place where you are squarely in the 4th Dimension of Knowledge and your trade promotion spending is a dependable piece of intelligence your company's shareholders can literally "take to the bank."

The Invisible Economy of Consumer Engagement is the more than $1 trillion in global spending to make sure you, as a consumer, fulfill your needs and become a loyal customer of a particular good or service. It is provided by the manufacturer/supplier and it is spent by the companies that comprise the various channels of distribution. It is typically the second largest line item in the corporate financials, and it is one of the most difficult issues facing any company selling their goods and services through channels of distribution.

And it fails all too often.

This book has been about how to make that money work better. It is about the methods, practices, policies, procedures, and initiatives that must be enacted to improve the top and bottom lines of both manufacturer/supplier and channel partner.

For most of my career, trade promotion, and its so many various names and forms of channel incentives, has been treated as a necessary evil—a pot of money used to wave in front of the buyer to get them to agree to buy huge volumes of products.

It seems that it has been nothing more.

Those of us fortunate enough to have been in this business for so many years, have worked hard to help companies improve the perceived value of this incredible ocean of money spent every day in every corner of the world, and across virtually every industry and line of business. It has not been as glamorous as being on the corporate marketing teams, working with ad agencies, media, and production companies making great commercials, building beautiful ads, and living the fascinating world of the advertising account executive.

Instead, it's been heads-down in the trenches, working out problems with claims, managing deductions, calling hundreds of customers to respond to complaints about how long it is taking to get their funds or arguing why the fund is lower than the retailer or distributor thought. It's not glamorous, and neither is working in the turbines of a generator plant, but we all must have the electricity it takes to live our lives. Trade promotion management has, in the past, been very much like that.

The unsung, hard-working managers, supervisors, auditors, processors, and customer service people who have the task of making sure this money is managed and accounted for, are the true lifeblood of this business. If there is one thing I would ask any of you making it to this point in the book, please thank your teams of people who carry out these missions—on both sides of the channel.

After more than four decades in this business of helping companies to improve their revenues, profitability, consumer loyalty and operational effectiveness in and around channel incentives, trade promotion, co-op advertising and all forms of market development funded programs, it is very gratifying to see the elevation of channel promotion to the level it should have always been—at the highest priority for every consumer products company employee.

The use of advanced technologies, increased communications, expanding trade organizations, the growing number of industry conferences and meetings dedicated to the Invisible Economy, is nothing short of exciting and heart-warming to see. And it's about time. That's my two cents!

Thank you for reading my book.

About the Author

Robert L. (Rob) Hand, Jr.

Rob Hand is an American executive consultant in the consumer packaged goods, high tech, automotive, fashion and retail industries. He is a domain expert and industry leader specializing in trade channel promotion, co-op advertising, supply chain, retail execution and revenue growth management processes, technology, and analytics. He has a 45-year history of working with and helping consumer products manufacturers improve their trade promotion spending ROI, performance analytics, consumer engagement efficiency and marketing effectiveness.

He is a pioneer in the channel marketing industry, founding and growing three highly successful and innovative companies providing services to the most successful global consumer products industries. He has created numerous educational and training programs, presented to global audiences, and has authored white papers, major magazine articles and blogs that have helped sales, marketing, financial and revenue growth management executives improve their companies' top and bottom lines.

Rob is a member of the Trade Promotion Management Hall of Fame and is a frequent contributor to books about co-op advertising, product management, and channel promotion. He is a favorite speaker on the topics of consumer products and trade channel promotion globally and has a highly successful podcast—The TradeScope Podcast.

Mr. Hand's background includes executive positions at SAP, Oracle Corporation, Capgemini, and Avanade, providing global leadership to consumer goods practices, software product management and industry strategy. He has served on the board of directors of both commercial corporations and non-profit organizations and provides ongoing direction to many venture capital and investment companies seeking to enter the areas of trade channel promotion, retail execution, analytics, and technology services.

Rob is based in the Austin, Texas area and is an avid musician and sailor. He is a graduate of the University of Memphis and is a veteran of the United States Navy, having served in aircraft carrier-based fighter squadrons and anti-submarine warfare units. The Invisible Economy of Consumer Engagement is his first book.

Endnotes

1. US Census, *Estimated Monthly Sales for Retail and Food Services, by Kind of Business*, 2021, Monthly Trade Report, May 2021
2. Heraldkeepers, *CPG Market Size, Share, Value and Competitive Landscape 2024*, , MarketWatch. com, Accessed March 19, 2021, Trade Management Software Market Projection by Latest Technology, Global Analysis, Industry Growth, Current Trends and Forecast Till 2026 - MarketWatch
3. Hand Promotion Management, *Survey on Trade Promotion and Channel Incentives*, 2017, p2
4. Nielsen, Inc., *The Path to Efficient Trade Promotions*, February 2015, Accessed March 20, 2021, the-path-to-efficient-trade-promotions-feb-2015.pdf (nielsen.com)
5. CSIMarket.com, *Grocery Stores Industry Profitability by quarter, Gross, Operating and Net Margin from 4 Q 2020*, Accessed March 22, 2021, https://csimarket.com/Industry/industry_Profitability_ Ratios.php?ind=1305
6. Schweizer, Errol, *Why The Grocery industry Is Concerned With Mass Consolidation*, Forbes.com, Accessed March 22, 2021; Why The Grocery Industry Is Concerned By Mass Consolidation (forbes. com)
7. Ronald Reagan, 2 March 1977, Ronald Reagan - Wikiquote, accessed April 1, 2021.
8. Mackay, Adrian (2004), *The Practice of Advertising,* London: Butterworth-Heinemann, ISBN 0-7506-6173-9. p.70.
9. Crouse, Megan Corinn, 2010, *Business Revolution: The Ad Agency*, Accessed July 12, 2021, The Pennsylvania Center for the Book - First Advertising Agency (psu.edu)
10. Hand, Robert (1995), *The Evolution of Market Development Funding*, PowerPoint presentation to the National Association of Advertising & Promotion Allowance (NAPAA) Spring Conference
11. "Peace and sharing dominate festival". *Spokane Daily Chronicle*. (Washington). Associated Press. August 18, 1969. p. 10
12. *Supermarket Facts*, 2019, Food Merchandising Institute, Our Research, accessed April 5, 2021, https://www.fmi.org/our-research/supermarket-facts
13. Houk, Robert F, *Co-op Advertising, The Authoritative Guide to Promotion Allowance Marketing for Advertisers, Retailers and Distributors, Association of National Advertisers*, NTC Business Books, p. 177
14. FMI, The Food Industry Association, 2021, *History*, accessed April 6, 2021, https://www.fmi.org/ about-us/history
15. Houk, Robert F, Co-op Advertising, *The Authoritative Guide to Promotion Allowance Marketing for Advertisers, Retailers and Distributors, Association of National Advertisers*, NTC Business Books, p. 176
16. *FTC Revised Promotional Guides Under the Robinson-Patman Act*, March 2008, FindLaw for Legal Professionals, accessed April 6, 2021, FTC Revised Promotional Guides Under the Robinson-Patman Act - FindLaw
17. Houk, p. 176
18. Butler, Jessica, 2015, *Customer Deductions: 2015 Benchmark Survey*, Attain Consulting Group, Accessed April 20, 2021, https://www.friedmanllp.com/uploads/1441/doc/attain-survey-optimized.pdf
19. Butler, p.9
20. Post Audit Policies, Johnsonville, LLC, 2021, accessed 4/22/2021, Post Audit Policy - Johnsonville. com
21. Hand, Robert (1995), *The Evolution of Market Development Funding*, Hand Consulting Group, Inc., PowerPoint presentation to the National Association of Advertising & Promotion Allowance (NAPAA) Spring Conference

22. McKinsey Research, October 23, 2019 article, *How analytics can drive growth in consumer-packaged-goods trade promotions*, Our Insights, accessed 4/23/2021, https://www.mckinsey.com/business-functions/marketing-and-sales/our-insights/how-analytics-can-drive-growth-in-consumer-packaged-goods-trade-promotions#:~:text=Consumer%2Dpackaged%2Dgoods%20(CPG,States%2C%20it's%2072%20percent).

23. Costliest U.S. tropical cyclones tables update (PDF) (Report). United States National Hurricane Center. January 12, 2018. Archived (PDF) from the original on January 26, 2018. Accessed April 28, 2021.

24. Solomon, Dan; Forbes, Paula, "Inside the Story of How H-E-B Planned for the Pandemic" *Texas Monthly*, March 26, 2020. https://www.texasmonthly.com/food/heb-prepared-coronavirus-pandemic/

25. Digital Commerce 360, US Department of Commerce, *Charts: How the coronavirus is changing e-commerce*, February 2021, Accessed April 28, 2021, https://www.digitalcommerce360.com/2021/02/15/ecommerce-during-coronavirus-pandemic-in-charts/

26. Digital Commerce 360, US Department of Commerce, "Curbside Pickup," *Charts: How the coronavirus is changing e-commerce*, February 2021, Accessed April 28, 2021, https://www.digitalcommerce360.com/2021/02/15/ecommerce-during-coronavirus-pandemic-in-charts/

27. Field Agent, "Endcaps and Insights blog," August 2020, *Impulse Goods in the Covid-19 Age*, Survey of 1,000 shoppers. Accessed May 20, 2021, https://blog.fieldagent.net/impulse-purchases-in-2020-how-is-the-pandemic-influencing-shopper-habits

28. Berlyne D. *A theory of human curiosity*. 45, British Journal of Psychology; 1954, pp.180-91.

29. Blum, Kelly, July 2020, *Annual CMO Spend Survey*, Gartner. Accessed May 26, 2021, CMO Spend Survey: CMOs at Odds With C-Suite Colleagues Over COVID-19 Recovery (gartner.com)

30. MarketWatch, March 2021, *Global Trade Promotion Management and Optimization Solution market 2021 Industry Growth Analysis, Segmentation, Size, Share, Trend, Future Demand and Leading Players Updates by Forecast to 2026*, Press Release, Accessed May 26, 2021, Global Trade Promotion Management and Optimization Solution Market 2021 Industry Growth Analysis, Segmentation, Size, Share, Trend, Future Demand and Leading Players Updates by Forecast to 2026 - MarketWatch

31. Digital Commerce 360, 2021, *US ecommerce grows 44% in 2020*, Accessed June 4, 2021, US ecommerce grows 44.0% in 2020 | Digital Commerce 360

32. The Nielsen Company, LLC, 2018, *Connected Commerce Global Survey 2018*, Accessed June 7, 2021, https://www.nielsen.com/wp-content/uploads/sites/3/2019/04/connected-commerce-report.pdf

33. Brunson, Russell, *Expert Secrets*, 2017, Hay House Business Publishing

34. Oliver, Richard L. *Satisfaction: A Behavioral Perspective on the Consumer*, Routledge, 2nd Edition. February 15, 2010, Chapter 5.

35. Statista Research, 2021, *Social media marketing usage rate in the United States from 2013 to 2021*, Accessed June 9, 2021, https://www.statista.com/statistics/203513/usage-trands-of-social-media-platforms-in-marketing/

36. Oberlo, *10 Social Media Statistics*, April 2021 (Statista Research), Accessed June 9, 2021, https://www.oberlo.com/blog/social-media-marketing-statistics

37. Cision PR Newswire, *New Data Reveals that Brand Loyalty Is on the Rise Among Consumers*, Yotpo, November 2019. Accessed June 10, 2021, https://www.prnewswire.com/news-releases/new-data-reveals-that-brand-loyalty-is-on-the-rise-among-consumers-300957799.html

38. Redbord, Michael, "The Hard Truth About Acquisition Costs (and How Your Customers Can Save You)," *Hubspot*, Accessed June 10, 2021, https://blog.hotspot.com/service/customer-acquisition-study

39. Consumer Goods Technology, *Making It Real – The State of Trade Promotion Management*, 2018, Report, Accessed June 21, 2021, https://consumergoods.com/making-it-real-state-trade-promotion-management

40. Miller, Sergio "Malaya: The Myth of Hearts and Minds", Small Wars Journal, 16 April 2012, accessed 10 Jun 2014

41. American Heritage Dictionary, *Definition of Economy*, 1.a, Accessed July 13, 2021, American Heritage Dictionary Entry: economy (ahdictionary.com)

42. Promotion Optimization Institute, *The State of the Industry*, 2019, Report, p.10

43. Rajagopal, Alarice, and Johnston, Lisa, *CGT & RIS Retail and Consumer Goods Analytics Study 2020*, Accessed June 28, 2021, https://consumergoods.com/sales-marketing-report-2020?oly_enc_id=7910C5594389G6B&utm_source=omeda&utm_medium=email&utm_campaign=BONUS_ConsumerGoodsTechnology&utm_keyword=

44. Kondo, Marie, *The Life-Changing Magic of Tidying Up: The Japanese Art of Decluttering and Organizing*, 2014, Potter/Ten Speed/Harmony/Rodale.

45. Hand Promotion Management, LLC; *Survey on Trade Promotion 2021*, HPM Research, May 2021

46. Coupons in the News, *"Coupons.com Chief Predicts the Demise of Coupon Inserts."* February 2020, Accessed July 6, 2021, https://couponsinthenews.com/2020/02/19/coupons-com-chief-predicts-the-demise-of-coupon-inserts/

47. Statista, *"Millennials who use paper coupons while shopping in the United States as of June 2020, by type."* 2020, Accessed July 6, 2021, • Millennial paper coupon use in the U.S. 2020 | Statista

48. Chapkanovska, Evangelina, *"Coupon Statistics: Is Couponing Growing or Slowing?"* May 2021, SPENDMENOT blog, Accessed July 6, 2021, Coupon Statistics - Is Couponing Growing or Slowing? (spendmenot.com)

49. Brown, Pam, *"Reset and Re-Plan,"* State of the Industry Report, 2021, Promotion Optimization Institute, LLC, P 26

50. Rucker, Chad, 2018, *Monitoring Out-of-Stocks in a Fast-Paced Retail Environment*, Blog, Accessed July 20, 2021, https://blog.wiser.com/monitoring-out-of-stocks-fast-retail/

51. Yoshioka, Ricardo. 2019. "How to Ensure Compliance Trade Promotions." *Aglo Blog*. July 22,2021. https://aglo.io/blog/how-to-improve-promotional-compliance-by-monitoring-6-metrics/

52. Davis, Jessica. 2019 "Stalled AI Gets Unstuck from Surprising Source." *Information Week*, Accessed July 23, 2021.

53. Patrizio, Andy. 2018, "IDC: Expect 175 zettabytes of data worldwide by 2025." *Network World*. 2018. July 23, 2021.

54. Shqiperi Gazette. 2021. *Gartner CIO Report: IT spending expected to increase for cyber, analytics, cloud.* July 20, 2021. Gartner CIO report: IT spending expected to increase for cyber, analytics, cloud - Shqiperi Gazette

55. HPM. 2017. *Survey on Trade Promotion Planning and Execution.* p 10.

56. Norman, Jeremy. 2021. "Michael Aldrich Invents Online Shopping." *HistoryofInformation.com*. July 23, 2021. https://www.historyofinformation.com/detail.php?entryid=4528

57. Troy, Mike. 2021. "Pandemic-Fueled Record Growth in 2020: The PG 100" Accessed July 26, 2021, https://progressivegrocer.com/pandemic-fueled-record-growth-2020-pg-100

58. Rachel Dalton, Todd Szahun, Kerry Curran, Meghan Lavin, 2020, *The State of e-commerce 2021*, Kantar and Catalyst, Accessed July 22, 2021, https://f.hubspotusercontent00.net/hubfs/3788602/Kantar-Catalyst%20State%20of%20Ecommerce%202021.pdf?utm_campaign=The%20State%20of%20Ecommerce&utm_source=landingpage&utm_medium=email

59. Droesch, Blake. 2021. "Amazon dominates US ecommerce, though its market share varies by category" *eMarketer Inside Intelligence*. April 27, 2021. Amazon dominates US ecommerce, though its market share varies by category - Insider Intelligence Trends, Forecasts & Statistics (emarketer.com)

60. Lidiya Chappel, Catherine Fong, Maria Kuska, Megan Lesko Pacchia, Tatiana Sivaeva, and Isabella Maluf. 2021. "High growth, low profit: The e-commerce dilemma for CPG companies" *McKinsey & Company*. July 26, 2021. https://www.mckinsey.com/~/media/mckinsey/industries/consumer%20packaged%20goods/our%20insights/high%20growth%20low%20profit%20the%20e%20commerce%20dilemma%20for%20cpg%20companies/high-growth-low-profit-the-e-commerce-

dilemma-for-cpg-companies.pdf?

61. Orosz, Caitlin. 2021 "Trade Spending on Amazon and Other Online Channels" *Blacksmith Applications Blog*. July 25, 2021. https://blacksmithapplications.com/blog/trade-spending-on-amazon-and-other-online-channels/

62. Feigen, Marissa. 2019. "The Evolving CPG Marketing Mix" *Cierant E.vole Blog*. July 26, 2021. The Evolving CPG Marketing Mix | Cierant

63. McClelland, Calem. 2021. "What is the Internet of Things or IOT? A Simple Explanation." *IOTforall.com* February 1, 2021. https://www.iotforall.com/what-is-internet-of-things

64. Brian Kopp, "Industrial telemetry", in *Telemetry Systems Engineering*, pages 493-524, Artech House, 2002

65. HPM. 2017. 2017 *Trade Promotion Planning Survey*. September 2017. P11.

66. Snipp Research. 2017. "What's In Your Basket: Consumer Shopping Habits by Day of Week." *SNIPP Blog*. August 3, 2021, https://www.snipp.com/blog/2017-07-05/whats-in-your-basket-consumer-shopping-habits-by-day-of-week

67. Hand, Rob. 2018. "Consumer Goods Technology Trade Promotion Survey" Observations. *Making It Real – The State of Trade Promotion Management*, 2018. p3.

68. Dr. Thomas Gruen and Dr. Daniel Corsten. 2007 "A Comprehensive Guide to Retail Out-of-Stock Reduction In the Fast-Moving Consumer Goods Industry." August 5, 2021. p10. http://www.nacds.org/pdfs/membership/out_of_stock.pdf

69. Vassella, Victoria. 2018. "Poor Retail Execution Can Cost You Plenty" *TWICE* Blog, Accessed August 13, 2021. How Better Communication Between Retailers And Vendors Can Improve In-Store Execution And Help Everybody Make Money (twice.com)

70. Krishna, Manu. *Perfecting Instore Execution*, White Paper, 2018. Trax Retail, p2. Accessed August 14, 2021, Perfecting In-Store Execution - Trax - 319.pdf (hubspot.net)

71. Krishna, p3. Krishna, p3.

72. Krishna, p11

73. Hand, Robert. 2017. *Trade Promotion Management and Execution Survey*, HPM. p14.

74. Skorupa, Joe. 2019. "Store Execution Versus Chaos Battle Plan" *Targeted Research Report*, RIS News, Accessed August 14, 2021, https://fokoretail.com/wp-content/uploads/2020/04/RIS-Research-Study.pdf

75. Skorupa, p3

76. Thake, Max. 2018. *Blockchain vs. DAG Technology*. Accessed August 16, 2021. Blockchain vs. DAG Technology. A basic comparison. | by Max Thake | Medium

77. McKendrick, Joe. 2020. "Enter the Tangle, a blockchain designed especially for the Internet of Things." ZDNet. August 17, 2021. https://www.zdnet.com/article/the-tangle-or-blockchain-for-the-internet-of-things/

78. IBM, *What is Blockchain Technology?* IBM.com. Accessed August 16, 2021. What is Blockchain Technology? - IBM Blockchain | IBM

79. IBM. 2017. *Using blockchain to disrupt trade promotions*. Accessed August 17, 2021. https://www.ibm.com/downloads/cas/MJ3R0A4K#:~:text=Based%20on%20a%20variety%20of,on%20trade%20promotion%20spend%20effectiveness.

80. Hetzenecker, Lukas. September 2019. "Blockchain 5.0—Fusing DAG Ledgers With Smart Contracts." *IOTA NEWS*. Accessed August 17, 2021, https://iota-news.com/blockchain-5-0%E2%80%8A-%E2%80%8Afusing-dag-ledgers-with-smart-contracts/

81. Smolik, Sam. 2021. "The Power of Goal Zero". Quality First Publishing, Page 80.

Index

Symbols

1st Dimension 144, 145, 146, 147, 148, 150, 158, 182, 230
2nd Dimension 145, 155, 156, 158, 159, 160, 170, 173
3rd Dimension 145, 171, 172, 173, 174, 175, 179
4th Dimension 127, 145, 179, 181, 183, 184, 185, 227, 228, 251
2020 Retail and Consumer Goods Analytics Study 75

A

accountability 140
accrual 20, 63, 68, 70, 97, 98, 99, 100, 236, 241
ads 5, 8, 16, 17, 18, 36, 41, 78, 91, 114, 123, 178, 252
Advanced Analytics 75
Advertisements 78
Ahold Delhaize 120
Albert Guffanti xv
Albertsons 120
algorithms 52
Alibaba 114
Amazon 8, 41, 42, 113, 114, 119, 120, 121, 122, 123, 124, 259, 260
Amazon Go 123
A/P 108, 109, 110
Application Program Interface 138
A/R 108, 109, 209
artificial intelligence 52, 54, 66, 96, 143, 145, 168, 227
Art Roberts 1
"As Is" 241
Attain Consulting Group 24, 257
audit 3, 4, 18, 21, 23, 25, 26, 28, 62, 106, 108, 109, 110, 111, 117, 135, 136, 163, 166, 193, 198, 209, 237, 239, 241

B

B2B 61, 82, 179
B2C 61
backlog 22, 116
Backroom Inventory 106
bad data 128, 140, 141
barcode 148, 181
baseline 86
baselines 86, 96, 105, 139, 148, 150, 182, 183, 228, 230
BDF 82
Best Buy 8, 71, 203
big data 75, 129, 132, 134, 150, 233
Bitcoin 204, 207, 209
Black & Decker 113
blockchain 204, 205, 206, 207, 208, 209, 210, 211, 212, 213, 214, 216, 217, 218, 219, 220, 221, 222, 260

Blockchain 203, 204, 205, 206, 211, 212, 214, 215, 217, 218, 220, 221, 260
BOGO 78, 116
BOPIS 42
brick-and-mortar 8, 33, 36, 41, 42, 44, 45, 69, 89, 93, 95, 96, 104, 119, 120, 121, 123, 177, 188, 213, 231, 248
budget 11, 12, 16, 18, 25, 26, 42, 45, 57, 68, 73, 74, 77, 83, 90, 91, 120, 123, 124, 163, 211, 240
business development funding 82, 180
business-to-business 9, 31, 82, 179
Business-to-Consumer 61
Buy Online and Pickup In-store 122

C

Calem McClelland 124
cannibalization 231, 234
Capgemini 171, 178, 182, 214, 228
Carrefour 120, 203
CAS 112
category 8, 26, 60, 61, 65, 70, 74, 81, 83, 90, 100, 101, 102, 120, 138, 151, 152, 154, 168, 177, 192, 193, 212, 237, 240, 241, 245, 246, 247, 259
causal 76, 115, 117, 131, 133, 139, 147, 152, 153, 155, 159, 166, 183
CDO 129
CEO xi, xvi, xvii, 60, 70, 76, 81, 129, 132, 155, 163, 193, 210, 227, 246
CFO 25, 91, 123, 132, 210
CGT 76, 171, 228, 259
CGT/RIS 76
channel customer 24, 61, 62, 68, 87, 93, 97, 109, 179, 180, 220, 245
channel incentives xiii, xiv, 8, 28, 29, 31, 57, 61, 67, 71, 113, 114, 162, 173, 221, 242, 252
Chief Data Officer 129
Chief Digital Officer 129
Chief Revenue Officer 88
CIO 129, 205, 220, 243, 259
CMO 70, 76, 85, 86, 89, 123, 183, 184, 237, 246, 258
Coca-Cola 70, 235
COD 139, 140
companion display 40
compliance 18, 25, 26, 27, 28, 62, 63, 82, 92, 99, 105, 106, 107, 109, 111, 117, 125, 131, 157, 163, 164, 165, 166, 175, 182, 187, 188, 189, 190, 191, 192, 193, 194, 196, 198, 199, 200, 201, 202, 208, 209, 210, 211, 213, 215, 216, 219, 222, 225, 239, 241, 247, 248, 259
Connected Commerce Global Survey 2018 45, 258
consensus 154, 206, 207, 209, 210, 211, 213, 220, 221, 234
Consensus Algorithms 207
Consumer Brands Association 24
Consumer Chain 31, 34, 35, 37, 38, 39, 41, 42, 43, 44, 46, 48, 50, 51, 53, 55, 56, 57, 66, 76, 77, 85, 118, 119, 121, 137, 145, 148, 162, 163, 173, 179, 180, 181, 182, 184, 208, 219, 222, 227, 246, 249
consumer engagement xiii, xiv, xvii, 11, 29, 31, 48, 49, 57, 74, 86, 87, 90, 92, 93, 104, 112, 118, 139, 141, 163, 165, 177, 179, 181, 218, 219, 220, 223, 226, 227, 237, 238, 244, 245, 249, 251
"Consumer Engagement" 83
Consumer Goods Technology xv, 67, 75, 150, 182, 258, 260
consumer packaged goods xv, 5, 8, 18, 21, 23, 26, 28, 68, 129, 199, 237
consumption 34, 46, 50, 53, 54, 55, 57, 83, 85, 101, 148, 149, 150, 185, 213, 216, 217, 219, 238, 245

COO 91

co-op xiii, xiv, xvi, 3, 4, 5, 7, 9, 18, 19, 21, 28, 31, 62, 63, 68, 70, 85, 98, 99, 107, 110, 112, 120, 133, 144, 146, 147, 179, 180, 200, 205, 211, 213, 221, 235, 236, 237, 252

co-op advertising xiii, xiv, xvi, 3, 4, 5, 7, 9, 18, 19, 21, 28, 31, 62, 68, 70, 85, 99, 107, 110, 112, 120, 133, 146, 147, 179, 180, 200, 211, 213, 221, 235, 236, 237, 252

co-op advertising programs xvi, 4, 237

co-operative advertising 4, 5, 20, 82

cooperative advertising 18, 19, 204, 209

Corporate Marketing 83

Costco 5, 8, 71, 119

Cost of Data 139, 140

coupon 45, 80, 81, 84, 89, 104, 118, 124, 153, 157, 163, 164, 201, 225, 246, 259

Coupons.com 81, 259

Covid-19 xvi, 11, 13, 32, 33, 37, 41, 44, 75, 117, 119, 138, 201, 227, 258

CPGToolBox xvi

CRaP 121

CRM 96

cryptocurrency 204, 209, 210, 213, 214, 221, 222

Cryptopromotion 213

CSO 89, 91, 184, 246

C-suite xiii, 88, 90, 112, 114

CTO 129, 211

Curbside Delivery 42

curbside pickup 33

Customer Service 83

CVS 119

D

DAG 206, 207, 208, 209, 211, 212, 213, 216, 217, 218, 219, 220, 260

Dale Hagemeyer xvi

Daniel Berlyne 38

DAO 210

Data Decision Vector Workshops 138

data hub 132, 133

Data Value Vector 134, 136

deal 1, 5, 27, 42, 47, 49, 50, 51, 57, 61, 62, 63, 64, 65, 66, 69, 77, 80, 84, 129, 149, 153, 155, 156, 179, 183, 188, 190, 191, 192, 217, 225, 237

Decentralized Autonomous Organization 210

deduction xiii, 22, 23, 24, 25, 26, 27, 28, 63, 108, 109, 110, 111, 126, 187, 198, 208, 209, 236, 240, 247, 248

deduction of promotional cost 22

Demand Creation 92

demand planners 83, 86, 135, 230

demand planning 31, 83, 88, 102, 105, 147, 150, 182, 212, 228, 232, 234, 243

Demand Planning 96

Demonstrations 78, 80

Design Thinking 136

Détente 121, 124

Dick Biondi 1

Digital couponing 123

digital media 89, 96, 121
Digital transformation 96, 104, 111, 126
Digital Transformation 96, 97, 100, 105, 107, 112
digitization 102
Dimensions 143, 144
Dimensions of Knowledge 143, 144
Directed Acyclic Graph 206, 207
direct mailers 34
direct store 162
Direct Store Delivery 188
direct-to-consumer marketing 83, 100, 177
discount 7, 16, 41, 63, 84, 109, 116, 126, 153
discretionary 10, 21, 244
display 25, 40, 57, 78, 84, 109, 111, 117, 120, 126, 151, 152, 153, 166, 168, 183, 191, 192, 193, 200, 201,
      213, 216, 248
Displays 78, 106, 109
distributed ledger 204, 208, 209, 211
distributor 7, 16, 19, 20, 27, 31, 47, 70, 76, 92, 98, 104, 110, 117, 172, 175, 180, 192, 208, 211, 213, 220,
      245, 252
DIY 8, 24, 82, 190, 237
Doritos® Brand Nacho Cheese Tortilla Chips 154
DSD 188, 194, 201

E

EDLP 60, 167
Eligibility 19
end-cap 78, 120
EnsembleIQ xv
Epiphany Bridge 46
equal and proportionate 59, 62, 67, 68, 69, 71
ERP 98, 138, 173, 213, 233, 238, 243
Every Day Low Price 167
Every Day Low Pricing 59
Exceedra 112
Excel® 112
Execution and Compliance 97, 105
Extract, Transform and Load 138

F

fast moving consumer goods 62
fast moving consumer packaged goods 18
favor 25, 39, 45, 122, 197, 248
fences 20
field merchandiser reps 27, 175
FMCG 5, 8, 28, 45, 62, 63, 68, 69, 70, 78, 79, 82, 84, 88, 90, 98, 109, 120, 145, 148, 166, 174, 182, 187,
      190, 194, 237
FMI 22, 23, 24
Food Marketing Institute 22
Food Marketplace Inc. 22
forecast 10, 11, 12, 26, 32, 52, 61, 79, 81, 83, 87, 89, 90, 91, 98, 135, 146, 147, 148, 149, 150, 176, 180,

182, 183, 227, 232, 247
foundational 28, 147, 158, 173, 215, 230
Foundational 145, 150, 182
Fred Meyer Guides 63
Free-Standing Inserts 81
Frito-Lay 113
FSI 81, 84
FTC 23, 25, 60, 63, 257
Funding and Budget Allocation 97

G

Gartner xvi, 113, 114, 117, 258, 259
Go Live 242
governance 19, 20, 98, 99, 108, 109, 129, 133, 208, 236, 239, 241
Grocery Manufacturers Association 24
"Guides" 63
Guides for Advertising Allowances and Other Merchandising Payments and Services 63, 69

H

Halo 231, 234
Hanes 113
Hans Van Delden xv, 244
Harris Fogel xvi
"hash." 206
"hashes" 206
H-E-B 32, 33, 122, 258
Hewlett-Packard 113
Hurricane Harvey 32
Hurricane Katrina 32
Hyperledger Fabric 214

I

IBM xviii, 113, 214, 221, 260
IDC 113, 259
Immutable Records 207
incentives xiii, xiv, 4, 8, 9, 10, 19, 26, 28, 29, 31, 37, 57, 61, 63, 67, 71, 82, 92, 100, 113, 114, 118, 162,
        173, 214, 221, 242, 252
Information Resources Inc. 101
in-store flyers 165
Intel 113
Internet of Things 124, 181, 208, 260
Inventory Tracking 103
Invisible Economy iv, xvii, 31, 39, 46, 48, 51, 54, 57, 68, 69, 74, 82, 96, 100, 105, 110, 117, 123, 125, 126,
        127, 146, 191, 200, 202, 203, 223, 244, 251, 253
IoT 111, 124, 125, 126, 148, 165, 181, 182, 208, 222, 248
IOTA 208, 216, 260
IRI 101, 157
Ivory Soap 17

J

Jeff Beckett xv, 233, 244
Joe Skorupa 196, 202
John Wanamaker 128
Joint Industry Committee on Deductions 24
Journal of Consumer Research 103
Journey Mapping 136

K

KAM 21, 26, 64, 84, 87, 90, 91, 102, 108, 115, 116, 117, 124, 146, 151, 167, 168, 183, 184, 192, 198, 240
Kantar 81, 112, 259
Katrina 32
Kawasaki 2, 3, 4
key account manager 61, 68, 80, 84, 98, 101, 115, 135, 146, 150, 166, 192
key account managers xiii, 21, 23, 24, 26, 42, 62, 64, 65, 68, 74, 76, 83, 101, 104, 106, 113, 125, 151, 182,
     225
Kimberly-Clark 88
KonMari Method™ 76
Kroger 8, 71, 119, 203

L

Loblaw's 120
lockdowns 32, 119, 120, 122
logistics 83, 92, 111, 129, 148, 162, 170, 176, 197, 198, 222, 233, 248
Logistics 83, 96, 166, 170

M

Machine Learning 113, 233
Macy's 8
Manufacturing 96
Marie Kondo 76, 77
market development funds 85, 120, 209
Marketing Alignment 103
mass merchandisers 5, 8, 121, 137, 197
Max Thake 204, 260
McClelland 124
McKinsey 120, 259
MDF 68, 70, 82, 144, 236
MEDIANET xv, 23, 107, 113
merchandiser reps 27, 175, 232
merchandisers 5, 8, 76, 121, 137, 197, 248
Metro 120
Michael Aldrich 118, 259
Microsoft 112, 113, 173
ML 113, 114, 145, 150, 151, 153, 158, 159, 195, 232, 234
mobile 31, 81, 96, 106, 107, 122, 124, 150, 163, 165, 196, 199, 200, 201, 202, 204
Mondelez 88

N

national ad budget 123
"national rates" 16
needs fulfillment 55
network 124, 192, 196, 197, 204, 205, 207, 208, 211, 217, 244
newspaper 3, 17, 18, 19, 41, 78, 81, 124, 165, 187
Nielsen 9, 45, 67, 74, 101, 105, 109, 145, 149, 157, 258
NPD 145, 149, 157

O

Omnichannel 118, 226, 227
one version of the truth 132
Optimization xi, xv, 74, 103, 145, 170, 184, 211, 239, 244, 258, 259
Oracle xviii, 112, 113, 173, 217, 218, 220
out-of-stock 117
Out-of-stock 103
Out-of-stock conditions 103
out-of-stocks 249, 259
"over and above" 63, 68

P

Pam Brown xv, 239
pandemic xiii, 11, 32, 33, 37, 41, 42, 44, 45, 56, 75, 76, 81, 88, 113, 117, 119, 120, 121, 122, 138, 167, 201,
      227, 258, 259
Pandora's Box 20
"pay-to-play" 123
PepsiCo 88
POC 165, 166
POI 213
point-of-sale 65, 101, 129, 137, 233
POP 211, 213
POS 49, 65, 66, 69, 96, 101, 102, 103, 105, 107, 111, 117, 135, 145, 148, 149, 150, 154, 159, 160, 161, 162,
      172, 173, 174, 175, 176, 178, 183, 192, 193, 201, 211, 212, 213, 216, 217, 219, 232, 233, 235, 238,
      240, 247
Post-audit Deductions 25
Post-Promotion 97, 112
PoW 213
PPG 154
predictive 69, 75, 76, 82, 103, 111, 114, 117, 145, 152, 158, 159, 164, 166, 170, 171, 172, 173, 174, 179,
      181, 182, 195, 210, 219, 244, 245
predictive analytics 69, 82, 103, 159, 166, 210
preprinted inserts 34, 149
prescriptive 69, 113, 145, 172, 173, 174, 176, 178, 179, 181, 182, 195, 219, 222, 233, 244
price reduction 7, 40, 79, 80, 81, 114, 116, 151, 153, 178
"Prime Day" 121
process mapping 110
Procter & Gamble 17, 70, 161, 235
product margins 10
Product Sampling 78

profit iv, 10, 11, 21, 28, 40, 41, 42, 45, 64, 65, 79, 90, 146, 155, 225, 231, 235, 240, 259
profitability 10, 11, 26, 64, 69, 79, 91, 96, 122, 140, 156, 162, 163, 164, 172, 174, 188, 190, 196, 197, 225, 230, 231, 252
profit margin 10, 40, 65, 79
program sponsorships 34
Promoted Price 106
Promoted Product Groups 154
Promotion Mechanics 78
Promotion Optimization Institute xv, 74, 211, 239, 259
promotion plan 26, 27, 28, 64, 68, 105, 109, 159, 174, 175, 216
Promotion Plan 25, 150
promotion planning 12, 28, 57, 60, 63, 66, 68, 69, 76, 79, 82, 90, 91, 101, 102, 103, 104, 105, 112, 117, 118, 131, 145, 150, 151, 156, 158, 159, 168, 174, 181, 182, 193, 199, 211, 220, 221, 222, 240
Promotion Planning 79, 97, 100, 215, 221, 247, 259, 260
Promotion Settlement and Closing 97, 107
promotion timing 26
proof of concept 165
proof of performance 17, 18, 19, 21, 26, 28, 62, 82, 99, 166, 187, 193, 209, 241, 248
Proof of Performance 213
Proof of Work 206, 213
PwC 244

R

repository 130
reseller 16, 21, 27, 47, 61, 62, 76, 83, 85, 92, 98, 99, 110, 172, 175, 208, 210, 211, 245
resellers 5, 7, 15, 34, 60, 62, 82, 92, 95, 107, 110, 143, 162, 175, 196, 203
Retailer Information Systems 75
retail execution 88, 92, 104, 107, 111, 117, 131, 164, 167, 174, 188, 190, 195, 196, 198, 199, 200, 239, 246, 248
Retail Execution 107, 117, 164, 165, 188, 189, 190, 191, 194, 201, 202, 215, 216, 260
Retail Solutions, Inc. 145
Retail Velocity xi, 145, 233, 244
Retail/Wholesale Channels 83
REX 117, 164, 165, 166, 188, 190, 191, 192, 193, 194, 195, 196, 197, 199, 201
RFID 148, 181
RFP 190, 242, 243
Richard Oliver 48, 51
Rick Pensa xvi
RIS 76, 196, 197, 200, 201, 202, 259, 260
Robinson-Patman 25, 59, 60, 62, 63, 68, 257
Roddy Martin xvi, 180
ROI xi, xvii, 9, 12, 60, 75, 76, 82, 84, 87, 91, 98, 100, 101, 102, 115, 120, 122, 131, 132, 133, 134, 136, 138, 141, 144, 146, 147, 151, 152, 153, 154, 156, 158, 159, 174, 185, 191, 193, 210, 213, 219, 223, 224, 225, 226, 227, 228, 230, 231, 233, 234, 235, 238, 240, 241, 245, 247
ROI formulae 138
Ronald Reagan 15, 257
Ron Riley 1
Roots 17
rules 20, 25, 63, 99, 108, 109, 133, 208, 209, 215, 239, 241
Russell Brunson 46

S

sales and operations planning 83
Sam's 5, 8, 119
Sam Smolik 251
SAP xviii, 112, 113, 173, 238
Satoshi Nakamoto 204
Sealy 113
Security Permissions 207
"Sell-In" 64, 155, 156
Sell-In 61, 64, 66, 155, 156
"Sell-Out" 64, 155, 156
sensor 96, 111, 148
sensors 96, 124, 125, 126, 143, 165, 181, 182, 248
sentiment 53, 54, 56, 83, 85, 135, 178, 179, 213, 219
settlement xiii, 21, 23, 28, 63, 64, 100, 108, 109, 110, 111, 126, 131, 148, 166, 198, 201, 208, 209, 214, 216, 217, 221, 236, 239, 240, 241, 242
settlement processing xiii, 236
Shelf stock 106
shelf tags 34, 126, 200
shell game 67, 69, 71
"Shell Game" 79, 146
shipment 28, 120, 148, 161, 162, 169, 170, 245
shipments 22, 125, 178, 198
shippers 109, 165
"Shippers" 78

shipping 25, 27, 28, 31, 32, 42, 61, 96, 106, 109, 120, 121, 125, 138, 148, 162, 166, 170, 197, 198, 203, 230, 248
siloed operating units 133, 139
siloes 139
single version of the truth 133, 147
Sir Gerald Templer 73
SKU 84, 125, 126, 154
SKUs 154, 185
slotting 123
"Smart Contract" 208
Smart Contracts 208, 215, 218, 221, 260
smart inventory 96
smart pantry 126
Smolik 251
social media 31, 34, 46, 49, 52, 53, 54, 60, 85, 96, 104, 111, 119, 133, 165, 178, 179, 185, 226
S&OP 102
spark joy 77
specific curiosity 38
spreadsheet 98, 114
stakeholder 227
stakeholders 110, 118, 135, 177, 196, 212, 224, 225, 234, 241, 246, 247, 249, 250
Steven Boal 81
stock 32, 36, 43, 56, 103, 106, 115, 117, 125, 130, 131, 139, 148, 151, 161, 162, 164, 165, 166, 168, 176, 191, 194, 195, 197, 200, 210, 216, 222, 230, 260

Stock Keeping Units 125
supply and operations planning 102, 182
Supply Chain Management 96
sweet spot 19, 38

T

tactical activities 21, 26, 65, 68, 70, 76, 79, 82, 99, 108, 109, 110, 114, 152, 154, 219, 247
tactics 5, 19, 26, 27, 34, 42, 52, 67, 70, 75, 77, 78, 79, 82, 84, 86, 87, 91, 101, 102, 103, 104, 105, 106, 109, 111, 116, 117, 124, 151, 152, 153, 154, 156, 157, 163, 164, 174, 177, 190, 211, 216, 233, 240
Tangle 208, 216, 217, 218, 219, 260
Tangle EE Working Group 208
Target 120, 203
tearsheets 18, 19
telemetry 127, 143, 203, 218, 260
Telemetry 127, 260
temporary price reduction 7, 40, 79, 114, 151, 153
Temporary Price Reductions 78
Tesco 120, 123, 203
The Linux Foundation 214
timing xiii, 19, 26, 65, 67, 86, 90, 91, 93, 101, 102, 103, 104, 108, 111, 148, 151, 156, 163, 174, 177, 182
Tim Moore xv
"To-Be" 242
"touchpoint" 119
touchpoints xi, 119
TPM 98, 99, 109, 110, 112, 114, 115, 117, 131, 144, 147, 152, 153, 154, 155, 156, 157, 158, 164, 173, 189, 212, 221, 237, 239, 243, 245
TPO 115, 117, 145, 151, 152, 159, 160, 170, 171, 239, 244, 245
TPR 40, 78, 79, 80, 81, 84, 115, 116, 117, 131, 151, 153, 167, 168, 178
TPx 27, 144, 145, 156, 158, 159, 162, 169, 189, 205, 211, 213, 221, 225, 233, 235, 236, 237, 238, 239, 241, 242, 243, 244, 250
Trade Channel Promotion 17, 78, 79, 215
trade channel promotions 37, 39, 78, 79, 180, 223, 224, 226, 249
Trade Channel Promotion Tactics 78
trade promotion fund 62, 99
Trade Promotion Optimization 145, 244
transportation 83, 123, 129, 222
truth xvii, 46, 61, 132, 133, 147, 163, 174, 188

U

Unilever 88

V

Valassis/Vericast 81
value-added reseller 208, 245
value chain xiv, 51, 54, 88, 93, 172, 184, 185, 227
Value Chain 12, 13, 184
Van Delden xv, 244
vector 134
Vector 134, 136, 138
Virtual Shopping Walls 123

270

Vistex 112
Volney Palmer 16
VSW 123

W

Walgreens 119
Walmart 8, 59, 67, 71, 119, 203
warehousing 31, 32, 83, 121, 125, 162, 170
Warehousing and Logistics 96
Watt 127
WHBQ 2
Whole Foods Markets 41
wholesaler 7, 31, 47, 76, 92, 98, 110, 162, 172, 175, 180, 192, 208, 211, 213, 220, 245
wholesalers 5, 62, 63, 82, 95, 98, 99, 100, 107, 127, 143, 170, 175, 203, 211
wholesalers/distributors 82
William Taylor 16
WLS 1
Woodstock 20
workshops 110, 136, 137, 177, 241, 242, 243

Z

Zenith 113

CPSIA information can be obtained
at www.ICGtesting.com
Printed in the USA
JSHW042050220222
23221JS00002B/14